Praise for the original *Dog*

"This wonderful book will help break the cycle of animal suffering caused by wrong-mindedness and harmful training methods. Paul Owens' nonviolent process will help prevent dogs from developing various behavioral and psychological problems, which can be difficult to treat later in life. It also helps us develop our empathy and understanding, making us more humane—and more human—and thus more deserving of the company of dogs whose virtues we so often fail to live up to."

—From the Foreword by Dr. Michael W. Fox
Senior Scholar, Bioethics
The Humane Society of the United States, Washington, D.C.

"Paul Owens has done dogs and dog lovers a real favor. He has given dog lovers permission to be kind, and as a consequence helped them to become more humane. He has given the dogs the chance to escape the brutal techniques that are so often imposed upon them 'for their own good.' This book provides us with a much needed modern reminder of the value of individual compassion, and shows us that love and learning can be fun and that they don't have to hurt."

—Karen L. Overall, M.A., V.M.D., Ph.D.
Diplomate, American College of Veterinary Behaviorists
ABS Certified Applied Animal Behaviorist

"I enjoyed this book immensely. Paul Owens reveals the mystique of the dog and that unique bond we all strive to share with our previous canine pets. While other trainers snap, crackle, and pop, Paul creates an atmosphere of social cooperation. Everyone should enjoy *The Dog Whisperer*."

—William Campbell, BehavioRx Systems
Author, Behavior Problems in Dogs *and*
Better Behavior in Dogs

"After working for years to expose trainers' cruelty to animals in the production of movies, I applaud a book that encourages the compassion and nonviolence that dogs so richly deserve."

—Bob Barker, Host
The Price Is Right

"How refreshing. Paul Owens offers us a well-thought-out, enjoyable, holistic text, which always has the physical and mental well-being of dogs at its heart. And, as added bonus, *The Dog Whisperer* has many useful tips to promote the physical and mental well-being of dogs' human companions."

—Dr. Ian Dunbar
Author, Dog Behavior, *and founder, Association of Pet Dog Trainers*

"The Dog Whisperer delivers a big message. With easy-to-follow lessons Paul Owens guides pet owners in raising cooperative, happy dogs. His techniques involve motivation rather than force. Well done, Paul. Your book leads the way to a better relationship with dogs."

—Terry Ryan
Author, The Toolbox for Remodeling Problem Behaviors

"This book is a must read for all dog lovers. Paul Owens offers a practical, heart-based approach to dog training filled with joy and love."

—Allen Schoen, D.V.M.
Author, Love, Miracles and Animal Healing

"Lately dog owners have become aware of the superiority of training systems based on kindness rather than harsh corrections. *The Dog Whisperer* shows them a very effective method that works everywhere, not just in the owner's backyard. It also offers guidance for the owners themselves. This enables the owner to achieve the balance in their own life that allows the deepest bonding with their dogs. I recommend this book to anyone who has ever had problems training their dog and to anyone who wants to learn the best way to train their dog."

—Nancy Scanlan, D.V.M.
Holistic Veterinarian

"Having worked with animals as a professional trainer over many years, I well understand the importance of changing human attitudes. Now, this book has changed my behavior. It has reminded me of many things I already knew but had somewhat lost touch with. Simply put, as I continue working with animals, including my own dog, I am having a lot more fun!"

—Mollie Hogan, Executive Director
Wildworks Wild Animals Nature Care Center
Topanga Canyon, California

"Paul's teaching methods adapt to working with schools, veterinarians, pet owners, and animals, creating order out of seemingly uncontrollable situations."

—Nancy Disbro, D.V.M.

"In the name of countless animals, thank you for your optimism and vision."

—Brian Forsgren, D.V.M.

THE DOG WHISPERER

2nd EDITION

A Compassionate, Nonviolent Approach to Dog Training

Paul Owens with Norma Eckroate

Adams Media
Avon, Massachusetts

This book is dedicated to my Mother.
–Paul Owens

Published by
Adams Media, an F+W Publications Company
57 Littlefield Street, Avon, MA 02322. U.S.A.
www.adamsmedia.com

J I H G F E

Printed in the United States of America.

Library of Congress Cataloging-in-Publication Data
Owens, Paul
The dog whisperer / Paul Owens with Norma Eckroate.—2nd ed.
p. cm.
Includes bibliographical references and index.
ISBN-13: 978-1-59337-598-0 (pbk.)
ISBN-10: 1-59337-598-0 (pbk.)
1. Dogs—Training. 2. Dogs—Behavior. 3. Human-animal communication.
I. Eckroate, Norma, 1951- II. Title.
SF431.O866 2007
636.7—dc22
2006100882

This publication is designed to provide accurate and authoritative information with
regard to the subject matter covered. It is sold with the understanding that the publisher
is not engaged in rendering legal, accounting, or other professional advice. If legal
advice or other expert assistance is required, the services of a competent professional
person should be sought.

—From a *Declaration of Principles* jointly adopted by a Committee of the
American Bar Association and a Committee of Publishers and Associations

Many of the designations used by manufacturers and sellers to distinguish their product
are claimed as trademarks. Where those designations appear in this book and Adams
Media was aware of a trademark claim, the designations have been printed with initial
capital letters.

Cover photograph by Brian Stemmler Photography, Los Angeles, California.
Illustrations on pages 7 and 271 courtesy of Aris Kakkis.
All photos courtesy of Harvey Branman of Photography As An Art, Burbank, California,
except photos on pages 9, 237, 239, 241, 243, and 245, which are by Brian Stemmler
Photography, Los Angeles, California.
Illustrations of The Professor on page 155 and Betty on page 271 courtesy of Jacci
Stincic. Illustration of Gentle Leader head collar on page 89 used with permission of
Premier Pet Products.

This book is available at quantity discounts for bulk purchases.
For information, please call 1-800-289-0963.

Contents

Part 1
The Basics of Dog Training

Part 2
Training Essentials

Part 3
The Lessons

Part 4
Problem Behaviors

Acknowledgments

Years ago, my great friend Jane Holland taught me about the "expanding heart." She said, "Just when you think your heart is so full of love that you can't possibly conceive loving more than you do, your heart expands. And it keeps on expanding until you come to the realization that love is infinite." That is how I feel about all those who made this book possible.

For inspiration and her infinite and truly divine support, my sincere thanks and all my love goes to my twin sister, Pam and the rest of the Owens clan, Peg, Pat, Tom, and Ruth.

For her unbelievable patience and enlightened gift of awareness, coupled with her metaphysically astute way with words, I offer my deepest respect and appreciation to my coauthor, Norma Eckroate. Without her, it is doubtful this book would have appeared in this incarnational round.

To our agents, Lisa Hagan and Sandra Martin, thanks for your dogged pursuit and support. And to Jennifer Kushnier, Kate Epstein, Shoshanna Grossman, Meredith O'Hayre, Jere Calmes, and everyone at Adams Media, many thanks for your undying belief and conviction in this philosophy and work.

Heartfelt thanks go to my friends. It is truly an honor to be able to put your names in print for the world to see. I wish I had space to tell the story behind each name. As I write this, know that I am thinking of you individually and how special you are to me: Sister Donna Hawk; John and Carolyn Zenisek (go Joncar!); Holly Merriman; Linda, Lynley, and Stacy Turnbough; Arnie Ritchie; Bill Kennedy; Tim Leslie; Donna Estes; Maureen Williams; Helen Waldes; Robbin Herman; Pat "You Know Who You Are" Brooks; Rebecca Stack; Steve Hays; Elizabeth Walton; Bill, Mary, Cameron, and Murphy Needle; Tom McGuckin; Pat McGuckin; Tom and Cindy Fello; Jenina Schutter; Carol Cupp; Nathan, Andrea, and Katrina Wilson; Linda Eller; Bill Marquardt; and Clay and Diane Williams.

For your supreme consideration and help in getting the words to match the thoughts, I wish to especially thank Marcie Goodman, Jane Wiedlin, Robyn Polashuk, and, of course, my sister, the Sister, Pam.

To Michael W. Fox, D.V.M.; Nancy Disbro, VMD, Ph.D.; Marilyn McCort, D.V.M.; Brian Forsgren, D.V.M.; Ian Dunbar, Ph.D., MRCVS; and William E. Campbell: your work over the years with and for our beloved animals has truly been an inspiration. Thank you for your kindness, compassion, and dedication.

Special thanks go to Karen Overall, D.V.M.; Nancy Scanlan, D.V.M.; Mary Brennan, D.V.M.; Morgan Spector; Ken McCort; and Jerry Teplitz, Ph.D., for their invaluable professional input; to Jack Canfield for his "Soup-in-the Soul"–like assistance; and warmest regards and undying gratitude to Jim and Keelin O'Neill for their generosity and professional support.

To Jacci Stincic for her wonderful illustrations and Aris Kakkis for his brilliant creativity in translating thought to visual accessibility, thank you both so much. Special thanks to our excellent photographers: Harvey Branman at Photography As an Art in Burbank, California; Brian Stemmler at Stemmler Photography in Los Angeles; and Tara Olsen (as well as her supermodel dog, Lucy).

Finally, to those friends with their furry sidekicks, a great big wag of my tail and scratch behind your ear! You made it all possible: Barbara Holliday and the awesome Bozley Beagle; Nichola Ellis with the irrepressible Conner and Tyson; Claudia Madrid with the ever-bounding Emily; Rosanna Lyons and the "I never met a human I didn't like" Angus; Renate Pless and "Mr. Energy" Joseph; Marcie Goodman and the wonder Weimaraners, Jackson and Spalding; Holly Merriman and Marble (cake); the beautiful and very generous Leah Meyer; Tom O. and "If that's a water puddle, I'm not moving" Thunder; Robyn Rosay and Merlin "The Merlinator"; Jane Wiedlin and Orbit, the Queen of the Universe; Wendy Parrish and Judah. Thank you all so very much.

And, finally, to seven of the greatest representatives of love ever incarnated in furry form, Tara and Molly, Buddy, Buck, Grady, Sid and Charisse.

Foreword

It is simply not necessary to break an animal's spirit in order to live together in harmony. The old methods of training dogs and other animals by controlling them through domination—in a misguided desire for "absolute obedience"—foster an attitude of human superiority and justified violence, rather than kinship and mutual respect. I believe it is harmful for all of us, and especially for children, to observe and take part in such methods. Fortunately, these ways are becoming a thing of the past as they are now being challenged by less harmful methods of establishing control.

In looking at our relationship with animals, it's helpful to consider how wild animals relate to people. If a person suddenly came face to face with an animal and found himself in the animal's "personal space," the animal might panic and flee, become catatonic and play dead, or turn and attack. In all too many cases, those wild animals who are captured are at the mercy of a trainer whose methods eventually break his spirit. Finally, the animal reaches a state of conditioned helplessness. In time the animal actually attaches himself to the trainer, who not only provides occasional relief from the beatings, but also represents his source of food, water, and security. Tragically, the animal learns to seek relief and solicit attention from the very trainer who abuses him.

We must ask ourselves, do the ends justify the means? When people applaud circus animal performances, they are not aware of the violent training methods that many of these animals have suffered through. Such training puts limitations on the human spirit and potential, just as it does on the animal's. Can any end justify breaking an animal's spirit?

Now we are entering a more empathic age and compassionate stage. As people mature, they look for ways to educate our animals with compassion and love, in order to establish a relationship and bond based on mutual affection, understanding, and trust. Much skill, patience, and understanding are needed with animals to establish this bond.

Dogs have been domesticated for over 100,000 years and the domestication process has resulted in most of them losing their "wildness," which includes a high level of vigilance and fear of strangers and unfamiliar places and stimuli. This process of domestication manifests in the readiness of pups to bond with their caretakers or "parent-pack leaders" during their formative early weeks. During this critical period, between the ages of about five to ten weeks, pups develop their primary social attachments. In the wild it would be to their littermates, mother, father, and other pack members. In the domestic environment pups attach instead to their human family. It is on the basis of this attachment early in life that dogs are naturally amenable to nonviolent training.

This book by Paul Owens is at the opposite end of the old-school moral spectrum and makes the nonviolent way of training a shoe-in. It is as much about dog-human education as it is about dog training. It advocates educating our dogs with affection and understanding. Paul Owens helps us open up to dogs and relinquish control so dogs can actually "train" us to understand their ways, their needs, and their language.

This wonderful book will help break the cycle of animal suffering caused by wrong-mindedness and harmful training methods. Owens's nonviolent process will help prevent dogs from developing various behavioral and psychological problems, which can be difficult to treat later in life. It also helps us develop our empathy and understanding, making us more humane—and more human—and thus more deserving of the company of dogs whose virtues we so often fail to live up to.

Dr. Michael W. Fox
Senior Scholar, Bioethics
The Humane Society of the United States
Washington, D.C.

Preface

Years ago a friend of mine, a priest actually, suggested that I write a book about Jesus's dog. That idea began to percolate. It's hard to imagine Jesus or Buddha or Krishna or Moses "owning" a dog. But I'm sure at least a few four-legged furry personalities could be found hanging around the throngs. So how would an Enlightened One—a person who lives a truly conscious life—deal with a dog trying to steal a loaf of bread or a fish? "Sit, you miserable cur!" doesn't seem very likely. Nor can I imagine one of these people swatting the dog on the nose with a scroll. But, would he simply let the dog eat the stolen tidbit? And how would he train the dog? Maybe telepathy? I can just imagine Buddha under the Bodhi tree or Jesus on the mount saying, "Nothing up my sleeve. For my next trick, I will stand behind this tree and, using just my mind, I will send my dog, Sparkus, visual images. He will roll over, get up, and go fetch my sandals."

We have all had moments in our lives in which we felt consciously connected to the universe—when we thought or willed something and voila, it happened. It is in these moments that intuition, creativity, and productivity flow. My first experience of this "connectedness" occurred when I was seven. Somewhere in the night I awoke to a half-asleep, half-awake consciousness—like I was in a dream and watching it at the same time. Suddenly my body seemed to be frozen. I felt a split second tingle and then I exploded. A tremendous flash of incredible white light burst within my body. Every pore seemed to expand and grow. The light flooded my entire room and expanded outward.

Suddenly I felt whole and connected to absolutely everything. And everything was love. Unbelievable, unconditional, infinite love. In that microsecond of time, there were no questions, there were no answers. Everything was perfect as it was. I was in tears. All I felt was gratitude. The experience of infinite, unbridled joy left me wanting everyone to experience it. The next day I couldn't think of anything else and I couldn't wait to go to sleep that night. Life was wonderful. I've been blessed with many other wonderful experiences since then, but this childhood taste of unconditional love was the ultimate.

Since then I've had my ups and downs like everybody else. This one experience of "connectedness" didn't lead to a life free of problems. However, as one great teacher said, "Pain is a prod to remembrance." Now when I look back at the most challenging moments in my life, I realize the support has always been there and many times animals were providing that support.

And that brings us to this book. The message of this book is not that nonviolent dog training is a new, groundbreaking path to enlightenment. It is our capacity to love, however, that opens the doors to the evolution of our intelligence, not the other way around. We adhere to the philosophy that the result of training your dog to sit is not as important as the process you use to get there. It's the "whys" and "hows"—the methods we use to train our dogs—that distinguish us as compassionate and loving beings. With this in mind, this book attempts to link intuitive and scientific methodology, all under the spiritual vehicle of nonviolence.

Dog training is ever-evolving, with new training ideas and tools popping up every year, helping us to educate our dogs and make the learning process easier and more fun. Since the first edition of this book was published in 1999, it has become a bestseller and spawned a DVD of the same title. This edition includes more in-depth training protocols and additional notes, hints, and problem-solving tips which make our Three-Step Process of shaping behaviors even more accessible. A new section on tricks makes training even more fun for you and your dog. We also offer a new, more comprehensive look at how to deal with and help dogs who are ultra-sensitive to the world's sights, sounds, and smells. And, we have increased our recommended foods list and added commentary on raw food diets.

Also, since the first edition was published, I've had numerous queries about the title itself. The term "Dog Whisperer" has been used by a number of trainers around the globe. It is at this point that I must make a distinction, however, because not all trainers agree on what the term Dog Whisperer means. To me, the word whisperer connotes the use of gentle and positive methods. Some trainers use negative, physical-force methods which are in stark contrast to the positive, nonviolent methods that I and other reward-based trainers advocate.

What I've found is that most people who wouldn't pin a dog to the ground, hang a dog in the air by a leash or collar, or jerk a dog to force him to submit, wouldn't do those things anyway, even after attending a dog training class or viewing a TV show that presents physically aversive methods. No dog training method should ever be used if it conflicts with how you feel about your dog and how he should be treated. And no advice should ever be heeded if it supersedes your own common sense and intuition.

From the practical point-of-view, more and more scientific studies are emerging to support the use of positive training over negative training. Top behavioral scientists at the leading veterinary schools, including the University of Pennsylvania, Tufts University, Cornell, the University of California at Davis promote only positive behavior modification methods and believe that negative training and physical force methods are unsafe, unnecessary, and ineffective in the long run.

With this revised edition we happily restate our commitment and philosophy that treating animals with kindness is directly linked with treating each other as human beings with kindness. Thank you for joining us on this journey!

PART 1

The Basics of Dog Training

Chapter 1

Positive Training Works

Within weeks after their birth, dogs know how to put their behinds on the floor (sit), lie down, stand, stay, bark and not bark, run and walk toward us (come), walk by our side (heel), and find things with their noses (track). We don't have to teach them any of this. All we have to do—mostly for safety purposes—is ask them to please inhibit their biting on certain objects, go to the bathroom outside, and do what they do naturally—run, dig, jump, bark— when and where we request.

Reward-Based Training

Basically there are two ways to train an animal—with physical force and coercion, which is often aversive, or with rewards, which is certainly easier on both dog and human and actually personifies kindness. It's the age-old idea of getting an animal to do something by beating her with a stick or rewarding her with a carrot. I tell people that the choice they have to make is to either jerk, hit, shock, and/or shake heir dog to get desired behaviors—or give rewards. Which is more humane? Which is easier, quicker, and, in the long run, more effective? Over the last few decades, thousands of dog trainers have discovered that the use of positive training answers these questions. In addition, there are many positive behavior modification programs now in use at the leading veterinary schools of behavior at the University of Pennsylvania, Tufts University, Cornell, University of California at Davis, and many others. They have found negative training to be unsafe, unnecessary, and ineffective in the long run. A study in England by the Department of Clinical Veterinary Science at the University of Bristol in 2004 strongly supports the value of positive training over aversive methods, which include physical punishment: "Because reward-based methods are associated with higher levels of obedience and fewer problematic behaviors, we suggest that their use is a more effective and welfare-compatible alternative to punishment for the average dog owner."

This book is about using "carrots"—that is, praise, food treats, toys, massage, social interaction, play, affection. The *process* we use to teach our dogs to sit is as important as the result. The training methods we use are important not only because of what we are doing to our dogs, but also because of how they affect us as human beings.

Aversive training says to the dog, "Do this or something bad will happen to you." *Positive* training suggests the opposite, "Do this and something good will happen." The difference between the two types of training is the consequences that are involved. In reward-based dog training fear, pain, force, and submission do not exist.

With aversive methods, you are taught to jerk, hit, pin, shock, or shake the dog to correct him when he does something you *don't want* him to do. You also jerk, hit, shock, or shake him every time you *want* him to do something. Eventually he does what you want him to do because he wants to avoid the pain and/ or discomfort. Then you gradually reduce the number of times you jerk, shock, hit, pin or shake him because he starts "behaving." Aversive training fosters fear.

Sometimes jerking on the leash is referred to by euphemisms such as *leash correction* or *jerk correction*. But a jerk on the leash is a jerk, no matter what you call it. If too much force is used, dogs can get injured. If the jerk is poorly timed or if the collar is placed incorrectly, once again the dog can get injured. Mistimed jerking often communicates messages that have nothing to do with the dog's pulling or other "misbehaviors" that the handler is trying to correct. Often it is used as a result of the human's frustration and hence becomes redirected human aggression. The result is confusion and frustration for both the dog and the handler. Sadly, the frustration often leads to anger and even more force is usually employed. It's a vicious cycle.

Jerking can lead to injuries such as neck and spinal damage, which can sometimes take years to manifest. Jerking also creates the potential for emotional trauma, which, of course, translates into even more behavioral problems. According to behavioral expert William Campbell, a jerk on the leash doesn't have to be forceful to inflict an injury to your dog. He says that tests indicate that even a normal jerk can inflict 15 pounds of concentrated shock at 33 feet per second to a dog's spine and throat. Campbell also quotes a landmark survey by Anders Hallgren in 1992 which revealed that 252 out of 400 dogs examined by a chiropractor had misaligned spines. Among the 252 dogs with spinal problems, 65 percent also had behavior problems, while only 30 percent of the dogs without spinal injuries had behavior problems. Of the dogs in the survey that were labeled as aggressive or hyperactive, 78 percent had spinal problems.

While some training methods limit the use of aversive force to a jerk on the leash, other methods include extreme abuse. They include hanging in the air by a choke collar until the dog actually passes out, holding the head under water to keep the dog from digging in a hole, rubbing the nose in excrement, kicking to hurry the dog along, hitting the dog's nose with a rubber hose, pinching the ear with a contraption that places the ear between a wooden dowel and a bottle cap, zapping the dog with electricity, and much worse. Several years ago there was a court case against someone accused of animal cruelty because he corrected his dog by biting him. His defense was that it is natural for one dog to bite another dog as a form of correction and he was just doing what he felt Mother Nature intended. He lost his case. Although rare, this was not an isolated instance as I've heard of other cases in which people actually bit dogs as part of the so-called training process. Using physical punishment with fearful or aggressive dogs is dangerous and unnecessary. Behavioral science has shown that suppressing behavior, especially through physical force or the threat of force, does nothing to bring confidence to a fearful dog or calm an aggressive dog, it only suppresses that behavior (out of fear) in that particular situation. Physical punishment involves applying a physical aversive to reduce the probability of the behavior continuing. "Flooding" refers to physically forcing a dog into an overwhelming situation he is afraid of until the dog "shuts down" or the behavior is suppressed. I do not promote or advocate these methods.

The alternative to this type of training—the choice that I advocate—is positive training. Positive training uses rewards and gentle persuasion to get your dog to do what you want. For example, if you reward a dog every time you want him to do something, he'll start responding more and more to get the reward. That's what dogs do. Gradually you stop rewarding him every single time and, eventually he'll continue doing what you want just on the chance that a reward is coming his way.

Think of it this way: If I gave you $10,000 every time you sat on a particular chair whenever you came over to my house, where would you sit? And how often would you be visiting me? To keep you motivated, I might decide to offer other great stuff from time to time, such as an expensive watch, tickets to the Super Bowl, or a vacation in Bermuda. Eventually you might decide it's really worthwhile visiting me and sitting on that particular chair. Even if I don't give you stuff you might decide you actually like my company because, besides being generous, I'm a great guy! So let's say I then start giving you something really great every second or third time you come over. Just the anticipation of a possible reward would keep you coming. After all, did you ever see a person in Las Vegas being forced to play a slot machine? In the end, the possibility of a reward is all that's needed to keep people coming back.

It is up to every individual to observe for themselves the methods a trainer uses and then decide whether they are comfortable using them with their dog.

Read the Label and Follow the Directions

Dog training, as it is currently practiced by many, is turned upside down. The primary reason people train dogs is *to keep them from doing things that come naturally.* They want to keep their dogs from using their teeth. They want to keep them from running. They want to keep them from eliminating. They want to keep them from jumping, digging, and barking. It's like putting them in behavioral straitjackets. So what can we do? The goal is to create an environment to let our dogs simply be themselves within the framework of our lifestyle.

Why dogs do what they do never changes. They do what they do for one reason—because it's in their best interest and it feels good. Getting a reward—praise, food, or freedom—is the payoff. Avoiding danger is a payoff too—like getting someone to stop hitting or jerking them if they "sit." Dogs learn to anticipate these consequences.

Positive training is based on proactively teaching your dog to do what you want . . . not on reactively getting your dog to stop doing something. We repeat this over and over again throughout this book. If the human doesn't know what he or she wants their dog TO DO, the dog can't figure it out either. It isn't, "How do I get my dog to stop jumping?" Instead, the question should be, "What do you want your dog to do?" One possible answer is, "I want my dog to lie down whenever someone comes in the door." Lying down becomes the substitute behavior and, as a result, the dog can't jump and lie down at the same time.

I believe that dog training in the next century will evolve more and more toward kindness through positive methods as trainers use less and less physical force to shape their dogs' behavior. The key is harnessing your focus and willpower and then directing that energy through specific, proven, scientific training techniques. When this happens and you channel your goals through these methods, you will get exactly what you are looking for. Specifically, this is done in measured movements, that is, the less you react, the more of a leader you are. A dog's world is rooted in economy of motion. This book explains how to do just that. Once the commitment is made, all you need to do is read the description and follow the directions on the label.

Figure 1

DOGGUS FRIENDLIUS

I pee, poop, chase, jump, dig, bark, and bite.
Training is required.
Batteries (food) not included.
Health care mandatory.
Total yearly cost: $750 to $3,000.

Additional Recommendations:
I prefer to sleep in the bedroom with you.
Please provide a minimum of 2 hours a day of
play, exercise, socialization and employment.
Education must include emotional, mental,
and physical stimulation.

Benefits: *I will accept you as you are,*
unconditionally love you,
work with you, grow with you,
and together we will form
a living, loving bond.

Please read label before adopting and follow directions.

Taking the Lead in a Gentle, Empowering Way

Positive dog training allows you to create a partnership with your dog using gentle persuasion based on kindness, respect, and compassion. With this philosophy you use gentleness with a flexible, yet strict, uncompromising attitude. Positive training is not permissive, but it is fun. So if you aren't going to hit, kick, shock, shake, pin, or jerk your dog, how will he learn to "obey"? How is this possible? It is done through proper communication.

The spoken word is actually full of power—and part of this power is based in the silence before, after, and between the spoken words. The less you speak, the more power you have. Throughout history there have been many leaders who have eloquently expressed the power of gentle persuasion, including St. Francis of Assisi, Mahatma Gandhi, and others. Martin Luther

King, Jr. once said, "If peace is our goal, then our means must be peaceful." Another example comes from the plant world. The famous botanist Luther Burbank was the first to develop a cactus without thorns. He told the great yogi Paramahansa Yogananda how he did it, which Yogananda shared in his book *Autobiography of a Yogi*: "I often talked to the plants to create a vibration of love. 'You have nothing to fear,' I would tell them. 'You don't need your defensive thorns. I will protect you.'"

Positive training is based on this same philosophy. We are here to protect our dogs; not the other way around. Positive training is not a new concept, but it is now taking root at a deeper level than ever before. Just as it is no longer acceptable to many people to punish a child by spanking, so, too, we are evolving as a species to eliminate violence in other areas. For many years there has been a movement toward the use of nonviolent, "cruelty free" products—such as cosmetics that do not include animal products or involve animal testing. Now it is time to totally eliminate violence in the training of dogs and other animals.

The point of this book is that we humans have an equal role in the behavioral give-and-take equation. The fact that we can get a dog to sit or lie down when we ask is not the entire picture. In this philosophy, which is certainly not new, how we go about it is equally important. Our desire to elicit behavioral responses that correspond to our limited view of what is right, wrong, or simply appropriate doesn't justify violent methodology. The end never justifies the means. And might does not make right.

Responding Versus Reacting to Your Dog

Sometimes all that is necessary to tilt the scales toward positive training is simply to become aware of the obvious. A few years ago a couple called me to do a consultation for their dog, Lucky, who was exhibiting aggressive behavior. When I arrived at the home, I learned the wife was a psychiatrist and the husband was a psychologist and yet they didn't know what to do with poor Lucky, who was locked in the basement. This couple knew more about operant and classical conditioning than I could ever hope to know in this lifetime. Yet, there I was setting up a behavior modification program for them and their dog, which was, in principle, similar to the ones they design and implement every day of the week for human beings! Fortunately the light bulb went off in their heads and they quickly realized they had not been using their expertise with their own dog. A few weeks later when I checked back, Lucky was well on her way to becoming a well-mannered member of society.

Like this couple, all of us have blocks in our awareness. It's as if we sometimes forget to "connect the dots." Often it's just a matter of finding the trigger to release and remember what we already know. To do this, we have to pause before we act and learn to *respond* rather than *react*. "Reacting" denotes an emotionally based knee-jerk behavior to a particular situation. On the other hand, a "response" means we bring all of our wisdom, creativity, intuition, and emotion to the situation. Why learn to respond rather than react? For one thing, when you stop and consider what you are about to do with your dog, you are able to focus on how to deal with the problem rather than the symptom.

Let's say a dog is barking at the mail carrier walking toward the house. The knee-jerk reaction is to react to the symptom, which is the barking, rather than respond to the cause, which is probably excitement. Most people never think about what is causing the dog to bark; he might be afraid, he might simply be saying hello. In essence, he perceives that he's doing his job. In most cases, people deal with the barking by yelling at the dog, hitting him with a newspaper, or jerking him on the leash to get him to stop. Regardless of the reason the dog was initially barking, he now associates the mail carrier walking toward him as a danger because of the bad things that happened to him when he barked at that person. So now the dog has a growing aggression problem toward people in uniforms approaching the house. Imagine, on the other hand, if every time the mail carrier showed up and the dog started barking, you interrupted him with a phrase like "Who's that?" and then gave him a treat. You will have ended the barking and the dog will have associated the mail carrier with something positive. So, by using this nonviolent, positive approach, you've stopped the barking and, in the process, you've made the dog more social.

Every dog deserves respect and consideration. You should do your best to find out why a dog is doing what he is doing before you take any action. Otherwise, it is easy to inadvertently fly off the handle and react in a way that might harm the dog and actually compound the behavioral problem. Reacting blocks respect; responding fosters respect.

Consideration also includes the recognition that every dog learns at his or her own rate. People often ask me how long it takes to train a dog. The answer is—it takes as long as it takes. In many ways, training a dog is like raising a child. No parent would ever expect a child to learn to behave perfectly within three months or six months or even three years. Yet many people expect a dog to learn to sit or walk by their side reliably with just a few days' training or after only a few sessions. It just doesn't happen that way.

What Is Violence?

Each person has to decide what violence is for themselves. Everyone looks at the world differently. And we look at dogs differently. To many of us a dog is a loved, cherished being with her own distinct personality. Our dogs are members of our families and our partners in life. They teach us patience and love and allow us to see these qualities reflected back when we look at them. Yes, to some, dogs are mirrors of our most exemplary human characteristics. Their presence increases our feelings of self-worth and helps to heal us emotionally and physically. In their role as service dogs, they help us stand and see, both figuratively and literally. They tell us when the phone is ringing or when someone is at the door. They predict epileptic seizures and can even smell diseases—and so much more.

To others, a dog is an extension of *machismo*; if a dog is big, tough, and mean, it must mean that the dog's owner is that way too. In some people's eyes, dogs are simply possessions that are disposable. Many people give up on dogs with behavior problems such as eliminating in the house or excessive barking, and drop them off at the shelter. In the United States alone, apathy, ignorance, and superstition are significant causes of more than four million dogs being put to death annually—not to mention the cruelty and the suffering of countless others.

People have dropped out of my classes because, as one guy put it, "I need to work with a more 'hands-on' approach." Read "jerk and shake" in that comment. "He's a Rottweiler," another guy said after punching his dog in the face. "He can take it." I then reported the man for this abuse. I felt sorry for the poor dog.

Violence is any behavior or thought that is harmful and stops growth—emotionally, physically, and mentally. Nonviolence is the opposite—any behavior or thought that promotes and fosters self-awareness, health, growth, and safety in these areas. All dogs are individuals with their own unique personalities just like humans. *And every situation in which a dog and a human interact is unique for that time and place. It is up to each one of us to determine what is violent and what is not at that moment in time.* This holds true for behavior directed toward animals, the environment, and, as common sense dictates, ourselves. It takes lots of practice.

Here are some examples, a frame of mind, to clarify the differences and help you draw the nonviolence/violence line in the sand. To interrupt a dog that is climbing on the dining room table or chewing an electric cord, you can distract him with sound and motion and redirect him to do something else. Can you see the difference between interrupting him and whacking him with a newspaper? Would yelling and hitting a dog or a child deter him from chewing an electric cord? Absolutely. But what principle have you then taught? In the same vein, you can encourage your dog (or child) or you can punish, physically force, and intimidate him by jerking, hitting, shocking, or shaking. You can create an environment where your dog learns by his successes or teach him fear. Does that mean there is no anger in the training of dogs? Let's face it, we're human beings and anger is a human emotion. Every now and then we humans get angry.

But there is a difference between ethical anger and violent anger. Ethical anger is anger in which emotion is expressed appropriately and with full awareness of the consequences of that expression. It means expressing oneself without causing harm. In its best expression, anger is a prod to positive change. Violent anger has no regard for consequence. At those rare times when you find yourself angry, reward-based dog training takes the violence out of that anger. This means that in no situation whatsoever do you ever harm your dog. And that takes awareness.

A nonviolent approach doesn't victimize. Nonviolence is proactive. It fosters the principles of love, respect, and compassion. A nonviolent approach also means not taking on the role of a victim, although there are times when we must put ourselves in harm's way to protect or care for a loved one or for a greater good. For example, Gandhi practiced peaceful resistance in India's struggle for independence. The point is, a commitment to nonviolence doesn't preclude using our good old common sense, as well as wisdom, humor, and other nonaversive conflict resolution methods. We are the intelligent, compassionate, intuitive, creative species, are we not? Certainly we can figure out how to shape a dog's behavior without the use of aversive methods.

Aversive training methods are not only harmful to animals; I believe they are at least part of the reason that animals sometimes exhibit violent behavior toward humans. According to recent statistics, there were 4.5 million dog bites in the United States last year and 75 percent of the victims were children. In fact, dog bites are the leading cause of children being taken to the hospital. The link is clear.

The Cycle of Violence
So, why do people still continue to harm or threaten to harm their dogs? There are three major reasons: (1) it's always been done this way, (2) the sense or need of the person to be in physical control of a situation, or (3) wanting to punish the dog. If a person is using aversive methods with a dog because "it's always been done this way," habituation and familiarity have set in. Changing things can be a threat to the status quo. To less secure

individuals it also might mean that they would have to admit they had been violent in the past. This would be like looking in a mirror and seeing themselves as different from who they thought they were. Scary! The other reasons people continue to use harmful training methods—their need to be in physical control and wanting to punish the dog—are usually associated with anger and frustration. As I said earlier, anger has no place in dog training. It shuts off and restricts wisdom, creativity, and intuition. Both the person and the dog suffer. To quote from the sacred text, the *Bhagavad-Gita*: "From unfulfilled desire comes frustration; from frustration, anger; from anger, ruin."

The tendency to use aversive techniques—violent force or the threat of force—is ingrained early in life. For example, whenever a child sees another person demonstrating brutish behavior, she learns that we "win" by being bigger, stronger, and tougher. In nonviolent dog training there is no "winning" because there is no competition.

When we use aversive training methods instead of nonviolent alternatives, we risk ensnaring our dogs and ourselves in a downward spiral of aggression and we desensitize ourselves to the higher aspects of who we are as humans. There was a recent article in a newspaper about a fourteen-year-old girl who had just killed a deer for sport. An accompanying photo showed the dead animal strapped to the hood of her father's car. The girl was asked, "How did you feel when you killed the deer?" She said, "Well, when I killed my first one last year I felt pretty bad. Now it's easier and *I don't think about it at all"* (emphasis added).

Studies have shown that humans who are violent toward animals often extend that behavior and become violent toward other humans. In the last decade, a number of news headlines have repeated the same tragic facts in story after story—a child who exhibited violence toward animals had turned to murdering people.

Reward-based dog training, through its nonviolent approach, promotes compassion and encourages our true nature as sensitive, empathic, loving beings. It acts as a bridge and fosters human-to-animal and human-to-human *nonviolence.*

Dogs Are, Well, Dogs

In theory, training a dog is easy. You form an image in your mind, such as the dog in a sitting position, choose the appropriate training tools, and shape the behavior to match the picture in your head. It just takes time, patience, and a little bit of skill. And that's the rub. Many people don't take the time. Out come the choke, prong, and shock collars—and the jerking, hitting, pinning, kicking, shocking, shaking, and ear pinching. The message is "You'll do this now or else!"

Let's face it, dogs bite, they eliminate, they bark, and they jump. They are themselves. They are not morally good or bad. They are not guilty nor are they heroes. They just are. And we are still discovering the fullness of what that means. In recent years scientists have postulated that we humans use only 15 to 20 percent of our brain power. That's on a good day, I think. Given this human limitation, it seems arrogant and downright silly for us to think that we know all there is to know about dogs and their behavior.

This book proffers an approach to mainstream dog training by focusing on the training *process* as the actual goal. It is when you lose sight of the process as a goal that the invisible leash of your will power is weakened. Your training becomes unclear, imprecise, and poorly timed. When this happens your bond with your dog is also weakened and she is either confused about what you want her to do or the payoff just isn't big enough for her. In other words, your dog thinks, in essence, "Without motivation, why bother?"

As a species we humans have accomplished some amazing things. We've tapped into the intelligence and bravery to put a person on the moon. We've been inspired to create outstanding works of art, thrilling books, awe-inspiring movies, and songs of joy. We've developed the stamina and physical ability to run a marathon, lift a thousand pounds, and jump 8 feet in the air. And we've found the inexhaustible hope and faith to heal life-threatening illnesses. Certainly with all of these abilities, it is also possible for us to teach a dog to walk by our side without having to hit, kick, shock, shake, or jerk him.

The methods we choose to raise and train our dogs determine not only behavioral responses, they also shape our own emotional, physical, and intellectual growth. And they help to define and shape who we are as individuals and as a species. This book is a presentation of positive training and nonviolent partnering with your canine pal. The goal is to enable you to learn and grow together and to experience unbelievable joy. It all starts by addressing the concept of nonviolence: kindness, respect, compassion, responsibility, and love.

Chapter 2

The Nine Ingredients for Optimum Health and Growth

It was the philosophy of holistic health contained in the eight steps of an ancient philosophy called Raja Yoga that inspired me to formulate a model for the optimum care and training of dogs. Most disciplines have a set of rules, which, if followed with perseverance and effort, provide measurable results in physical, mental, and emotional growth. The "nine ingredients" of dog care fit right in. They are: a high-quality diet, play, socialization, quiet time, exercise, employment, rest, step-by-step training, and health care.

Overview of the Nine Ingredients

When I present my Paws for Peace programs in elementary schools, I try to make the nine ingredients accessible to the students by teaching them a little poem:

Food and play and socialize,
Quiet time and exercise,
Give your dog a job to do
And lots of rest when day is through.
Train with love, respect, and care,
And see your vet throughout the year.

These nine ingredients comprise a holistic picture of all the factors that contribute to and influence your dog's behavior. Each of these ingredients is a piece of the puzzle needed to shape the environment in which optimal learning takes place. When you create an optimum learning environment, training is easier, it's quicker, and it's a more pleasant experience.

Think for a minute about your own requirements for optimum health. If you are tired, hungry, sick, or had a bad day at work, you simply aren't going to be at your best. This illustrates the value of looking at and modifying behavior from a "big picture," or holistic, point of view. It is not only the quantity but also the quality of each ingredient that affects behavior.

When you incorporate all nine ingredients into your dog's life, a synergy develops. I love the concept of synergy. It occurs whenever the sum of the total is greater than the sum of the parts. In other words, it's like 2 + 2 + 2 equals 10 *or* 20 *or* 30 *or* 100. The result is greater than that which would have manifested if any one ingredient was applied singly or even when several of the ingredients are applied but others are missing. One example of synergy at work might include the Beatles—they were great individually, but as a unit, they ruled. The same goes for any championship sports team. Applications of great synergy in the dog world would include dogsled teams and animal-assisted therapy groups that take teams of humans and dogs into hospitals and nursing homes. In your home, synergy is also at work between you and your dog. Scientific studies have proven that a person's well-being, both physically and emotionally, benefits from positive interactions with dogs and other animals. It has also been proven that an animal's well-being is enhanced by positive human contact.

When you read about each of the nine ingredients, keep in mind that these ingredients are structured to make dog training easy and part of your everyday routine. Additionally, you will probably note that these are the same ingredients humans need to maintain health, happiness, safety, and growth. This whole philosophy is based upon pure common sense. It's just a matter of daily practice. The practice will become a habit and once it's a habit, it will become part of your daily lifestyle and routine. As a result, there's no sense of dread or weight of responsibility in *having* to train and care for your dog. It becomes a natural process.

If your dog exhibits behavioral problems, I suggest taking a mental snapshot of all the aspects of your dog's life and then review each of these nine ingredients to determine which ones might be out of balance. Many behavioral problems just disappear when this nine-part holistic approach for optimum health and well-being becomes the focus. In addition, when all of these ingredients are provided in a balanced way, dogs are much easier to train. (Part 4 of this book deals with the most common problem behaviors. Some severe behavioral problems are beyond the scope of this book. If a problem persists, please call a professional dog trainer who is versed in positive training methods. Remember, it's always better to err on the side of safety.)

Ingredient Number 1: A High-Quality Diet

This section may include more than you want to know about your dog's diet and what's in most of the popular commercial dog foods. If that's the case, simply jump ahead to the suggested diet recommendations:

🦴 **Option 1:** Canned food and/or kibble made from "human grade" ingredients with extras (see page 25)

🦴 **Option 2:** Raw Diets (see page 26)

🦴 **Option 3:** Molly's Favorite Gourmet Dinner (see page 27)

🦴 **Option 4:** Homemade diet with all the options (see page 27)

No one diet works for all dogs. Your dog's age, lifestyle, size, metabolism, and health influence his dietary needs. That being said, you'll see how easy it is to provide the highest quality diet for your dog. The bottom line is, your dog's stool, coat, behavior, and energy level will let you know whether the diet he is on is the one for him. Growing puppies, especially the giant breeds, and pregnant bitches will need some dietary modifications, but that holds true no matter what diet you use. The following information will get you started.

"A dog is what she eats." I'm going on record here to say if a dog is genetically sound, there is really no reason most healthy dogs can't live to be twenty, even twenty-five years old. In fact, this is not unrealistic. Holistic veterinarian Nancy Scanlan, D.V.M., reports a recent case of a dog that lived to be twenty-seven. Today, the average dog's life span is ten to fifteen years. (My Portuguese Water Dog "Molly" is sixteen and still going strong.) I truly believe more and more dogs would live much longer if we integrated all of the nine ingredients—and it starts with good nutrition.

When I'm consulted about a particular behavioral problem, one of the first things I ask the client is about the dog's diet. Food is fuel. The health of your dog's immune system and resistance to disease, his energy level, his behavior, his ability to process and figure things out, and his quality of life are directly affected by the quality and type of food he eats. A dog's diet affects his mood, his stamina, and, of course, his life span. In addition, behavioral problems can often be linked to a low-quality diet, eating too much, eating too little, or food allergies or sensitivities.

Good nutrition for your dog is actually pretty easy to attain; however—to put it bluntly—not if you buy what Madison Avenue is selling. Since the first edition of this book appeared, more and more companies have sprung up offering high-quality foods. Unfortunately, many of the bigger companies still produce commercial dog foods that are not as nutritious as the public is led to believe.

Most large pet food companies want you to think their foods are "scientifically formulated," "completely balanced," and "100 percent nutritionally complete." The government allows these claims to be made based on feeding trials that are done for a limited period of time. The fact is, no one really knows the nutritional requirements of a cat or dog to the extent that those claims could possibly be valid.

Veterinarian Dr. R. L. Wysong argues that pet food companies should not be allowed to use the "100 percent complete" claim. He uses a human parallel as an analogy: "How many parents would take the advice of a pediatrician who placed a packaged food product on the exam table and told the parent that this is the only product they should feed the child day-in, day-out, for the child's lifetime, and further that they should be sure to not feed any other foods because that might unbalance the product? Even if the pediatrician gave assurances of nutrient analyses that exceeded required minimum levels, feeding trials, and even if the label guaranteed '100 percent complete and balanced,' how many parents would accept such counsel?"

Of course, one of the main reasons we wouldn't buy into the idea that any single packaged food product is nutritionally adequate for a person is that it lacks the health-giving properties of food that is eaten closer to its natural state. The canning or drying process strips food of its life energy. We get the greatest benefit from food when it is in the freshest and most natural state.

Let's look at the problems with many commercial pet foods on the market today.

Problem No. 1: Where's the Raw Food?

Only raw food contains "life energy." Most commercial foods have little or no "life energy." A great example of this for humans is the typical hot dog. Hot dogs have virtually no nutritional value compared to, say, a dinner comprised of a fresh green salad, baked potato, and a homemade soup. When the phrase "life energy" is used to describe food, it relates to a subtle but powerful aspect of elements that are not listed on any food label. It is present in all fresh foods, especially raw foods, and is represented in beneficial bacteria, enzymes and bio-available (defined as "the ability to be of use to a living organism") proteins, vitamins, minerals, and carbohydrates. Here's a look at these components not available in processed food:

Beneficial bacteria are the "good," or friendly, bacteria that are naturally present in the body. They are used for the digestion of food and they also help to suppress undesirable bacteria and yeast. Sometimes the body's own supply of beneficial bacteria is depleted. When this happens, the bad guys can multiply, creating an imbalance. To insure a plentiful supply of the "good guy" bacteria, beneficial bacteria can be added to the diet in supplement form. A number of natural pet products companies offer products specifically formulated for dogs that contain beneficial bacteria.

Enzymes are protein molecules that break down and digest our food. Without them, food is not properly digested; therefore, nutrients are not fully absorbed by the body and metabolic deficiencies can result. Enzymes are present in all raw foods, including raw meat. The body has its own stores of enzymes so when you, or your dog, eat enzyme-deficient food, the body must draw on its own enzyme reserves from organs and tissues. Research studies support a strong correlation between enzyme deficiency and diseases, both acute and chronic. You can overcome this problem by feeding your dog more raw foods, either mixed in with his usual food or as a treat, and you can also purchase enzyme supplements to add to his food. Several manufacturers market digestive enzymes for dogs; others include digestive enzymes in their dog supplement formulas. One of these products can be particularly helpful if your dog has a digestive problem, if he has been on a poor quality diet, or if he is getting on in years.

It might be a tad "out there" for a dog training book, but here's a well-known tenet of Eastern philosophy you can play with: Life energy in its most subtle form is rooted in thought. For example, when a carrot is just a seed, it cannot sustain an animal. Picked at the optimum moment of growth, however, the carrot is a great source of vitamins and minerals. There is a perfect moment for carrots to be pulled from the ground and eaten—the perfect moment of optimum health-giving properties. But what if you can't pick and eat a carrot at the perfect time? According to Eastern thought, humans are unique in that they can actually infuse health and energy *into* food. It's a matter of thinking good, healthy thoughts and willing those healthy thoughts into the food you are preparing or eating. Does this work? Some studies indicate that focused thoughts can be transmuted into health-giving medicine. The best example of all this is the scientifically measured results of placebos. Whenever you prepare food for yourself or your dog, imagine infusing the food with health and "life energy." This is really not so different from a belief in prayer or the power of a deity to heal. Whatever you believe, what have you got to lose?

Problem No. 2: Processing Destroys Nutrients

In addition to the lack of beneficial bacteria and enzymes, there are other problems with processed food. As we mentioned, our goal is to feed the highest quality food to our dogs, which means presenting them with the least processed foods we can find. Whether it's canned, dry kibble, or semimoist, processing destroys a good deal of the nutritional value of the food. Of these three choices, canned food is the best because fewer nutrients are destroyed in the canning process than by the other methods. Most kibbles are low-quality foods that have undergone more processing than canned foods. They are pressure cooked, flavored, colored, dehydrated, and then sprayed with fat to make them tasty. In addition to the loss of nutrients due to all of this processing, Alfred J. Plechner, D.V.M., says in his book *Pet Allergies* that he finds many animals have a food intolerance or allergy to kibble. He writes, "I believe the reason is because kibble is a concentrated collection of many of the foods that are the most allergenic for animals. Practically everything on my allergic HIT List is found in those sacks: beef, milk, wheat, corn, yeast, fish meal, plus a bountiful array of chemical additives. There's probably some mold, hair, and other impurities in there as well." All of that being said, there are some pet food manufacturers that have taken great effort in producing the freshest, highest quality kibble possible.

Semimoist foods are the poorest quality foods. They contain a large amount of artificial flavorings, preservatives, and sugars, which are required in order to keep them in an ever-moist state. Finally, in all processed foods, but particularly with most kibbles and in all semimoist foods, the protein is of low quality and difficult to digest.

Problem No. 3: Most Commercial Pet Foods Are Made of Low-Quality Meats

Most commercial dog foods don't contain "human quality" ingredients, which they consider too expensive. Therefore, most pet food manufacturers use ingredients such as meat by-products that are not considered fit for human consumption. The term the U.S. government uses for these meat ingredients is "4-D," which stands for dead, dying, diseased, and disabled. Much of this 4-D meat has actually rotted (they called it fermented) and has phosphoric acid added to stop the rotting process. You certainly wouldn't want your dog to eat a cancerous tumor that the government calls "safe" because it has been sterilized but, in fact, this is the case with many commercial dog foods. And it's not just grocery store brands; even some "premium" brands sold by veterinarians are not so premium when you know what they contain.

Andi Brown, author of *The Whole Pet Diet: Eight Weeks to Great Health for Dogs and Cats*, and the Director of Halo, Purely for Pets, which makes pet foods good enough for humans to eat, explains it this way: "Many pet foods, even the so-called natural ones, may include by-products, which are foodstuffs rejected for human consumption but permitted in pet foods. This includes beaks, feet, feathers, hooves, hair . . . and bones. Meat rendering plants purchase and process one hundred million pounds of waste material every year, including roadkill, ground-up diseased animal parts, and fecal matter, which can then be incorporated into pet foods and labeled 'by-products.' 'Meat meal' (including chicken meal or fish meal) is a more pleasant-sounding name for such by-products. Saddest of all, and as truly awful as it sounds, over the years several pet food manufacturers have been caught processing the remains of dog and cat carcasses that had been euthanized, obviously with highly toxic substances, including their pet tags and collars."

I have no idea how widespread the practice of selling euthanized animals as an ingredient for pet food is, but years ago a professional working in an animal shelter told me this was happening at his shelter. According to Ann N. Martin, in her highly researched and acclaimed book *Food Pets Die For*, some veterinarians and rendering plants say it is common, while pet food manufacturers vehemently deny it.

Problem No. 4: Many Ingredients in Commercial Foods Are "Not Fit for Human Consumption"

Commercial pet foods often contain many other ingredients of the lowest quality, such as rancid or moldy grains, rancid oils, and other refuse from food processing plants that is not considered fit for human consumption. This includes the so-called natural flavor that is sprayed onto dry food to make it tasty and appealing to dogs. In addition, pet food companies sometimes include other items you wouldn't consider to be food. Even peanut hulls have been added to food and labeled as "vegetable fiber." Why should our beloved companion animals be subject to eating non-nutritious foods that contain any of these ingredients?

Problem No. 5: Additives, Flavor Enhancers, Sugars, and Chemical Preservatives Are Not Good for Fido

Many commercial pet foods also contain dyes, stabilizers, thickeners, "flavor enhancers," and chemical preservatives, such as sodium nitrite, sodium nitrate, butylated hydroxyanisole (BHA), butylated hydroxytoluene (BHT), monosodium glutamate (MSG), sodium metabisulfite, and ethoxyquin. Some of these preservatives, such as ethoxyquin and sodium nitrate, have been linked to cancer. These preservatives must be listed on the label if the pet food manufacturer adds them to the food. However, pet food manufacturers often buy ingredients that already contain preservatives such as ethoxyquin and, in those cases, are not required to list them on the label. Various forms of sugar, including corn syrup, and excessive salt are also added to the food to entice a dog to a particular food.

So . . . What Should You Feed Your Dog?

The very best diet for your dog is a homemade food made of organic ingredients, along with quality supplements. This means meats and other ingredients that are free of pesticides, antibiotics, and hormones. However, since time and money are prime considerations for many people, below you'll find several options to raise the nutritional bar. As I mentioned earlier, a number of factors determine your dog's unique nutritional requirements, including her age, breed, size, daily activity level, emotional make-up, physical sensitivities, and tolerances. Most veterinarians, like most medical doctors, have studied only rudimentary nutrition. Many veterinarians actually sell brands of food that contain questionable ingredients. A veterinarian who is trained in holistic modalities is more likely to be the one to help you tailor the highest quality diet.

*Option 1: Canned Food and/or Kibble Made from
"Human Grade" Ingredients with Extras*

While homemade food is the absolute best, for many people it's just not something they want to do. So, the next best alternative is to find a wet food (in cans or pouches) and/or kibble made by a manufacturer of natural pet food. Then mix in a few of the raw food items and nutritional supplements listed on page 31 as "The Extras."

When selecting a commercial food, remember that even though a company advertises "all natural," its pet food may contain questionable ingredients. Short of visiting the pet food processing plant—and tracing the suppliers of meats, grains, and other ingredients—it is extremely difficult to judge the quality of manufactured pet foods. One indicator of a higher quality is the use of "human grade" meats that are labeled USDA (United States Department of Agriculture) and other human grade ingredients and no by-products. While very few companies use human grade ingredients, if a label or product brochure indicates this, you can be pretty sure the quality is much higher than other pet foods. Of course, it also means the food will be more expensive than other brands.

Remember, a wet food is always nutritionally superior to a dry kibble, however, as we mentioned earlier, there are high-quality kibbles available from companies that use pure, natural ingredients. Many veterinarians believe that kibble has an additional benefit in that it helps to keep teeth clean, exercise the jaws, and promote the health of the gums. My dog Molly's diet consists of half canned food and half kibble with the extras (including raw ingredients) and she just loves her daily treat of a nice big raw carrot that she holds between her paws while devouring. This proportion of half canned food and half kibble is acceptable, but any amount of canned food is superior to none.

Option 2: A Raw Diet
Raw meats include beef, fish, poultry, venison, lamb, and rabbit. Many people have two concerns when they consider switching to raw meats:

1. Can the uncooked bones cause breaks or punctures to the stomach and intestines? I had this concern myself and was assured that raw bones, even chicken and turkey bones, can't harm your dog. But cooked bones or frozen raw bones can. It seems the cooking or freezing makes the bones splinter and that's what does the damage in your dog's stomach and intestine. Many of my friends have been feeding raw meat bones like chicken necks and backs to their dogs for years, and they've never had a problem.
2. Another concern is the possibility that bacteria in raw meat can cause illness. A dog's digestive system in not like a human's. Dogs have developed a digestive system that is short and acidic, making it ideal for dealing with bacteria. Even the bacteria found in old buried bones don't prove problematic. There is a rare exception, since some hot dogs contain the bacteria listeria which is a potential hazard for dogs. In the book *Becoming the Chef Your Dog Thinks You Are*, authors Micki and Yogi Voisard explain: "If you are using ready-to-eat hot dogs as a treat for your dog, cook them first. There is no nutritional value in hot dogs anyway,

so cooking will not compromise their use but it will kill the chance of the bacteria listeria. If your dog has a weakened immune system, dealing with listeria is the last thing he needs." They suggest buying nitrite-free hot dogs (and bacon) without fillers and preservatives. All this being said, our digestive systems are another story. Always be sure to wash your hands after touching uncooked meat.

Option 3: Molly's Favorite Gourmet Dinner

¾ cup brown rice cooked in 2 cups water (Note: other grains can be substituted; see "Grains" in Option 4 below)

1¼ cups cubed (¼- to ½-inch cubes) organic free-range turkey or chicken (preferably raw)

¼ cup raw grated zucchini

¼ cup broccoli in small pieces (lightly steamed because raw broccoli sometimes causes gas)

1½ teaspoons extra virgin olive oil
Vitamin and mineral supplement (according to label directions)
Enzyme supplement (according to label directions)

1. Put the water into a pan along with the rice. Bring to a boil and then reduce heat to a simmer, cover, and cook as directed. You want it to be slightly overcooked so it is more digestible for your dog.
2. Mix all of the ingredients and serve.

Option 4: Homemade Diet with All the Options
The following homemade diet is courtesy of Mary Brennan, D.V.M. She has updated the homemade diet that was given in her book *The Natural Dog* as she now believes that grains should be limited in a dog's diet, according to more recent understandings in canine nutrition. It is a good basic diet for adult dogs. To make homemade food for a puppy or a dog who is overweight, suffers from food allergies, or requires a restricted protein diet

(such as kidney patients), refer to Dr. Brennan's *The Natural Dog, The Whole Pet Diet: Eight Weeks to Great Health for Dogs and Cats* by Andi Brown, *Natural Nutrition for Dogs and Cats* by Kymythy Schultze, and *Becoming The Chef Your Dog Thinks You Are* by Micki and Yogi Voisard.

Dr. Brennan's diet gives you a lot of range to pick ingredients that you prefer or that your dog particularly likes. I suggest multiplying the indicated quantities to make large batches of the food. Then keep three or four days' supply in the refrigerator and freeze the rest. However, don't freeze more than three or four days' supply in any one container. Be sure to allow a day or so to defrost a container before you need it.

If you're cooking the meat portion of the ingredients instead of using it raw, you'll see that it can be cooked in a couple of different ways. One method I recommend is to prepare chicken, for example, by simmering it in water in a pot on the stove. Then you can mix the cooking water in with the food and end up with a stew-like consistency that most dogs just love. So it is easily digestible, the grain should be overcooked. Use 2½ cups of water for each cup of uncooked grain. Bring to a boil and then turn to a simmer, cover, and cook for up to an hour.

Grain: Many nutritionists suggest limiting or avoiding grains altogether, so this is an optional ingredient. Brown rice and oatmeal seem to agree with my dogs, especially in helping with allergies and to keep their stools firm. That being said, grains have been reported to exacerbate some dog's allergies and, as mentioned previously, dogs don't need carbohydrates in their diet. If you are using grains, I suggest cooked brown rice, oats (usually in the form of oatmeal), quinoa, amaranth, or spelt. (*Note:* Although brown rice is preferable to white rice, some dogs may suffer from digestive problems and do better on a mixture of half brown rice and half basmati rice until their systems get used to the extra bulk of the brown rice. Basmati rice has more nutrients than most white rice.)

Protein: Use lean hamburger, chicken, or turkey (preferably raw). Choose lean meat with a little fat. If using raw meat, you can minimize the possibility of harmful bacteria such as salmonella by making sure it is fresh and taking precautions in your care and handling of it. If using cooked meat, preferred cooking methods are broiling or boiling. However, if you cook the meat remember to remove all bones because cooked bones can be a choking hazard.

Vegetables: Experiment to find the vegetables your dog likes best. Try grated raw zucchini, yellow squash, or carrots; chopped alfalfa sprouts; lightly steamed broccoli, asparagus (most dogs love it), green beans, turnips, parsnips, or peas. Try other vegetables to see how your dog responds, but avoid onions and cabbage because they can cause digestive upsets. If your dog doesn't like the vegetables at first, try chopping them finely and mixing well into the food.

Oil: Choose any high-quality vegetable oil: safflower, corn, sesame, wheat germ, sunflower, flaxseed, or extra virgin olive oil. Or buy an oil supplement for pets from a natural pet food company. Dream Coat by Halo, Purely for Pets contains a full spectrum of essential fatty acids and can be used as a substitute for any of the combinations of oils I recommend. Omega Nutrition manufactures a high-quality flaxseed oil that's an excellent source of the Omega 3 fatty acids. During the winter months give an extra dose of oils a few times a week to compensate for the drier skin and coat. *Note:* High-quality oils are cold pressed and should be refrigerated after opening. Wheat germ and flaxseed oil are extremely high in nutrients but turn rancid easily. These oils should be refrigerated as soon as you get them home—even before opening.

Vitamin and Mineral Supplements: Choose a vitamin and mineral supplement formulated for dogs from a natural pet food company. Be sure it is made of natural whole food ingredients and contains no preservatives or artificial ingredients. Use according to directions on the label. I'm especially fond of Anita's Vita-Mineral Mix. This powdered blend of delicious, raw foods is great for the coat and skin, and since it contains an abundance of B vitamins, it helps to calm the nerves of a dog under stress. It's a beneficial supplement during stressful times of dog training.

Enzyme Supplement for Dogs: Use according to directions on the label. I really like "Missing Link." I also like the products by Probiotics.

Antioxidant Supplement for Dogs: Use according to directions on the label.

FIX-IT-YOURSELF BASIC DIET—QUANTITIES
Use the following chart to determine how much food to make per day. Multiply these quantities to make food for more than one dog or to make more than one day's supply. Remember that each dog's metabolism differs and these are only approximate amounts.

When you serve the food, you can add additional nutrients as well as variety by mixing in a few extras from the list that follows.

A more scientific explanation of which meats and grains are best for their dogs according to traditional Chinese medicine can be found in the book *Four Paws, Five Directions* by Cheryl Schwartz, D.V.M. This thorough book explains how certain meats and grains can be better depending on the dog's constitutional type. Without going into detail here, this simply means that a dog's diet can be tailored to help counteract imbalances in his physiology. The factors that are used to determine the best types of foods for your dog include whether she is sluggish, laid back and calm, overweight, assertive, wanting attention, and so on.

The Extras
By adding some raw foods or high-quality supplements, you will be upgrading the quality and adding energy and nutrients to

Dog's Weight in Pounds	5	10	25	40	60	80
Grain	½ cup	1 cup	2 cups	2½ cups	4 cups	5 cups
Protein	2½ T.	⅓ cup	⅔ cup	1⅛ cups	1⅓ cups	1¾ cups
Vegetables	1 T.	⅛ cup	¼ cup	⅓ cups	½ cup	⅔ cup
Oil	¼ tsp.	½ tsp.	1 tsp.	1½ tsp.	2 tsp.	2½ tsp.
Vitamin & Mineral Supplement	Use according to directions on the label.					
Enzyme Supplement	Use according to directions on the label.					

the diet. This is especially important if you are feeding canned food or kibble (or a mixture of the two). *At the very least, include some raw vegetables daily.* Here are some of the raw foods Dr. Mary Brennan recommends:

Raw vegetables: Add ⅛ to ¼ cup of raw vegetables for each 10 pounds of your dog's weight. Choose one of the following that your dog likes best: grated carrot, zucchini, chopped lettuce, green beans, or lightly steamed broccoli. (Or give a whole raw carrot as a treat from time to time.)

Raw fruits: Give a small amount of raw fruit such as apples and watermelon a couple times a week.

Organic meat: Add ⅛ to ¼ cup of raw, broiled, or baked organic meat for each 10 pounds of your dog's weight. Choose from chicken, turkey, beef, or lamb; free range is the best. However, if you cook the meat remember to remove all bones because cooked bones can be a choking hazard.

Raw egg: Eggs are a great source of antibodies. Feed a raw egg once a week or so. To minimize the possibility of salmonella poisoning, use fresh organic eggs from range-fed chickens. How do you know if an egg is fresh? It will sink to the bottom of a bowl of cold water. If it floats, it's a bad egg.

Garlic: Add ½ clove of minced fresh garlic to the food for each 10 pounds of your dog's weight or give a capsule of Kyolic or other high-potency garlic. If desired, garlic can be added daily.

Acidophilus: Add ¼ to ½ teaspoon acidophilus liquid or powder or the contents of one capsule once a week. Acidophilus is found in the refrigerator section of natural foods stores. This will help the body keep a proper balance of beneficial bacteria.

Yogurt: Give ⅛ to ¼ cup for a small dog or ½ to ¾ cup for a large dog. Use a plain, natural culture yogurt from the health food store. Add to the food or serve as a treat occasionally, up to several times a week.

Cottage cheese: Cottage cheese is an excellent source of protein that is easy to digest. Add a small amount to the food up to three times a week. If your dog is ill, cottage cheese can be fed daily.

Goat's milk and cow's milk: Goat's milk is naturally homogenized and therefore easy to digest. It also has a more complete nutrient balance than cow's milk. *Do not feed cow's milk* in the form of cream, half-and-half, or whole milk as these forms of cow's milk *often cause diarrhea*. Some dogs don't have the proper enzymes to digest these products.

Cheese: I use cheese for treats and almost all of my clients do also. But every dog is different. If you choose to use cheese, slowly acclimate your dog by adding three or four small pieces to his daily meals to make sure there's no problem. If your dog becomes constipated or has loose stools after eating cheese, use meat products and high-quality dry treats that are made by reputable pet food companies instead of cheese.

Vitamin and mineral supplements: Choose a vitamin and mineral supplement for dogs made from high-quality natural ingredients by a natural pet products company. These products come in powders that are added to the food, such as Anitra's Vita-Mineral Mix (from Halo, Purely for Pets), Body Guard (from Pro-Tec), or Good Gravy (from Pet Nutrition). Other products, such as Vita-Dreams (from Halo, Purely for Pets), come in the form of tasty chewable supplements.

Antioxidant supplements: Antioxidants are supplements that combat the body's toxic invaders called free radicals. Beta-carotene and vitamins C and E are called antioxidant supplements because they play a supportive role in this process. In addition, there are products on the market made from whole food sources such as sprouted wheat that promote the body's own antioxidant enzyme supplies. These products include Bioguard and Vitality from Biogenetics. (Even dogs that have food sensitivities to wheat are generally able to take these supplements with no problem because the protein gluten found in the grain of wheat is not found in the wheat sprouts.)

Changing Your Dog's Diet

When you put your dog on a high-quality diet, it's likely you will notice the difference in a few days or weeks. Ongoing health problems may disappear. The dog will have more energy, a shinier coat, less "dog odor," fewer bowel movements, and less gas.

However, it sometimes takes a few days or a week for a dog to adjust to a radical change in the diet. A high-quality, *nutrient dense* diet can cause a temporary cleansing process. The most common short-term symptoms of this adjustment are looser stools and more gas. You can minimize any upset to the dog's system by gradually incorporating the new diet over a ten-day period. Unless your dog has a sensitivity or allergy to one of the ingredients in the food, the transition to the higher quality diet will lead to a more youthful, energetic appearance in short order.

> If you think your dog is suffering from a food sensitivity or allergy, check with your veterinarian or use the muscle checking method of testing the food as described in *The Natural Dog,* by Mary Brennan.

Ingredient Number 2: Play

A bridge of communication between you and your dog is created and strengthened with the introduction of fun and humor, which are the very essence of play. Your dog will learn much more quickly if your attitude is playful. Certainly both your own as well as your dog's stress levels are reduced when you're having fun. A smile, a laugh, a good-natured grin speak volumes. Just as humor can bring down communication barriers among people of different cultures, so too does it bridge the gap between species.

Humor is a release valve for the ever-present stresses of everyday life. The idea is that fun, playfulness, and humor play a huge role. With the "ingredient" of play, you make the training process a game.

> A Great Pyrenees falls out of a tenth-story window. He is lying there, surrounded by a crowd, when a police officer comes up and asks, "What happened?" The dog responds, "I don't know. I just got here myself."

Patty Ruzzo, a well-known dog trainer, aptly stated that there is no such thing as commands in training—it's all about tricks. From the dog's point of view, that makes perfect sense. If you make it fun, every behavior you ask for is like performing a trick to your dog. Sitting, lying down, coming when called—it's all about getting your dog to do things because it's in her best interest. Playfulness is an attitude that benefits both you and your dog not only for the joy it creates, but because it also teaches the dog to focus on you as the source of all good things. This helps create reliable behavior in other areas.

Did you hear about the Border collie that went to see his veterinarian? The vet told him to stick out his tongue and go stand in front of the window. The dog followed the directions and then asked, "What's this for?" The vet said, "Nothing. I just don't like that Springer spaniel in the house across the street."

I suggest a minimum of two 15-minute play periods each day. If your dog initiates the play period, such as nudging you with a ball and asking you to throw it, this is a wonderful way to practice positive dog training. Simply ask her to do something, like sit or lie down first, and then throw the ball as a reward. Besides fetch, games include hide-and-go-seek, tracking and scent discrimination (teaching a dog to identify one object from another by its scent), identifying up to 100 different toys and putting each one in a toy box, jumping up to chase bubbles (nontoxic) and tug. I am currently working with a one-year-old Australian Shepherd who likes to push a volley ball around with his front legs. So we're teaching him to push the ball into a soccer net. This brings up an important point: if you see your dog doing something that looks like a game to you . . . it is a game. Work with whatever your dog shows you.

Playing Tug

Tug is a great game as long as it is done correctly. In each play session, you will sometimes ask your dog to drop the object and other times let him take it from your hand. However, he can take it only with your permission. Say "okay" before you release the object. Seven out of ten times you might ask your dog to "drop it" and three out of ten times you give your dog permission to "take it."

Here are a few rules for playing tug:

- When your dog is holding an object in his mouth, do not lift him off the ground by holding onto the other end of that object.
- Avoid jerking the object back and forth.
- The dog must learn "drop it." (See page 233 for the "drop it" rules.)
- Before releasing the tug object, always say "okay."

Games to avoid include chasing laser lights, which can quickly turn into an obsessive-compulsive behavior, and roughhouse games, including face grabbing and "gitcha-gitcha" teasing games played with your hands or feet. Teasing games can inadvertently teach a dog to mouth and bite, which is obviously something you want to avoid.

Play affects the development of the physical, mental, and emotional life of your dog. Proper play helps to develop your dog's coordination, timing, and the skills needed for hunting and self-defense. You can provide all kinds of playful stimulation by enrolling in agility, flyball, herding, the aforementioned tracking or water work classes. See more on this later in this chapter under Ingredient Number 5: Exercise.

Play also includes the use of toys. But toys should not be left around for the dog to play with by herself. If you provide the toys, your dog's attention is directed to you as the source of entertainment. If you're the source, your dog will more readily listen to what you have to say because she can access the toys only through you. You may, however, permit an exception to the rule and leave one or two chew toys around to relieve boredom.

A dog had a dream that God told her to get her act together. So, she joined a 12-step program, bought some new clothes, and started practicing yoga. She now had a healthy glow and looked like a new canine. Suddenly, she was struck by lightning and wound up in heaven, where God didn't talk to her. She shouted to God, "You told me in my dreams to better myself! I joined a 12-step program, got a new wardrobe, and took weekly yoga classes. Now you don't even talk to me!" God responded, "Don't holler at me. I didn't recognize you."

Suggested Toys

Chew toys: Although there are lots of chew toys available for dogs today, a few of them are in a class by themselves. I suggest Nyla bones, Kongs, Bully Sticks, and chicken strips to keep your dog's interest and massage the gums. They also tend to last awhile. Whatever you give your dog to chew on, make sure you supervise. The last thing you want is for your dog to choke on anything that can break into small pieces. For that reason, I discourage chewies made from hooves, rawhides, and pig ears.

Smart toys: I also recommend so-called smart toys that you can fill with treats before you go to work, such as Kongs, Buster Cubes, and food-dispensing plastic balls. Dogs can have hours of fun playing with these toys and intermittently being rewarded when a treat falls out.

People toys: Soft Frisbees, tennis balls, and virtually anything else your dog might have fun with as long as it's nontoxic. One of my favorite toys is the "Go-Dog-Go," which is a tennis ball–retrieving machine. You simply teach your dog to put the tennis ball into the bucket and a motor throws it out again for the dog to retrieve. This super device allows you to sit on the porch and watch your dog run back and forth retrieving! It's great for any dog who has a big enough jaw to fetch a tennis ball and is especially good for energetic pups and dogs who have lots of energy.

Squeaky toys: Squeaky toys are great but make sure you strictly supervise their use as many dogs love ripping them open to find the squeaker inside, which can be a choking hazard.

Bubbles: Some dogs love playing with bubbles. So buy some nontoxic bubbles and have a ball!

Before I forget, what vegetable do dogs like the most? *Collie-flower.*

So let the games begin. Start with hide-and-seek, which is described on page 181. And, by the way, be sure to tell your dog a joke every day, too. He may not comprehend the words, but he'll sure get the feeling!

Ingredient Number 3: Socialization

We ask our dogs to live with us under our terms and conditions. Therefore, it's important to socialize them so they can more easily adapt to their human family, neighbors, and other animals. Socialization deals with stimulating the five senses. It is the exposure to sights, sounds, smells, tastes, and touch. Socialization is interaction with life and all it has to offer, and being able to adapt to its challenges. "It's about surviving errors," as Dr. Karen Overall puts it.

Figure 2.1

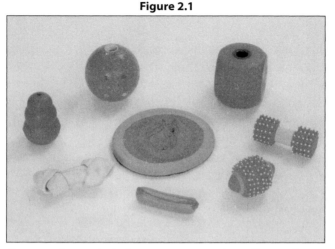

Suggested toys include smart toys such as Kongs, Buster Cubes, and other treat-dispensing toys, as well as soft Frisbees, Nyla bones, squeaky toys, and tennis balls.

If a dog is deprived of social stimulation, both physical and emotional health are compromised. A lack of socialization can lead to health problems, as well as obsessive behaviors such as tail chasing, self-mutilation, scratching, biting, destruction of the environment (including walls, floors, and furniture), interminable spells of barking, chewing, and various manifestations of aggression. Because of the lack of physical, emotional, and mental stimulation, many domesticated animals don't get along well with others.

The first sixteen weeks of a dog's life are the most influential in shaping the adult dog's temperament and behavior. All through puppyhood, the mother dog socializes her pups through tactile stimulation, using her tongue to massage her puppies to teach them how to control elimination. She talks to them in a language made up of sounds, touches, smells, and body postures. And as the pups grow older, the bond of social familiarity is strengthened through this network of communication. Pups become aware of brothers and sisters vying for their mother's milk and learn the language Nature patiently teaches them.

There are two types of socialization—active and passive. You are involved in actively socializing your dog when you introduce her to toys, games, neighbors, friends, and strangers. With passive socialization, nature is involved to a greater degree. Dogs learn by interacting with the sights, sounds, smells, and touches of other animals, plants, and environments while away from you. They learn the consequences of their actions as individuals on their own. Obviously, it's important to provide an environment in which you avoid life-threatening situations, such as putting your dog in a room with a literal or figurative pack of wolves. But the more she can learn and experience about herself on her own, the more she develops confidence, learns to adapt, and is able to bounce back from stressful situations.

Your dog is socialized through playing, being groomed, training, and the everyday challenges you place before her. Take your dog everywhere—in your car and to the office, supermarket, park, dog training classes, and visiting friends and relatives. Take her to the veterinarian's office for a visit even when she doesn't have an appointment. (However, wherever you take your dog, do not leave her unattended!)

The following will give you a general idea of what to look for in your dog's behavior during various stages of his maturation. These periods can vary somewhat depending on size and breed. And you'll also see some overlap between the periods. It's important to remember that every dog is unique and not to ask more of your dog than she can possibly do. Physically, mentally, emotionally, and socially, each dog has his or her own individual personality, ability, and unique way of doing things. The skill is learning when to challenge, when to back off, and how to balance the two.

Stages of Maturation
The following is a breakdown of the stages your puppy will pass through in the first three years of his life.

Eight Weeks to Ten Weeks
This is called the critical imprint or fear impact period. It is said that during these two weeks sharp noises and rough handling can have more of a negative impact on future behavior. It can take months, and in some cases, years, to recover from experiences that frighten a puppy during this time period. That being said, life happens and sometimes a puppy is exposed to frightening experiences before we adopt her or as a part of everyday life, such as the sound of a vacuum cleaner, a child who is having a tantrum, or a banging kitchen pan. You can help shape your puppy's future reactions to things in life that startle or scare her by your own reactions. How you act when scary things do occur during this period, as well as throughout the first year of your dog's life, can have a tremendous influence in shaping your dog's temperament. Let's say you unintentionally drop a kitchen pan on the floor. Your dog's immediate response might be to run and hide. *Your* immediate reaction is to want to coddle your dog and run to her saying "Oh, I'm so sorry. Are you okay? Everything's okay, don't worry." And you pick your little puppy up and hug and kiss her. What your dog learns in this situation however is that: (1) loud noises are to be feared, and (2) my human is reinforcing my fearful behavior. Although our normal compassionate reaction is to support our puppy and try to lovingly assuage her fear, we are actually reinforcing it. So what do you do when the pot falls? You immediately launch the "happy-treat" routine. You become a great actor and say, "Yay! The pot fell! Here's a piece of turkey! Wasn't that fun!" And then feed more yummy treats. What you've done is changed the way the dog feels about the pot by redirecting her attention away from her fear. This is done by your happy reaction and by associating the sound with the food. Over the weeks to come, you can practice desensitization exercises with your puppy using falling pots and other unexpected sounds. Eventually she'll say, "ho-hum, a pot dropped." See desensitization to sound protocols on page 282.

Eight Weeks to Fourteen Weeks

This period overlaps with the previous one because it is from eight weeks to fourteen weeks that your puppy goes through what is called the primary socialization window. Also, no two dogs experience changes at the same rate. I repeat that it is during this period of time that socialization, or the lack of it, has the most impact on the shaping of your dog's temperament and behavior. It's very important that you continue to socialize and train your puppy during these formative weeks, as well as throughout her adult life. Socialization builds your dog's self-confidence and really develops her emotional "bounce-back" ability. This means the more she interacts with her environment and is provided the opportunity to learn from her mistakes, the more even-tempered she will become. Training includes housetraining (see Eliminating, page 257) and beginning to work on behaviors such as sit, lie down, stand, stay, come when called, heel, go to your spot, and so on. It's also very important that you teach your dog to control his biting during this period (see Mouthing and Bite Inhibition, page 262). Even at this early age, puppies respond well to clicker and target training.

Many veterinarians suggest keeping your dog indoors or on your property during the first four months of her life until she is fully immunized in order to avoid health risks. This premise actually threatens the growth of sound temperament and non-aggressive behavior. The primary socialization window is small and you want to do all you can to teach your dog to love people and animals. Obviously you want to protect your puppy from health risks so you must avoid neighborhood dogs you are unfamiliar with or those you know have temperament problems (dogs who are aggressive or play rough) or health issues. You should avoid dog parks and anyplace your puppy isn't welcome . . . not everyone likes puppies (hard as that is to believe!).

The idea is to control your puppy's environment to the best of your ability for safety and provide opportunities for your puppy to safely explore his new life. I suggest you make up a list of your intended puppy socialization exposures. Each day you'll be able to check off the socialization experience and this will encourage you to keep going.

Puppy Socialization Exercises
Here are some suggestions for ways to socialize your puppy.

Handle Your Dog: Lift your dog in the air while gently stroking her and speaking to her. Begin this handling and verbal communication as soon as you bring the puppy into your home. Continue safe handling for very short periods several times a day, occasionally associating a yummy treat while you are touching and stroking. Gradually extend the snuggling time until your dog trusts you for as long as you hold her. (See Handling on page 272.) Each day introduce one new person, including children, adults, men, women, and everything in between. Have each person repeat what you are doing. The key here is short periods of handling, using treats, being gentle, having fun and exercising safety. Make handling a positive experience!

Environment Enrichment Exercises: As the puppy grows, let her explore safe surroundings, both inside and outside and put toys and novel stimuli, such as balls of different sizes (baseballs, basketballs, beach balls), stuffed animals, and lawn tools, on the living room floor and in the yard. A good trick is to play the Hansel and Gretel game. This is done by leaving a trail of treats leading up to the strange new object. If the environment is safe, leave your dog alone to figure out what to do without you. Dogs can use this time to learn to be brave on their own rather than always leaning on you for support.

Introduce Other Animals: You should introduce other animals to your puppy, using strict supervision, of course. (Review the safety precautions in Chapter 7.)

Introduce the Collar: Just before offering a meal, put the new collar on your dog's neck. When she's finished eating, remove it. Do this for three days and then just leave it on her all the time. Caution: if you have another dog in the house and they like to grab each other when they play, REMOVE THE COLLARS for safety. Puppies and older dogs can get their jaws caught in a collar, sometimes resulting in a dog being choked to death.

Puppy Kindergarten Class: Remember, the more you socialize your dog early on, the more you shape her temperament and establish a loving bond. Find a puppy kindergarten class where your puppy can romp and roll with others.

Four Months to Eight Months

This stage is called the "first independence" window, during which it's a dog's job to really begin to "test" the reward hierarchy pyramid of life. Basically this means the dog is figuring out who or what provides the greatest rewards in life: you or the sights, sounds, and smells of Mother Nature. Although your dog may have remained close to you for the first six months, all of a sudden he will be off running and not listening to your repeated calls to return. With this in mind, always keep your dog safely tethered or leashed to you. I have had many clients who boasted that their six-, seven-, or eight-month-old dog was reliably staying by their side and coming when called. Next thing you know, I hear their dog has run away, chasing a squirrel or another dog.

It is also during this period that the second set of teeth begin to appear. Make sure you provide plenty of proper chew toys to help avoid chewing and biting problems during this teething period. To sum up, keep your training routine fun and maintain socialization exercises but be sure to go at your dog's own learning pace. And keep your dog safe!

In multiple-dog households, it's normal for both puppies and dogs to exhibit some non-injurious aggression as part of their maturation process. Play aggression teaches dogs to inhibit their bite, and injuries are rare. If you feel the intensity of play is getting too intense, such as one puppy or dog yelping and the other continuing to bite and even drawing blood, separate them and call a professional. This degree of aggression, in which one dog intentionally injures another, is abnormal behavior. It can be attributed to genetic factors and/or a lack of proper socialization during the first fourteen weeks of the dog's life.

Six Months to Eighteen Months
Although I don't like to anthropomorphize, to help explain these stages I am using terms more related to human stages of development. So said, this is the "teenage period" in a dog's life, the period of sexual maturity. Your dog continues his life-long journey of experimentation, learning what behaviors produce positive consequences and what situations are to be avoided. But during this period, based on what was passed along genetically and how much socialization was accomplished up to this point, it's possible his experimentation might be a bit more assertive and even aggressive. For other puppies, there may be moments when he may suddenly seem reluctant to try something new. It is your job to be your dog's guardian and teacher—which means no matter what he does at any given moment, you will maintain your loving, patient, and consistent direction.

This is the period during which neutering or spaying has traditionally been done. However, these days, many veterinarians are neutering and spaying dogs much younger than in the past, starting at the age of eight weeks. I do not have enough data to comment on this so you might ask your veterinarian at what age neutering or spaying should be done. And remember, if you are going to breed your dog, be sure you are in the position to take responsibility for every puppy.

Around the eleventh or twelfth month of age, your dog may severely try your patience and act like a teenage bozo. Don't worry—it's just part of the growing up process. There will also be moments when he seems to be God's gift to dogs. For months, he may do a Jekyl/Hyde thing, as he bounces back and forth between acting out of control one moment and then go back to being his happy, jovial, "I'll-do-anything-for-my-human" self.

The bottom line is to be patient, be consistent, and continue your compassionate role as guardian and protector.

Eighteen Months to Three Years

It is during this stage of maturation that reliable behavior starts to take hold. With an optimum training environment you can get reliable behavior in less time; however, in the typical busy household in which training is inconsistent, it is only when your dog reaches emotional maturity at approximately eighteen months that she can be expected to reliably respond to your requests. Smaller dogs mature more quickly than larger breeds. Some dogs reach social maturity earlier than eighteen months while others don't reach this stage until the age of three.

There will be ups and downs in the training process but if you maintain an even keel, you will find that, with consistency, your dog really does get the picture of who she is as a member of the family and what is expected of her. Because of your dog's increasing reliability at this stage, this is a good time for her to be introduced to animal-assisted therapy—with plans to visit hospitals, nursing homes, and schools.

Sometimes two dogs who have been friendly in the past may suddenly seem to be at odds. This happens most frequently with female siblings and even two females who aren't related. Two males also may prove more testy. Consistent training and socialization will go a long way in helping dogs to learn how to live harmoniously. In most cases, they learn that they can get what they want without the need for aggression. However, if you are having problems with aggression, call a professional trainer immediately.

SOCIAL FACILITATION

It is helpful to look at a concept from the world of psychology called "social facilitation." If one dog is chewing a bone, the second dog will want to join in—normally by stealing the bone, even if he already has one. If one puppy goes to get a drink from a bowl, all the puppies decide to get a drink. If one dog starts digging, others seem to think, "What's so good over there? I better start digging with her." This is the way you get a dog interested in toys. Make a huge fuss over a new toy and watch your dog's interest grow.

Of course, social facilitation also occurs in other ways between humans and dogs. Dogs often pick up on our emotions and behaviors and follow suit. When I am called to do private consultations, I often find problems are directly related to people inadvertently teaching their dogs to be aggressive because of their own fears. In her book, *Excel-erated Learning,* Dr. Pamela Reid says, "People socially transmit fears to their dogs via social facilitation all the time. Women who are wary of passing by men at night may quickly end up with a dog that barks ferociously at men. Some people have a hard time because of tentativeness or fear when someone is following behind. The dog, feeling the tension, quickly develops the same fear and, sometimes generalizes the fear to all strangers or all dogs. This sort of problem is extremely difficult to treat." In short, there are many subtle ways in which we communicate our emotions to our dogs that directly affect their behavior. And, of course, many positive emotions are also transferred from human to dog.

Ingredient Number 4: Quiet Time

Just as humans sometimes need a time out from the day's activities, dogs also need a place where they can go to get away from it all. Find a place where she can go and not be disturbed and then create a safe spot such as a large cotton rug or mat, a kennel, a place underneath the table, or a doggy bed. The Go to Your Spot behavior in Part III provides instructions to help your dog learn to absolutely love going to her spot.

If you have children, teach them to respect your dog's safe area. This is especially important over the holiday season if your house is packed with partying people.

Ingredient Number 5: Exercise

For optimum health, dogs require the same four types of exercise that humans need—aerobic exercises, strength exercises, stretching exercises, and balancing exercises. The most common aerobic exercise for dogs is running. Of course, aerobic exercise can easily be incorporated in play since a dog runs while chasing balls, Frisbees, and bubbles. Flyball and agility training are also great opportunities to run. A dog should have a minimum of two 15-to-20-minute aerobic exercise periods each day. It is the one sure way to provide your dog with the top nutrient he needs: oxygen! You can combine this with the play period to make it fun and easy.

Strength exercises are easy to include in your dog's daily routine. They include running up a hill, running through snow or sand, and, of course, swimming. You can help to maintain your dog's muscle tone and strength by teaching him to carry items in a pack strapped to his back or by hitching him up to a cart or wagon and having him pull your child down the street. Obviously, this must be done with a great deal of discernment. Whereas a Malamute can pull a child's sled, it wouldn't really benefit a Chihuahua to pull a sled—even if you had a miniature toy sled that would match his size. Physical capabilities, age, health, and the way in which you train your dog all influence his strength level and how the various strength exercises will benefit him.

Stretching exercises are extremely helpful in keeping your dog's ligaments, tendons, and muscles supple, flexible, and healthy. Anyone who lives with animals is aware of their natural inclination to stretch. Most people recognize the value of stretching before they begin to exercise in order to minimize the possibility of strains and muscle pulls. When you ask your dog to fit into your daily exercise routine, it's important to keep his own stretching needs in mind so he won't get hurt either. The best way to help your dog stretch is to give him a daily massage. It doesn't have to take long—five minutes of massage a day is extremely beneficial.

In addition to the obvious therapeutic benefits, massage is also a terrific way to bond with your dog. In his book *The Healing Touch,* Michael Fox, D.V.M., says: "The tender loving touch is essential for well-being and for the normal growth and development of all socially dependent animals. It would seem that their nervous systems require such stimulation either from the gentle licks of their mothers' tongues or the strokes of a caring human hand. As a seedling cannot thrive without the light of the sun, so, too, do our animal kin suffer without the energy of love. And it is through touch especially, that this energy can be given and reciprocated."

In addition, massaging your dog also benefits you. In her excellent book *Four Paws, Five Directions,* Cheryl Schwartz, D.V.M., relates: "It has been shown through projects developed and publicized by Dr. Leo Bustad, while Dean at Washington State University Veterinary School in the 1980s, that stroking and touching an animal can help lower a person's blood pressure, increase self-esteem, and establish a feeling of well-being."

Among the massage techniques Dr. Schwartz shares in her book is the following: "The type of massage stroke you may be most familiar with is the long stroke using the flat of the hand and finger tips. This is known as 'effleurage.' Long strokes are good for the abdomen and larger muscle groups along the neck and back. Most animals enjoy these strokes. The pressure should be regulated according to what the animal tells you. He will move away if it is too hard or closer if it is not hard enough.

"Another useful stroke is like a rubbing motion, called 'friction.' Use the tips of your fingers and apply pressure in a forward and backward motion, usually beginning slowly, about 1 per second, and gradually increasing to 2 per second. I usually recommend that this be done between the shoulder blades and over the rump area or along the midline of the chest between the front legs extending down toward the abdomen."

For more information and additional massage techniques, I suggest both Dr. Fox's and Dr. Schwartz's books.

The final category of exercise, balancing exercises, includes, among other exercises, walking on planks and balance boards, balancing on teeter-totters, and swinging on porch swings. These exercises are wonderful confidence builders. For some dogs, you can add sitting up in the begging pose, walking on hind or front legs, and climbing ladders. However, use common sense here; there are limitations on the balancing exercises that can be done by puppies, older dogs, and larger dogs. The best way to teach your dog how to balance is to enroll in an agility class in your area, where the necessary equipment is provided.

Ingredient Number 6: Employment

If you don't give your dog a job to do, she will become self-employed. Dogs become gardeners and replant all the flowers and vegetables in your yard; they become official greeters and jump on and lick every guest who walks in the door; they become alarm systems that go off in the middle of the night when the wind attacks your house; they become home decorators and rearrange the look and placement of pillows and furniture; and they become firefighters, putting out all the imaginary fires throughout your house. The lack of a proper balance of mental, physical, and emotional stimulation is one of the main reasons that people have problems with their dogs. Bottom line, they're bored. Employment is important because it not only provides stimulation but also promotes and develops a sense of purpose and pride.

To help explain and illustrate the importance of dogs "working" for their living, I developed the concept of "canine currency." All animals are genetically encoded with the instinct to expend energy in order to survive. This comes in the form of the hunt for food, safety from predators, and safety from the elements. They even have to work to mate and certainly to provide for their offspring. In most cases, when we take dogs into our homes, they no longer have to work for anything. This creates a situation where the dog is unemployed. So, to fill the vacuum, she may herd the children or retrieve the neighbor's newspaper. She may guard her food and toys or protect the home from the mail carrier and even nice Aunt Minnie. An unemployed dog might express her boredom by exhibiting manifestations of stress such as chewing on the furniture or even herself, ripping up linoleum, and destroying houseplants.

When you institute the concept of canine currency, you *pay* your dog in response to appropriate behavior, which is looked at as his work or his job. A dog then works for the currency, which is represented by food, affection, play, and special privileges. Having to work for a living challenges dogs and engages them in life. It eliminates boredom and gives them purpose. Once you institute the rule that "Nothing in life is free," your dog will work for almost everything and be happy to do so. Jobs include retrieving toys, doing tricks, and playing games. My dog Molly can answer the phone and throw it in the wastebasket if it's a bill collector. She can run an agility course, retrieve a ball under water, guard my car (nonviolently, of course), and demonstrate twenty different tricks when we visit elementary schools as part of our Paws for Peace animal-assisted therapy program. Not a bad job!

Ingredient Number 7: Rest

Where should your dog sleep? Dogs are social animals and they are healthiest when they are with their family. When humans domesticated dogs, we became their family. Therefore, the ideal location for your dog's bed is around the smells and sounds of a family member. If you desire, it's okay to permit your dog to sleep on your bed. However, allow the dog on your bed only with your permission. This is a great training opportunity. Before allowing your dog on the bed, ask him to sit or lie down. When he does it, invite him onto the bed as a reward. Sleeping in the bedroom really strengthens the human-animal bond. I can't say enough about the benefits this provides.

Dogs sleep for up to sixteen hours a day. Again, just as with humans, undisturbed quality sleep is of utmost importance. It's important to teach children not to awaken a sleeping dog. When a child sees a dog running and whining in his sleep, she sometimes wants to wake him because "he's having a nightmare." However, this behavior while sleeping is part of a dog's natural sleep state, referred to as rapid eye movement (REM) sleep, where dreams abound. As with humans, REM sleep is important because it is the part of the sleep cycle in which some of our stress is resolved. REM sleep comes before, as well as between, the stages of sleep referred to as the dreamless states. The body enters its deepest relaxation during the dreamless states. Both the REM stage and the dreamless states of the sleep cycle are important for health. In short, let sleeping dogs lie.

Ingredient Number 8: Training

Since most of this book is about training, I'll say just a few words on how training fits in with the other eight ingredients. Positive training respects a dog's physical and emotional abilities. Your dog will learn whatever behaviors you want to teach him but you will go at your dog's learning speed. In essence, training takes as long as it takes. How long are training sessions? Four or five short sessions of three to five minutes per day are better than two long sessions. I suggest two sessions in the morning and two or three in the evening. Many people find a great time to do training sessions is during commercials while they're watching television.

Ingredient Number 9: Health Care

Health care needs vary with age, size, breed, and genetic influences, so check with your veterinarian for specific recommendations on the care of your dog. Proper grooming is an important part of your dog's health care regimen. The dog's coat, skin, nails, and ears should be cared for on a weekly basis at a minimum. Some veterinarians actually recommend brushing your dog's teeth on a daily basis, if possible. It is helpful if more than one member of the family learns to take care of the family dog since the time spent on these needs is a wonderful opportunity for socialization and bonding. (Also see Chapter 7, "Safety for Your Dog and Family")

Since Western medicine is generally more invasive than alternative healing modalities and often utilizes pharmaceutical drugs that cause negative side effects, I prefer a veterinarian who includes holistic health care in his practice. Many times health problems can be more gently corrected through acupuncture, homeopathy, chiropractic, herbal medicine, and so on. You might also inquire at your local natural foods store, yoga school, or holistic medical doctor for referrals.

Vaccinations

As I discussed in the socialization section of this book, it is vital that puppies be exposed to as many sights, sounds, and smells of the world as possible during the first fourteen weeks of their lives. This includes letting them interact with other dogs and puppies in areas you are familiar with, such as the homes of your friends and family members or puppy classes. This is a bit of a Catch-22 because it's also important to keep him away from any area that a dog who is infected with a contagious disease may have visited. If you find yourself in an area that concerns you, err on the side of safety and carry your dog until his immune system is protected by vaccinations or other protective measures according to your veterinarian's recommendations. There is some controversy among holistic veterinarians as to which vaccinations should be given or if they should be given at all. Sometimes they also recommend homeopathic nosodes as a more natural immunization or as an adjunct to conventional vaccines. Some believe that vaccinations actually cause diseases or trigger adverse immune reactions, which is called vacinnosis. Others question the frequency of vaccines and booster shots. According to Dr. Jean Dodds, a leading veterinary researcher into vaccination protocols, "Studies are now showing the duration of immunity from vaccination is now accepted to be at least five or more years for the clinically important diseases of dogs and cats. . . . In the years between or instead of boosters, serum vaccine antibody titers can be measured to determine the adequacy of immune memory." Vaccine antibody titer testing measures antibodies to determine whether an animal's previous vaccinations still provide immunity from any infectious diseases that the animal may be exposed to. It is much safer to have the dog's immune titer levels tested rather than automatically giving booster vaccines.

All this being said, it is up to every individual, in consultation with his or her veterinarian, to decide on the best course of action regarding vaccinations.

I suggest that you read more on health care for your dog in *The Natural Dog* by Mary Brennan, D.V.M., and Norma Eckroate; *Dr. Pitcairn's Complete Guide to Natural Health for Dogs and*

Cats, by Richard H. Pitcairn, D.V.M., Ph.D., and Susan Hubble Pitcairn; and *Four Paws, Five Directions*, by Cheryl Schwartz, D.V.M.

Combining the Nine Ingredients

Establishing a daily routine is very helpful in developing your puppy's or your new dog's sense of security and confidence. And it's also great for housetraining! Here is a sample of a daily routine you might try with your dog. It's just an idea of how Sparky's day might go. Obviously, everyone's schedule is different and many variables exist. Select the parts that are realistic for you and your family and try your best to be consistent. If you have a problem, contact a professional dog trainer who uses nonviolent training methods.

Suggested Daily Routine

7 A.M.–8 A.M. Take Sparky out of his kennel. Have him lie down or sit before opening the kennel. (The reward is the door opening.) Say "okay" before releasing him. Begin by asking for a 1 second sit or down and gradually increase the time he must hold the position before you open the door.

Take Sparky outside. As he begins to circle/ sniff/gets that gleam in his eye that tells you he needs to urinate, call or "label" the elimination process with a phrase like "Hurry up." Praise and offer him a treat when he is successful. Bring him back inside the house and let Sparky investigate and say hello to people. Everyone should ask Sparky to sit or lie down before getting petted. Ignore him until he does. Some dogs, especially those who enjoy being out in the yard, learn quickly that elimination means all the fun ends, as they are brought inside right afterward. Those dogs then take longer and longer to eliminate! The trick is to wait until the dog eliminates, then play with him for at least two minutes so he disassociates elimination with the end of fun. Feed Sparky. Be sure to practice come, sit or down before putting his dish down. About 15 minutes after he's done eating, take Sparky outside to eliminate again and then take him for a walk. (Note: Puppies must have vaccinations before being walked outside of your own yard.) Practice walk without pulling, sit, and down, especially at streets.

Take Sparky back inside and allow him to explore a little. Practice the "magnet game" throughout the day. Put him in a kennel, exercise pen, or tether him in a supervised, social area. Give high-quality, yummy chewies like Bully Sticks, or toys filled with treats, such as a "Kong" (avoid pigs' ears, hooves, and rawhides).

9 A.M.–12 P.M. Rest time.

12 P.M.–1 P.M. Take Sparky outside to eliminate. (Remember to ask him to "sit" or "lie down" before going in or out the door.)

Inside or outside, practice 1 to 2 minutes of sit, down, stay, come, go-to-spot, or hide-and-go seek. Make it fun! Vary the routine. Vary the treats.

Throw toys and play with him. Have him chase you; do not chase him. Interact with other people in friendly, positive ways. Remember, Sparky must earn treats and affection.

1 P.M.–5 P.M. Rest time. If your dog is left alone for long periods of time, consider having a dog walker visit.

5 P.M.–6 P.M. Take Sparky outside to eliminate. Repeat the activities listed above.

Take him for a walk in the neighborhood; however, be watchful of stray dogs.

Practice heeling, walk without pulling, sit, come, down, stay.

Interact with people. Ask them to follow "approach and greet" protocols. (Explain to other people that he's in training). Praise his good behavior!

6 P.M.–10 P.M.   Give Sparky supervised free time or keep him kenneled or tethered in a social area of your home. Watch TV (especially *The Dog Whisperer* DVD!), read a book, or work on your computer while practicing the Magnet Game (see page 159). Give high-quality, yummy chewies like Bully Sticks, Chicken Strips, or toys filled with treats, such as a "Kong" (avoid pigs' ears, hooves, and rawhides).

Attend dog training class once a week.

10 P.M.   Take Sparky outside to eliminate.

Keep him in a kenneled or tethered in your bedroom for a good night's sleep.

Chapter 3

Stress and Your Dog's Behavior

Many years ago, at a large zoo, primates were getting sick and dying. After much study, stress management experts decided the monkeys' immune systems were being compromised due to a lack of stress. They weren't getting enough physical, mental, and emotional stimulation. In short, their lives were just too routine and dull. So the zookeepers constructed a life-size, lifelike predator in the form of a mechanical lion. On a random schedule, the lion would appear out of the bushes, growling away. The monkeys would run screeching to the safety of their trees. This simulated threat improved the health and longevity of the monkeys by stimulating them, thereby strengthening their immune systems. Because they were always successful in escaping from the "predator," these incidents proved to be a positive stress.

All of us, dogs and humans alike, need stress in our lives. We need to be challenged in order to stay healthy and evolve. We need to face challenges and successfully adapt to these challenges—physically, emotionally, and mentally. Studies have shown how animals raised without the stress of physical and emotional stimulation—stress that challenges but doesn't overwhelm—actually have less gray matter in their brains. This means their health and growth is actually impaired by a lack of stress.

For both dogs and humans, all stress—both positive and negative—is defined as the body's reaction to change in the environment or a perceived change in the environment. These changes include such everyday occurrences as being late for work, meeting a job deadline, paying bills, or making dinner by the time the family gets home. Of course, external stressors also include bigger events in a person's life, including job changes, such as being hired, promoted, or fired; getting married or divorced; moving; having a baby; illness; or exposure to extreme heat or cold.

Your body also reacts to changes in your internal environment. Stressors that impact you internally include emotions such as anger, worry, or anything that you perceive as a threat, real or imagined. This is an important point—it is how we perceive the world that affects us. If we can change how we feel about events in our lives, they will have less negative impact on our health and well-being.

What Is Stress, Anyway?

Balancing your checkbook might not cause you any stress at all; however, if you have trouble with bookkeeping or believe your checking account balance might be overdrawn, it might be a big stress. Stress is very individual—some people thrive on situations that other people perceive as overwhelming.

Any stressful event can trigger a survival instinct that has been part of our genetic code since caveman days. Referred to as the "fight or flight" response, this survival instinct tells us we have two choices: to fight our adversary or to take flight. Even though we rarely find ourselves in the life-or-death situations of our ancient ancestors, the nervous system reacts to any stressful situation with this instinctive response. Let's say a deadline is approaching. The heart begins to pound, the blood pressure spikes, the pulse races, and the amount of perspiration increases. The body releases adrenaline, which causes the digestive system to shut down, and steroids such as cortisol surge into the bloodstream to pump up the energy level and add to muscle strength. At the same time, blood flow is directed to the muscles and the pupils dilate. Stress can also cause us to unconsciously change our breathing rate from longer breaths to very short, shallow breaths. When this happens the volume of air we inhale is greatly reduced.

The fight or flight response kicks in whenever you are feeling threatened. But, as with some of the examples I mentioned earlier, the threat doesn't have to be extreme. If you are startled every time your boss calls your name or every time your dog starts to bark, your body automatically goes through this reaction. If the stress continues over a period of time, you maintain a level of tension throughout most or all of the day and can actually forget how to relax. After a while you go from what's called the resistance stage, where the body is able to handle the stress of everyday living and stay healthy, to the exhaustion stage, where your body just can't take it anymore. This is where illness and injury occur.

Stress Thresholds

When there are too many stressing stimuli presented all at once or, to put it another way, when too much stress accumulates, the stress threshold is compromised. In other words, there's just too much on the plate to deal with. Accumulated stress must be released and pent-up energy expressed in some way or you or your dog will become susceptible to illness and accidents. Think of it this way: Let's say you take your dog to the veterinarian. Upon returning home, a friend comes over to visit, along with her not-too-friendly Akita. Now the kids come home from school and one of them accidentally steps on your dog's foot. Someone turns the television on at a high volume and, at the same time, the Akita eyes your dog's bone. Then the doorbell rings and a guy in a uniform enters with a package. Get the picture? Overload for both you and your dog. Normally your dog is fine. But like building blocks being piled one on top of another, the stress accumulates and rises above the dog's stress management threshold. The dog needs to vent. If he doesn't, it's possible for an overload of stress to lead to acts of aggression. With some dogs, biting is the natural response.

One of the greatest stresses is not being able to predict the future. This means we feel hopeless or powerless over our own lives. Think of what it's like to be a dog. Dogs are geared for routines. So what happens if routine is missing from a dog's life? Imagine not knowing when and where your next meal is coming from, or not being able to go where you want, or wondering if another animal is just around the corner waiting to attack you. If an animal is continually in a state of "I don't know what's going to happen next," the stress can become unbearable. Getting to know your dog and his stress threshold is the first step in establishing a healthy environment. The second step is knowing what to do about it. Among other things, that's what this book is all about.

Stress management is the ability to cope with stress by minimizing its causes and/or by raising an individual's stress threshold. Each dog is an individual with his own unique ability to handle stress. However, a dog doesn't have the ability to consciously choose to handle stress overload, His stress threshold can be raised, however, with your help. For example, a dog's reaction to a child stepping accidentally on his foot might be to bite the child. Through systematic desensitization and counter conditioning, however, that same dog can learn to respond to the same situation by jumping up and looking for a treat.

Desensitization means getting the dog used to the threatening event gradually by increasing the stress little by little over a period of time, until she perceives the formerly stressful event as no big deal or even as something positive. Many species have been trained to accept experiences that are painful. Some animals are even taught to help facilitate the event that causes the pain. Baboons and other primates, for example, learn to put their arms out so veterinarians can stick a needle in and do blood tests. Killer whales slide out of the water and lift a fin for the same purpose. And elephants are taught to lift their massive feet through a fence so caregivers can file their nails. The training that is required to shape these behaviors takes time and requires an environment where an animal can build on success. The nine ingredients in Chapter 2 are the means to create a healthy environment to do just that.

Four Ways Dogs Manifest Stress

Dogs basically express or manifest stress in four ways: orally, vocally, physically, and/or viscerally. These manifestations of stress can include the following stress-induced behaviors.

Oral: licking, chewing on furniture, clothing, their own bodies, or people

Vocal: barking, whimpering, and whining

Physical: scratching, running around, pawing, digging, or jumping—as well as less demonstrable indicators such as dilated pupils, blinking, yawning, sniffing the ground, and moving in circles as well as a host of other displays

Visceral: an upset stomach, panting, sweaty paws, drooling, runny nose, eliminating, or vomiting

Many of these manifestations of stress have certain meanings to other dogs and are also used as language. Turid Rugaas, a Norwegian behavioral expert, labeled some of these behaviors as "calming signals." In psychology circles, they are called "displacement behaviors." Among the signals Rugaas labels as "calming" are blinking the eyes, looking away, sniffing the ground, turning to the side, licking the lips, and yawning. In other words, dogs learn to actually communicate how they are feeling by using the stress manifestations as signals. Watch your dog closely so you will learn to recognize what she is "thinking" and what she is "saying." All of these signals are recognizable to humans if we watch for them. Your dog may be reaching her stress threshold if she starts panting and drooling, or shivering, or if her paws become sweaty.

Why is all this important? When a dog reaches the threshold of distress, learning stops and the dog is in survival mode. This is why many shelter dogs have such a difficult time. In a shelter, their "fight-or-flight" responses may be triggered hundreds of times a day. With such an exhausting environment, it's easy to see why aggression rises to the surface and health becomes an issue. This also helps us understand why it can take so long for a dog to trust a new person or family who has adopted him. So once you learn to recognize your dog's stress threshold, you have entered into a new level of fluency in canine communication and life with Fido will be much more pleasant.

When a Person's Stress Leads to Abusive Situations

Of course, just as with dogs, distress is debilitating to us humans, too. It negatively impacts both our physical and emotional health when we internalize our stress and bottle it up. This bottled-up stress can result in headaches, ulcers, and other serious health problems or even alcohol or drug abuse. It becomes an even greater problem when it leads to hostility and manifests as physical or emotional abuse toward others. When a person's stress is directed toward a dog, he might be assuaging his own pent-up emotions, but in the process the dog is learning something the person probably doesn't want to teach. For example, let's look at a classic example of stress when it is displaced or redirected as aggression. We'll call it the scenario of "the old man has a bad day at the office and comes home and kicks the dog." It goes something like this:

1. The man walks in and the dog recognizes the visual, sound, and scent cues of the person by immediately associating his body language with past experiences. These physical cues include the person's shallow and restricted breathing, muscle tension, and the scent of stress hormones being given off.

2. The dog remembers that the person yells, hits, or does something else negative when he acts, sounds, and smells this way. The dog responds submissively by putting his tail between his legs, putting his ears back, crouching, rolling over, and licking his lips. Just as a person might act submissively in a threatening situation by cowering, shaking, or running away, the dog's behavior is a signal that he is doing everything he knows to do to tell the person that he "submits." In human terms, the dog's response says, "Okay, I surrender. You don't have to escalate the behavior and you don't have to hurt me."

3. Oblivious to what the dog is communicating, the person continues to fume about what happened at work during the day, slamming doors, yelling, and throwing the mail on the table.
4. Because the person continues to use the same body language, the dog sees that his submissive behavior just isn't enough and feels he must submit even more. He then urinates on the Persian rug, saying, in essence, "See, I defer to you even more."
5. The person now puts his attention on the dog urinating on the carpet and redirects his still unresolved anger. He yells, threatens, picks the dog up by the nape of the neck and shakes him, and then throws him out the door.
6. Now the dog really begins to have problems. He has done everything he could to communicate but nothing worked.

In this situation, the dog has learned nothing about what not to do, is thoroughly confused as to what he's supposed to do, and begins manifesting more behaviors that will get him in trouble, such as chewing, digging, escaping from the yard, or even biting. This is normally the point where I'm called in for a behavioral consultation. That's if the dog is lucky and hasn't been taken to be euthanized. In the next chapter, I'll share some additional tools so you can implement a stress management routine for the sake of your dog as well as yourself.

Chapter 4

The Human Emotion and
Dog Behavior Link: The Bridge of Breath

A few years ago I conducted an informal study, asking about thirty professional dog trainers what percentage of the dog's behavior is influenced by a person's emotions. Those I surveyed felt that at least 50 percent of a dog's behavior (in the typical family home environment) is related to the emotional state of his handler. These experts opined that how people feel and their emotional state of mind has a major impact on how their dogs behave. Their reasoning was that feelings influence what people do, what they say, and how they say it. In other words, communication is affected.

Most people have experienced this emotion-behavior connection with their dogs. When we're upset, our dogs get upset. When we're happy, they tend to be happy. When we're frightened, our dogs may feel threatened. Dogs learn to associate our behaviors with certain consequences, and the cycle starts with our emotions. From feelings of joy and happiness to frustration, despair, anger, and rage, our emotions are translated into physical expressions. Dogs are able to "read" even the most subtle of these human behaviors through our body language, odors, and breathing patterns.

When people bring their dogs to my classes for the first time many of them are pretty tense. The dogs, pretty excited themselves, feed off people's stress. They jump, bark, and pull them all over the place. As a result, the people get more anxious—and some of them get angry and frustrated. They mutter "I'm sorry. He's not this way at home," or "Fido, knock it off!" followed by a pop on the leash. Animal behaviorists and trainers, such as those who work with dolphins and killer whales, are well aware of how much their own stress affects their training ability. To minimize the degree to which a person's feelings can impact a training session, they establish precise training schedules in strictly controlled environments.

On the plus side, the strong emotional connection between ourselves and our dogs can also be used to benefit both of us. So let's explore ways to optimize this emotional link.

The Benefits of Complete Breathing

As a child and young adult, I was close to death a number of times due to asthma and severe food and environmental allergies. So I decided to explore alternative therapies to get a grip on my health problems, which led to yoga. I cannot express strongly enough what yogic breathing exercises did to improve my health. As a practitioner and teacher of yoga, I found that breathing exercises can lead to a new level of peace, self-control, uncommon aware-ness, and power. Years ago, my first yoga instructor told me: "Try my suggestions for a few months. If these methods work for you, continue to practice them. If you see a direct influence, continue to practice them. If they don't work for you, throw them in the lake and try something else." I say the same thing here. Try the suggestions I list in this chapter. If they don't work for you and your dog, try something else.

Among the many benefits of complete breathing are that more oxygen gets to the brain, the sympathetic and parasympa-thetic branches of the autonomic nervous system are balanced, and hormones such as endorphins, which increase your sense of well-being, are released. Now here's where the dog's amaz-ing sense of smell comes into the equation. A dog's sense of smell is connected to the amygdala gland in the brain, which processes emotional behavior, and hence, influences physical behavior. Dogs can smell hormones released by a person's body. Through past positive associations, which are learned behaviors, a dog can actually gain an increased sense of well-being simply by smelling a person's hormones. This is a simplistic explanation of a complex process, but the bottom line is that your breathing and all it entails not only benefits you but also your wonderful canine partner via your relaxed body language and your smell.

The complete breath exercise (which I'll share later in this chapter) helps to reduce stress and tension while it gives an increased ability to focus and concentrate. When you do the complete breath, you'll actually have greater control of situations as they occur while, at the same time, you'll find that your creativity and intuition are increased. A round of three complete breaths takes only a minute to do and is a great way to begin every training session with your dog. I do this exercise every time I begin a training session and I teach it at the beginning of every class. I find it does wonders to put people in a relaxed frame of mind and instill a feeling of control.

People attending my classes may have wondered what a breathing exercise had to do with dog training, but to this day no one has ever questioned it. Perhaps that's because the benefits are so obvious after you do it the first time.

Finding Your Power Through Breath

Why is it that one person can be totally inspiring when giving a speech while another person might give the exact same speech and bore you to tears? Or why can one member of the family tell the dog to sit and get an immediate response from her, while the same dog totally ignores another member of the family every time he says sit? In part, it's because of the dog's training and reinforcement history. Clearly, the dog responds to the member of the family who worked more with her and rewarded her for sitting. But another, more subtle, difference has to do with the person's words and actions being infused with power. Dogs are more responsive to people whose willpower is strong.

Dogs react not only to the gross manifestations of your body language, but also to the subtler energy manifestations of your will. When you start each training session with the complete breath exercise, you will find that it is easier to attract your dog's attention and that you are able to keep it longer. Dogs respond to the finer signals of your "mind-stuff" or thoughts. It's as if you've created a powerful magnetic attraction that draws your dog's attention. You've infused your words and actions with power. Really great animal trainers have developed this ability. Watch what happens when a skilled trainer walks into a roomful of dogs.

To understand how your will power can be heightened by a simple breathing exercise, it might be helpful to look at the Eastern view of what breath is and how it affects us. Breath actually carries with it a subtle but powerful energy. In yoga this energy in the breath is called "*prana*" and all the different breathing exercises are called "*pranayamas*." Other philosophies call this same energy "*chi*" or "*qi*," while Luke Skywalker knew it as "The Force."

Think of it this way: which light is more powerful—a streetlamp or a laser? The light that radiates from a streetlamp is diffused; it lights an entire area of the street. But when light is focused in a small direct beam as a laser, it is much more powerful. It can even burn through steel. In this same way, controlled breathing takes your own diffused energy and focuses it, making it laser-like.

When you focus on your breath, your concentration and your awareness of what's going on both externally and internally are increased. Your willpower is no longer diffused by myriad distractions, so, in the process, it is also strengthened exponentially. You can then focus and concentrate on a singular thought or image and give it shape and power.

When training a dog, focus your energy and your concentration on the image of the behavior you want your dog to do. Your now-focused concentration and enhanced awareness will enable you to observe your dog in much greater detail. Eventually you will be able to actually "read" your dog and anticipate his behavior. As a result, you become more confident and relaxed, more aware, more alert, and more focused. Imagine how all this is going to affect your dog.

In addition to enhancing your willpower, the state of relaxation that comes from complete breathing and visualization also puts you in the frame of mind to *respond* to your dog rather than having a knee-jerk *reaction*. As discussed in Chapter 1, this ability to respond rather than react opens you up so you can use your wisdom, creativity, intuition, and positive emotions. In short, it puts you in control of the situation.

Dogs are pure in their connection to nature—and nature is, after all, one big communication network. The breathing methods presented in this chapter will help reconnect you to that which you have known all along but may have forgotten—how nature communicates. And, there are added benefits—breathing exercises improve your overall health and studies show they also help relieve specific tension-related ailments such as headaches, chronic fatigue, asthma, and allergies. It's such a deal!

The Nuts and Bolts of Breathing

You've been breathing all of your life. But, if you're like many people, your breathing is shallow and, on occasion, you might even unconsciously hold your breath. The main goal of controlled breathing is to fully oxygenate your body. You need those oxygen molecules to travel down to the millions of tiny air sacs in the lung tissues. Once there, the oxygen passes through the membranes of the lungs and blood vessels to be picked up by the red blood cells. And at the same time—here's the important part—toxins and carbon dioxide are released through the lungs and oxygen is transported to the brain. This is why the complete breath makes you more relaxed while, at the same time, you become more alert and aware.

One of the reasons so many people have a shallow breathing pattern is that they breathe *exactly opposite* from the way that would give them the most oxygen. When asked to sit up straight and take a deep breath, most people do two things wrong. As they inhale, they puff up the chest like a frog and then draw the abdomen inward. Then, as they exhale, they slouch forward slightly as the belly area expands. Before reading further, take a deep breath and see if this is what you're doing. What moves first—your stomach or your chest?

If you're puffing up your chest, the air tends to fill only the upper part of your lungs. The small amount of air that is circulated to the lower portions of the lungs gets there through the force of gravity more than anything else. As a result, a lot of fresh, oxygen-rich air doesn't fully reach the bloodstream. This lack of oxygen affects everything you do.

With the complete breath you fill the lower portion of your lungs with air *first*, allowing your abdomen to expand, before moving the chest area. This allows your lungs to be completely filled with air, like filling a glass with water from bottom to top. Then, when you exhale, allow the lungs to slowly deflate until they are totally empty. It is not difficult to train yourself to breathe like this all the time. All it takes is practice, which will then retrain the muscles, and eventually this deep complete breathing will become natural. (Later in this chapter, I'll take you step-by-step through a complete breath exercise.)

The normal breath rate for both humans and dogs is between 10 and 30 times a minute. Many things, including the physical and emotional stimulation of a dog training class, affect this breath rate. For example, when humans and dogs pant due to excitement, fever, exercise, or heat, the faster breathing creates hypoxia, in which the tissues of the body become deficient in oxygen. And when you're tense, you just naturally take breaths that are shallower. As a result, the reduced oxygen uptake further restricts the amount of oxygen going into the bloodstream and to your brain. This lack of oxygen also restricts your mental, physical, emotional, and intuitive processes because oxygen is the most accessible and health-giving source of energy you have.

The whole process looks like this: First, we get tense and restrict our breathing. Then our restricted breathing limits the amount of oxygen feeding our body. This then makes us more susceptible to diseases—and round and round we go. It's a vicious cycle.

Breath to the Rescue

Breathing exercises can increase your physical, mental, and emotional health and awareness and, at the same time, elicit different behaviors from your dog. For example, the complete breath exercise helps an energetic or stressed dog relax (see instructions on page 72). On the other hand, if your dog is lethargic and you want him to be more active, a few rounds of a panting breath will get his attention. A panting breath is easy to do: quickly repeat "ha, ha, ha, ha, ha" as you do when laughing. (However, when doing the panting breath, be sure you don't blow air directly into a dog's face. Some dogs may perceive that action as a threat; therefore, children should never do this exercise.)

Breathing can actually be used as an "occasion setter." That is, you can turn your dog's "action switch" on through the use of a breathing pattern. Just like picking up a leash means going for a walk or opening the bag of dog food means food is on the way, breathing can signal "It's time to work" or "It's time to relax." The added benefit of using your breathing as an action switch is that you are also triggering your own physical, emotional, and mental power stations. You become more focused, your willpower is "lasered," and, as a result, your dog responds to your requests that much quicker.

If you want to see an example of the impact of the complete breath on dogs, walk into a shelter full of barking dogs and do a series of deep breathing exercises. In a short time, most of the dogs will calm down demonstrably. If several people walk in and do this breathing at the same time, the results will be that much more dramatic.

Total Relaxation Exercise

Before doing the complete breath exercise (which follows), it is helpful to do this relaxation exercise. It's difficult to focus on relaxed breathing if the body isn't relaxed, so the first step in learning any breathing exercise is muscle relaxation. This takes a few minutes to read but it only takes a minute or two to actually do it. However, don't rush.

Practice in a place free from distractions, including your dog and, if necessary, turn the ringer on your phone off and put a "do not disturb" sign on your door. Also, adjust the heat and lighting so you will be comfortable. That way, your mental and physical muscles won't be startled or distracted by a phone ringing, an unpleasant light, extreme heat or cold, or other intrusions, such as a slobbery canine tongue.

1. Sit comfortably on a chair, on the floor, or on a pillow, keeping your back straight. If it's more comfortable for you, lean against the back of the chair or wall.
2. You might find it helpful to close your eyes. Gently take a deep breath.
3. Now inhale for three seconds, tense your entire body, including your face, hold it for three seconds, and then relax completely while exhaling for three seconds. Let your body go limp.

Figure 4.1

In Step 3 of the total relaxation exercise, tense your whole body, beginning by "making a fist" with your face and hands.

4. Now, for deeper relaxation, imagine your facial muscles softening and let any remaining tension drain out.

5. Slowly move your awareness down your body and relax the muscles in groups, starting with your face and going all the way down to your feet. Go through a mental checklist. ("Okay. Hmm—there's my left bicep. Relax. Relax. There's my left hand. "Go limp hand, relax." And so on.) Observe and relax, if possible, every muscle except those helping your body to sit up straight. They'll take care of themselves. Be sure to go through your entire body, including your feet and even the lines on the bottom of your feet!

6. Now move your awareness slowly back up your body in the opposite direction, from feet to head, checking for any remaining tension—and let it go. You can let it drain into the floor or imagine it's just evaporating—whatever works for you. Once you've mentally returned to your face and find it relaxed, you're ready for the complete breath exercise.

Complete Breath Exercise

This is one of the easiest and most effective breathing exercises. It can be practiced anywhere at any time. The complete breath consists of smoothly inhaling and exhaling through the nose for equal amounts of time. (It is also called the relaxation breath or diaphragmatic breathing.) The benefits of this exercise include greater relaxation, increased ability to focus, and improved concentration. It also helps you to become more acutely aware of the present moment—something dogs are naturally attuned to.

If you feel lightheaded or dizzy at any time, STOP! Take a break and try later. Then do just one complete breath instead of a series of three breaths.

Figure 4.2

Use the complete breath exercise to take a refreshing relaxation breath at any time, not just before training sessions.

1. This exercise can be done with your eyes closed or open. If you're at home, close your eyes. If you are driving a car or walking across a street while doing the exercise, keep them open.

2. Picture your lungs divided into three sections: top, middle, and lower. Begin to breathe in through your nose. (Be sure your mouth is closed so you are breathing through the nose only.) Allow the breath to fill the lower part of the lungs first, like water filling up a glass. As you inhale, allow your stomach to push out slightly. (If you tighten the stomach muscles inward, as most people do when breathing, it may take a few practice breaths to reverse this process.) When your lower lungs are full, imagine the oxygen filling the middle part of the chest. Then fill the top portion of your lungs. Your chest will expand and your shoulders will draw upward and back a little as you fill the top portion of your lungs.

3. Without stopping when your lungs are full, begin to exhale smoothly, again through your nose. Imagine that your lungs are two balloons that are slowly deflating. Near the end of the exhalation, expel any remaining breath by gently pushing your stomach muscles inward and a little upward toward the spine.

4. Immediately after the exhalation, gently begin to inhale your next breath.

At first, do a series of three complete breaths, timing your inhalation and exhalation so they are equal in length. Most people start with a count of three or four seconds for the inhalation and three or four seconds for the exhalation. Remember, the goal is to move smoothly from the exhalation into the inhalation of the next breath. Think of this transition as driving around gentle curves rather than sharp turns in the road. Slowly and smoothly work up to three breaths.

Over a few weeks' time, gradually extend the time of each inhalation and exhalation up to ten seconds. Don't hold the breath in between the inhalations and exhalations. Don't strain—let the length of each breath increase naturally. While you're beginning with a round of three breaths, your eventual goal is to extend the length of time you spend doing the exercise as well as the length of inhalations and exhalations. Spend one or two periods of five to ten minutes doing this relaxed complete breathing each day.

Another hint to help you concentrate and relax while doing the complete breath is to wear earplugs and listen to the sound of your breath. You'll be able to hear yourself breathe and be able to relax even more.

It's usually best to do these five- to ten-minute sessions before beginning your day or at the end of the day. In addition, however, for practical, everyday purposes, practice taking a series of three complete breaths several times throughout each day— before a training session with your dog, before the kids get home from school, before that big meeting, or while the police officer is walking toward your car. Remember, the benefits accumulate. As you become more relaxed and comfortable doing the complete breathing exercise, you will begin to find previously ingrained stressful, reactionary habits are automatically replaced by a refreshing breath. This allows you more oxygen to help you think and it also gives you a second or two to consider more healthy responses to any situation at hand.

After three months, do an assessment. You will undoubtedly find that these daily breathing exercises have positively affected you and your environment, including your home life, work life, friends, and, of course, your dog. If you see even a tiny change, make a mental progress note. It will encourage you to continue to refine your breathing and incorporate it more and more into your daily life.

How to Handle a Stress Crisis

So, what should you do when you come home after a bad day? Here you'll find stress management tools for you, the human half of the human-dog partnership. I've included both a quick stress management routine for emergency situations and a more in-depth routine that takes a bit more time and exploration. You can use the quick fix when the "stress overload truck" seems to be running you over.

Whichever stress management routine you opt to use, get the breathing down first so it becomes second nature. Implementing your stress management plan will give you a new perspective on the problem so you can consider the healthiest response. Along the way, with persistence and commitment, you will improve not only your stress management skills, but also your communication skills. Your dog will begin to understand what is expected of him and you will begin to understand what your dog is saying to you.

The first step in handling any stress overload is to get control of yourself. Remember, you can't expect a dog to be in control if you're out of control. As soon as you realize that you are out of control, do the following easy exercise.

Quick Stress Management Routine for Humans

Stop, do one complete breath, tense your body, relax, do one more complete breath, and relax even more. Imagine the tension, anger, frustration—whatever—draining out of your muscles. Now apologize to your dog and give him a treat.

Chapter 5

How to Speak "Dog"—Opening Doors of Communication

Years ago, when I was going to school in Mexico, my aunt and uncle traveled all the way from Cleveland to pay me a visit. My uncle was a really nice guy who used to be a milkman—for those of you who remember having milk delivered to your door. Anyway, we were standing on a corner at Paseo de la Reforma. Rather than just asking me for directions, he walked up to an elderly woman and said, "Can you tell us where the supermarket is?" The woman responded, "Qué?" So my uncle spoke louder. The woman took a few steps backward and said, "No speak English." She repeated this phrase several times. Finally my uncle returned. He was really mad. "Can you believe it?" he said. "She doesn't speak English."

My uncle's attitude illustrates the major stumbling block people have in communicating with their dogs. They actually think that they, being human, are lords and lordettes of the universe. It's an incredible, egotistical superiority complex. They expect their dogs to understand what they want. Instead of learning the language and customs of dogs, people do what my uncle did—speak louder and louder and say the same thing over and over—as if volume and repetition are going to suddenly bridge the communication gap. In short, they expect dogs to speak English. This ignorance comes out in statements like "stupid dog" or "He knows it, he's just being stubborn."

The Communication Gap

Picture yourself in a foreign country, unable to communicate. You don't know the body language or etiquette of the culture you're visiting. You might notice that everyone at the dinner table burps after the meal. If you don't know it's considered impolite *not* to burp, you will be considered a rude visitor. Or, you may offer someone your left hand, not knowing that it is considered offensive to do so. Then, all of a sudden, someone comes along who speaks to you in your own language and also explains the etiquette of the culture to you. Your relief would be almost palpable; the ability to communicate and be understood opens the world and all its wonders for you.

As explained in Chapter 3, dogs communicate with one another through tactile, tonal, and postural body language, which ranges from the very subtle to the very obvious. This body language can include a look or stare, blinking the eyes, looking away, licking the lips, yawning, various speeds and locations of a wagging tail, sniffing the ground, scratching, mouthing, pawing, or marking the territory by urinating. Other body language includes the position of the body such as the play bow, turning the back or side to another dog, rolling over on the back, or blocking another dog's movement. Each movement is measured and exact—no more and no less than is absolutely necessary for the particular situation or moment of time. It's pure economy of motion.

Behaviors like these can be energy vents, helping to express built-up tension. As discussed in Chapter 3, these behaviors are called displacement behaviors. They are the result of competing motivators; that is, two desires that are pulling at the same time. Imagine, if you're a sports fan, being invited to see the Indians or the Browns, both playing on the same day at the same time. (Can you guess that I'm from Cleveland?) While you're trying to decide which game to attend, you might pace back and forth or chew your nails or eat something, or you might even feel a little stomach upset.

Figure 5.1

In this photo, both the dogs and the people
are saying hello in their own way. Notice how
one dog is turning his head sideways, averting
eye contact with the other dog.

Dogs, as well as most other animals, have an amazing ability
to notice the subtle movements made by other dogs as well as
humans and associate these movements with consequences. The
story of Clever Hans, an Arabian horse, which is well known
in psychology circles, is a fascinating example of this ability to
read subtle signals. In 1900, Hans was purchased by Wilhelm
von Osten, a retired schoolteacher, who spent a great deal of time
training Hans in order to prove his theories about the intelligence
of animals. The result was amazing—Hans could use a hoof to
tap out the correct answers to math problems written on a chalkboard. Hans became a sensation as people flocked to see the brilliant horse. Despite efforts by scientists and academics to determine whether von Osten was somehow signaling the animal, no
trickery was detected. Then, one of the academics had an idea.
What if Hans' owner was unconsciously signaling the horse with
subtle movements or tension or some other factor? Armed with

this idea, the horse was shown a math problem on the chalkboard while von Osten and everyone else in the room was positioned behind the chalkboard. Suddenly, the clever horse lost his brilliance. He could no longer do math. It seemed that Hans had always tapped out the correct answers to the math equations by reading subtle signals that von Osten had been unconsciously cuing to him, such as the raising of an eyebrow, when he reached the correct number of taps.

Just like Clever Hans, dogs learn associations. They learn to connect events with a "what happens when" perspective. That's why it's so important to develop a "clean" and precise body language of your own. Dogs can pick up on anything. What happens when you reach for the can in the closet? *I get fed.* What happens when the bell rings? *Someone comes in the door.* What happens when someone comes home, slams the door, and forcefully throws his coat on the chair? *I better hide so I don't get yelled at.* What happens when you put your coat on to leave for work? *I'm going to be left alone all day.* What happens when you put your coat on at night? *It's time to go for a walk.* Dogs can easily discriminate.

Because of the wide range of canine vocabulary, it's easy to see why most dogs are misread. People tend to anthropomorphize, giving their dogs human characteristics. "Oh, she peed on the bed *because she was mad at me.*" "*She was jealous* because I was hugging my boyfriend, so she bit him." Or, "She knew that knocking over the kitchen wastebasket was wrong *because she acted so guilty.*"

The extent to which people not only misread canine body language but have become inured to it was demonstrated by an incident shown on the television show *America's Funniest Home Videos.* Someone actually placed a defenseless little Chihuahua on a clothesline where she hung by her front paws. The dog's tail was between her legs, her ears were back against her head, and her entire body was shuddering. Then she began to urinate. The audience responded by howling in laughter at this poor scared little dog who was urinating out of fear. It's hard for me to imagine why people would think abusing this dog was funny. These are all examples of people who are unable to properly read the causes of the behavior because they just don't understand why dogs behave as they do or because they have become hardened to the point of insensitivity. When misperceptions lead to insensitivity, both animals and humans suffer. Education is the key to bridging the communication gap—and it also helps to open the heart to sensitivity and empathy.

Sometimes a dog's body language isn't very obvious. Just because a tail is wagging, that doesn't mean a dog is friendly. And, conversely, just because the hackles are up, that doesn't always mean a dog is going to bite. All individual body language expressions have to be taken in the overall context. No one feature can be translated into what's going on in the dog's mind and emotions.

Dogs can and do move from one expression to another in microseconds. Depending on what's going on in the environment, one moment he might be fearful, the next relaxed, and a second later he might bite. It is well worth the effort to attend a few classes and learn the subtle language of canine communication from an experienced trainer.

Dog Etiquette—How to Greet a Dog
Here are some ways to use canine body language in everyday situations when greeting dogs you are meeting for the first time or dogs you don't know well.

1. Keep your breathing easy and relaxed.
2. Until the dog learns to relax or is trained to enjoy "greetings," don't approach her straight on. Stand approximately 6 feet away. This amount of distance is sometimes referred to as the dog's "critical distance" or the amount of distance most dogs need to feel they can safely escape if necessary. Now imagine a curve on the ground like the letter "C" and approach along that curve. (See Figure 5.2) Once you are close to her, turn to your side rather than facing the dog head-on. Keep your hands by your sides. By doing this, your dog will look at the other person as less threatening. (See Figure 5.3.)

3. Instead of approaching a dog, let the dog come to you. Avoid sudden movements.
4. Once you determine that the dog isn't feeling threatened, pet him under his chin where he can see where your hand is going, not over his body. Then pet him gently on the chest or on the side of the face, away from the ears and eyes. Don't ever reach over the dog's body to pet him on the top of the head or back until you know him well and are sure he enjoys being petted there.
5. Avoid eye contact.
6. Speak softly in a monotone, friendly voice.

Figure 5.2

Figure 5.3

Children should be supervised when interacting with dogs, even when the dogs are members of their own family. Seventy-five percent of the dog bites sustained by children are by dogs familiar to them. In some cases, if a dog has food or a toy, and a child comes into his personal space, he may feel the need to protect it and that protection could manifest in biting. Dogs should be allowed to eat in peace but for safety purposes they should also be educated to allow family members to reach into their bowl at any time. This is a step-by-step process. If you have any qualms whatsoever, hire a professional trainer to show you how it's done. It is also important that we teach children to respect dogs and not to tease them with food or toys.

Opening More Subtle Doors of Communication

Almost all of us have had hunches that proved true. Have you ever received a call from a person you were just planning to call, had the same brilliant idea as another person, or had a sudden intuitive understanding of what an animal wants? One of the strangest experiences I've had happened in 1979. I was with a friend in India when a complete stranger came up and told him a number of things he had no way of knowing. The stranger told my friend, "Your girlfriend's name is Sue; you live in Cleveland, Ohio; you are an engineer; and your birthday is on the second of January." He went on to tell my friend his mother's name and a few other details of his life most of his friends didn't even know.

On another occasion, an Indian mystic told me, "Your mother recently had a terrible upset and you moved back in with her to take care of her." He was right, my mother had recently divorced and I had moved back in with her. Then he said, "You were very sick as a boy with lung problems and your twin sister has a back problem." Both statements were true. He proceeded to draw some lines that looked like railroad tracks on a piece of paper. "This is the spine. Here is her problem." It was true; she did have a back problem. And then he pointed to the exact vertebra that was causing her trouble. At no time did he ask me any questions. I know of yet another incident in which a teacher who spoke no

English suddenly understood everything that was said to him and even answered questions in English.

In all of these situations, a person is linked to information and abilities that he seemingly has no direct access to. Most of us would call this person psychic. Webster defines the word "psychic" as "beyond natural or known physical processes." In Eastern philosophy, this is called "direct knowing," which is the ability to directly access information without having to learn it from an outside source or through what most people would consider normal means. In other words, the information is just there—downloaded, so to speak, into your reality without the need to attend a lecture, read a book, or use any other method of learning. We all do this to one extent or another.

In Dr. Michael Fox's book *Superdog*, an entire chapter deals with animal telepathy and extrasensory perception. One amazing true story details the journey of two dogs and a cat that traveled across the country to a place they'd never even visited, to be with their relocated humans. How is this possible? In addition, how do dogs seemingly predict our comings and goings and do other out-of-the-ordinary stuff? And how can you learn to, in essence, read your dog's mind? Welcome to the world of subtle communication, intuition, and psychically derived knowledge.

So why am I presenting this information in a book on dog training? Well, it's fun, for one thing. For another, if we set limits on what's possible, we are only limiting our own potential. It also introduces one of the most powerful tools a dog trainer has at his disposal—learning to shut up and listen. When your mind is going a mile a minute, your thoughts keep you so preoccupied that you often miss what's right in front of you. It is only when you are centered and focused and your mind is quiet that the subtle realms of communication are open to you.

There is something to be said about developing your intuitive awareness as a tool to help keep your dog safe and healthy. I submit that dogs are not here for our amusement or to serve us. Maybe we're here to serve and amuse them. Maybe if we provide an environment where a dog can be all that she can be, whatever that is, we are helping ourselves to be all that we can be as humans. That's what this book is about—discovery. Don't limit what you can do with your dog and don't limit what your dog can do.

When I was in Aspen back in the '70s, I got a job working in a restaurant as a short-order cook. I decided to experiment by guessing what people would order. So, before the a customer even ordered, I would throw a hamburger on the grill or and drop chicken and fries in the basket. I must say I got pretty good at this. The waiter would drop the ticket off and thirty seconds later the lunch would be served. It was really funny seeing the look on the faces of the waiters and the customers. Some of the customers returned day after day because of the unbelievably fast service. But then, after a couple of weeks of almost perfect hunches, I found my guesses going sour. I'd have six or seven hamburgers frying and no one to eat them. Suddenly, my intuitive information was no longer flowing. The problem? A thought crept in that I was really good at this. Once my ego was involved, it was as if I started to "possess" the ability and the information no longer flowed. The trick is to tap into the more subtle aspects of intuition, which starts with getting your ego out of the way. Fun is one thing; a power trip is another.

Practice the following exercise before every training session and you will see synergy at work. Your intuitive ability to communicate with your dog will evolve tremendously.

Communication Exercise

Note: It is not necessary to spend more than ninety seconds on this exercise.

1. Open your awareness by closing your eyes and doing three rounds of the complete breath exercise. (See page 72.) Listen to the sound of your breathing.
2. Tense all the muscles in your body at once. Hold for three seconds and then relax and let your body go limp.
3. Do one more round of the complete breath exercise.
4. Now open your eyes and become an observer. Watch yourself watching your dog. Do this by pretending you are in

a movie and watching the movie at the same time. "Feel" your dog's mood, attitude, and energy level. The key here is to quiet your own mind so you can really tune in to what's going on with your dog. It's important to do this from your intuition, not your intellect. This process takes only seconds. Now you're plugged in to nature's rhythms. It's that easy. The more you concentrate and the more you rely on your subtle observational skills, the more accurately you'll be able to communicate with your dog.

5. Think about each of the behaviors you are going to work on in the upcoming session. With your eyes closed, spend ten seconds picturing your dog in the final position of each behavior. For example, picture your dog in a sit position for ten seconds, then a down position for ten seconds, and so on. Really use your imagination and focus in your mind's eye on each separate behavior; infuse each behavior with the power of your will. You do this by really imagining it as real. The more you can make it real, the quicker the behavior will take shape.

The technique of picturing the result in your mind's eye is the same one used by world-class athletes in both training and competition. People in my classes have reported some pretty amazing results when they take the time before each training session to do this simple exercise. You should notice progress within three weeks of steady practice. To accelerate the results even more, some people do this mental exercise not only before each training session but also at other times during the day, whenever they happen to remember. The more you practice, the greater the results.

Chapter 6

Training Gear: Collars, Leashes, Tethers, Clickers, Kennels, and Beds

Certain training equipment can really help create an optimum-learning environment—an environment that promotes safety, fun, and the driving motivation to learn.

Collars

With positive training, the commonly used choke collars, also referred to as training collars or slip collars, are not acceptable because of the potential for hurting the dog, especially while you are developing the skill to use them correctly. While the methods I teach involve no jerking at all on the leash and collar, it's important that I clarify here that it is possible for some professional trainers to give a gentle tug on the leash and collar to get information to the dog without inflicting any harm. I know several trainers who have the skill, touch, and timing necessary to use the leash and collar nonviolently in this way. But to get to that level of proficiency takes time and practice and necessitates learning to "read" each individual dog in order to know how much or how little intensity to use. Too much intensity and the dog can be injured; too little and the method proves ineffective. And timing is critical—too soon and the dog gets confused; too late and the dog gets confused.

A simple tug on the leash can and does easily get out of hand and is harmful to the dog. Most people immediately fall into a trap and feel that if a little "attention grabbing" jerk on the leash is successful—well, then a more serious pop will just hurry things along that much quicker. In the process, the dog acts as a guinea pig and could sustain injury. The line between a slight "pop" on the leash to get attention and a stronger "pop" that inflicts discomfort or pain can be difficult for most people to determine. The bottom line is that it is not necessary to use any jerking at all to get your dog to do what you want.

Prong and *shock collars* (also referred to as *electronic collars*) are unacceptable for the same reasons as choke collars. Prong collars look like medieval torture devices, while shock collars actually deliver an electric shock. Both of these types of collars are designed to deliver pain or discomfort, especially when the dog pulls on the leash. Many popular training systems actually tell you to use a shock collar and "set the degree of correction you want" to correct your dog when he is doing something you don't want him to do. Other, supposedly more gentle training methods promote the use of these collars to "get your dog's attention"; the rationale is that prongs and electric shocks don't inflict pain. However, the difference between a "static electricity charge similar to walking across a carpet" and a jolt that kicks the eyeballs loose can be blurry. That being said, it is also possible to use electronic collars without inflicting harm *as long as they are not used for correction.* You could certainly set a collar to a level to communicate to your dog which direction you'd like him to go, whether you wanted him to come to you, whether you wanted him to lie down, and so on. But these gentle, barely felt signals are a far cry from what these collars are presently used for. So I do not recommend them.

So what type of collars should you use? For a smaller dog, I suggest a body harness collar that fits around the front half of the body. For medium to large dogs, one type of Martingale-style collar, such as the one from Premier Pet Products, is preferable because it never closes completely around the dog's neck. These collars are ingeniously designed so they can never choke a dog.

If you have a problem with a dog that pulls on the leash, try a body harness called the Easy Walker by Premier Pet Products. The Easy Walker came out a couple of years ago and is very

Figure 6.1a

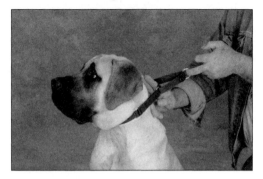

Premier's Martingale-style collar.

Figure 6.1b

Gentle Leader halter-style collar.

effective and easy to put on. The design of this harness includes a ring located on the dog's chest. The leash is attached to this ring so when he pulls, his body is gently turned to the side, thus inhibiting the pulling. I recommend trying the Easy Walker first.

Another collar I recommend is a head-halter-style collar (also called a nose harness collar). My favorite type of halter-style collars are called the Gentle Leader, which is also made by Premier, and another type called the Halti. There are also several styles that are similar which are sold at major pet stores. These collars work on the premise that where the head goes, the body follows. Most dogs get used to these collars without problems, although occasionally I find a dog who just can't get used to it. One problem that can develop with the halter-style collar is the way people use it. When the dog pulls on the leash to greet another dog and the handler doesn't allow enough slack, the dog is unable to use his doggie communication body language with the other dog. If you hold the dog's head up, for example, he can't go through the dog greeting ritual, which sometimes involves looking away, sniffing the ground, or turning his side to the other dog. You must remember to keep the leash slack to avoid these problems.

Almost every year I hear of a dog being injured or dying because he got his jaw caught in another dog's collar. If you are a multi-dog family whose dogs love to romp and grab each other around the neck, take off their collars or fit them with break-away collars. Obviously your house and yard must be 100 percent escape proof if your dogs are not wearing tags. You might also want to look into other identification methods such as identification chips or tattooing.

Another problem with the halter-type collar has to do with public relations because some people mistake them for muzzles. Hence, strangers perceive a dog wearing this collar as dangerous. Unlike muzzles, dogs *can* bark, eat, and drink, and even bite with halter-style collars on. However, you might find yourself repeatedly telling people, "Don't worry, this isn't a muzzle. He doesn't bite." This problem can be somewhat ameliorated by choosing a collar that blends with the color of the dog's coat or a brightly colored one that makes people think the collar is fun and nonthreatening.

Leashes and Tethers
When used properly as a management tool, the leash is a vital part of a safe training environment. For everyday purposes,

choose a leash that is 4 to 6 feet long and made of nylon. For distance training work, you'll also need a 20-foot leash and you might even want a 50-foot leash. I prefer nylon because it's light and flexible. Stay away from chain leashes because they are too heavy and get caught on things.

I'm a big fan of Bungee leashes. A bungee leash, because of its elasticity, buffers a dog's neck. It can help prevent stress or injury to the cervical area in the event that the dog should suddenly give his neck a sharp turn when he becomes aware of a squirrel or something else that captivates his attention. Another advantage of the bungee leash is that it doesn't hang as low to the ground, so it doesn't get tangled in the dog's legs.

I am not a fan of flexi-style leashes—the type that automatically retracts when the dog comes toward you and extends as the dog walks away from you. I really dislike them because of the lack of control. Sometimes the hold slips or breaks when the dog pulls or, if you are surprised, you can't stop your dog in time. Next thing you know, your little Shih Tsu is 15 feet away barking at a dog who is looking at lunch. However, if you live in a gated community with no aggressive dogs, they're fine.

The term "tether" is used for a leash or cable that holds a dog in place. If you hook one end of a leash to your belt, your dog is tethered. The late trainer Job Michael Evans called this an "umbilical cord," which is a nice metaphor. You can also tether your dog to a piece of furniture, clip a tether to an eye-hook that's secured in a baseboard, or wedge one end of the tether under a door to secure it. Another method is to hook a leash to a doorknob, open the door and slip the leash handle over the door handle on the other side. Drop the leash to the floor and slip it under the door. Close the door. The idea is to keep the leash flat along the floor so your dog won't choke herself or get tangled up in the leash.

Figure 6.2

The safest way to tether your dog to a door: Slip the leash handle over the doorknob on the other side of the door, drop the leash to the floor, and slip it under the door. Then close the door. Never tether your dog unless you are there to supervise.

Figure 6.3

Figure 6.4

Don't use a nylon leash as a tether. For one thing, some dogs chew right through them. Also, a nylon leash can get wrapped around the dog's leg, neck, or body and cause an injury. So instead of a regular leash, use a tether made of wire cable like the ones used to attach a bicycle to a bicycle rack. This wire cable is stiff so the dog can't chew through it or get wrapped up in it. It should be just long enough for the dog to move around—approximately 4 feet, depending on the size of your dog, of course. You can purchase a chew-proof tether from *www.dogwhispererdvd. com.*

Never tether a dog while she's left alone. If you tether your dog at night, only do so in your bedroom while you are in the room.

Clickers

As you'll learn in Chapter 11, the clicker can be a valuable training tool. Clickers are almost impossible to find in stores, but can be purchased on the Internet at *www.dogwhispererdvd.com* or by calling 800-955-5440.

Kennels

A portable kennel is an important training tool for managing your dog safely. Along with the proper use of leashes and baby gates, use of the kennel helps to keep your dog, your family, and the environment out of harm's way. Getting your dog to absolutely love going to the kennel—her "safe spot"—is your first priority. (See Go to Your Spot in the lessons in Part 2 on page 184.) Kennels, like anything else, are as helpful and useful or as cruel and negative as we make them. I love the use of a kennel as long as you take the time to introduce your dog to it in a gradual and positive way.

Your dog should be taught on a gradual schedule to love spending time in her kennel, so she views it as "home, sweet home." With correct use, most puppies get used to the kennel very quickly. For an older dog or puppies that are having problems adapting to the kennel, don't use it until the dog has formed a positive association with it. Instead, put the dog in the kitchen behind a baby gate or a dog pen, which is like a kennel without a top, similar to a baby's playpen.

Please be sure to take your dog's collar off before putting her in the kennel. Hard as it is to believe, I've known of dogs that have gotten the collar caught on something, causing them to almost choke to death. And do not leave rubber toys or rawhide chews in the kennel; I know of several dogs that have choked on them also.

Kennels come in two basic models. Some are open, like the wire-cage models, and others have solid walls, with wire only at the gate, like the airline travel models. Whichever type you choose, pick one that allows your dog to stand without stooping and lie down without curling her body. If you are buying a kennel for a puppy, be sure to get one that will be large enough for her when she's fully grown. If your dog is a pure breed, it's not too difficult to determine how large she will be as an adult. However, if your dog is a mixed breed, ask your veterinarian approximately how much your dog will grow before picking a kennel. While she's a puppy, you can block off part of the interior of the kennel so she doesn't have room to eliminate in it. As she gets bigger, simply remove the barrier.

Remember, the kennel is an item you will be keeping for years and years. It is your dog's "safe spot." It's worth it to spend a little more for a quality kennel that will last. There are some less expensive models on the market that can present problems. For instance, I've known dogs to catch a nail or get cut on the wires of the kennel or even get their head stuck.

Beds

I suggest purchasing a bed for your dog. This can range from a simple mat to an embroidered, plush cushion complete with your dog's name. Ideally, I recommend purchasing a bed that has a cover that slips off the padding so it can be washed. For those dogs who are prone to chewing, you can purchase bed covers that are more durable and, hence, more chew-proof. Once again, it can be used as your dog's safe spot and can be a wonderful security object.

Chapter 7

Safety for Your Dog and Family

Over four million people suffer from dog bites every year in the United States alone. If this statistic isn't bad enough, over two million of them are children. In fact, more children suffer from dog bites every year than from the combined annual totals for measles, mumps, chicken pox, and whooping cough. Children who are ages five to nine are the primary victims of animal bites. Seventy-five percent of these bites are from dogs that the victim knows. Injuries to the head, neck, and face are common in young children. These injuries often cause significant trauma and many require hospitalization.

Preventing Dog Bites

Education is the key to preventing dog bites. The risk of a bite can be reduced dramatically when children and adults are taught how to approach and handle dogs, read the warning signals, and avoid risky situations. In our society, we teach children how to telephone for emergency help, cross the street safely, and avoid threatening situations with strangers. It's just as important to teach them how to respect a dog and understand her needs, without instilling fear. In my Paws for Peace programs in elementary schools, I do just that.

Here are the safety rules I share with kids. Of course, they work for adults, too.

1. Always ask permission before approaching or petting a dog. This is especially important for children.

2. Don't pet or approach an unfamiliar dog, especially if food or toys are involved.
3. Don't approach or pet a strange, untrained, or injured dog. Also, don't approach a strange dog if the dog's exit is blocked or if the dog is up against a wall.
4. Stay out of other people's yards.
5. Never tease a dog.
6. Don't blow puffs of air into a dog's face, pull a dog's tail, or try to lift a dog off the ground.
7. Don't wake a sleeping dog.
8. Instruct children never to run through the house waving their arms. This can excite some dogs who then want to join in the fun and chase the children, which could lead to an accident.

(Also see Dog Etiquette—How to Greet a Dog on page 81.)

Keeping Your Dog Safe

You can "dog-proof" the environment to prevent or at least minimize the potential for accidents by removing or locking up chewable and toxic objects. Of course, there's no substitute for good old common sense when it comes to preventing accidents. Practice management by putting your dog in a kennel, behind baby gates, or in an exercise pen so he can't get to "illegal" objects or practice prevention by putting off-limits objects like the kitchen wastebasket in a safe place where he can't get to it.

Common Dangers—Items to Keep Out of Your Dog's Reach

Here's a list of some of the more common dangers to your dog's safety. You can also consult your veterinarian or the Animal Poison Control Center which is run by The American Society for Prevention of Cruelty to Animals on the web at *www.aspca.org/apcc* or call their hotline at 888-426-4435 for more specific information.

Chocolate: Though you may think you're giving your dog a nice treat, avoid giving chocolate or leaving it out where your dog could snatch it. A component of chocolate is toxic to most dogs and can even cause death; therefore, for safety, just don't feed chocolate.

Plants, plant bulbs, and plant water (including Christmas tree water): There's a long list of plants that are toxic and/or can cause gastrointestinal upsets. So keeping your dog away from plants is always a wise course of action. A note of interest, however, is that longtime concerns about poinsettias being toxic have been disproved. *However,* ingestion of poinsettias could cause stomach upset.

Medicines and household cleaners: Protect your dog from these items by keeping your cabinets locked. A small prescription bottle could seem like a fun toy that rattles; then, if your dog cracks it open, the medication inside could be extremely harmful to him.

Household and office items: Plastic bags, plastic ties, balloons, rubber bands, electrical cords, tinsel, string, paper clips, needles, pens, pencils, and any sharp object could be dangerous if your dog bites it or ingests it.

Food or leftovers such as cooked chicken and turkey bones: Your dog could choke on a bone if he gets into the trash.

Children's toys: Some toys can be dangerous, particularly if a dog could tear or chew off a part and choke on it. Instead of leaving children's toys out, use smart doggie toys like Kongs, Pedigree plastic balls, or Buster Cubes.

Electric wires and cords: A puppy or dog could be injured if he chews on a wire or cord.

Tablecloths: A puppy could pull on an overhanging table-cloth and be injured by a falling object.

Antifreeze: Dogs find the taste of antifreeze appealing. Unfortunately, it can be deadly. If your dog ingests even a small amount of antifreeze, call your veterinarian immediately. A safer type of antifreeze is available; ask your veterinarian about this.

Rat poison: This is another toxic and deadly substance that dogs have been known to ingest. If you suspect your dog has ingested rat poison, call your veterinarian immediately.

Toilet bowl cleaners: Don't use a toilet bowl cleaner that is placed in the tank. The toxic chemicals can cause illness if your dog should happen to drink from the toilet.

Preventing Heatstroke

Never leave your dog in a car in warm weather. Every year news reports abound with cases of both infants and dogs that were left in a car in hot weather with disastrous results. The popular idea of cracking a window so she'll get some air is fine if the temperature isn't too high and you're parked in the shade, but it really doesn't help at all when it's hot outside and the sun bakes down on a parked car. Also, remember that the sun moves—one minute your car might be parked in the shade and a few minutes later it might be in direct sunlight. If the temperature is 85 degrees Fahrenheit outside on a hot summer day, the inside of the car can reach 160 degrees Fahrenheit within half an hour. Your dog can suffer brain damage or death if her body temperature reaches 107 degrees Fahrenheit, which is only five degrees over her normal body temperature. Signs of heatstroke include: excessive panting, vomiting, a fast pulse rate, and high body temperature. If you suspect heatstroke, do not delay. Get your dog to a veterinarian immediately. If that's not possible, soak your dog in cool water until her temperature goes down. Ice packs around your dog's head will also help.

Don't take your dog along with you in hot weather if you're going to have to leave her in the car for even a few minutes. In those emergency situations when you have to take your dog with you in hot weather, I suggest leaving the air conditioning running. Another option is to make a bed of ice for the dog to lie on. You can do this by filling a large plastic tray with ice and covering it with a towel. But even in these situations, the bottom line is this—never stay away for more than a few minutes. In Florida and Michigan, it's actually illegal to leave your dog alone in the car.

Managing Your Dog

It is important to physically control your dog until she learns what to do and what not to do. Use of a leash and collar, as well as a kennel, will help immensely in this process. (See Leashes and Tethers, page 90 and Kennels, page 93.) Introduce these items to your dog using positive reinforcement. Always use leash management to keep your dog from running to the street and be respectful by keeping him off other peoples' yards. Since some lawns are chemically treated, you don't want your dog to be exposed to these chemicals.

Watch for broken glass on sidewalks. In hot weather, be aware of the temperature of the pavement or, at the beach, the sand. If it's too hot, your dog's paws could be burned. To test this, put your hand on the pavement or the sand. If it's too hot for your hand, it's too hot for your dog's paws. And be aware that your dog can get sunburned too, so take necessary precautions and avoid taking her outside during the hottest hours of the day. In the winter, salt that is used to melt snow and ice can also be a problem. You don't want her to ingest too much sodium when she licks her paws, so be sure to wipe her paws when you bring her inside.

Don't allow your dog to ride loose in the back of your pick-up truck. This seems like a commonsense notion, but I've actually witnessed a dog being flipped out of a truck and others holding on for dear life. I also suggest seat belts when your dog is in the car. Make sure your dog keeps his head inside the window to avoid injury from dust and stones from the street or from flying insects.

Chapter 8

Principles of Learning

Let me digress a bit here and clear up the often misused concept of "being dominant" as it relates to our relationship with our dogs. While it is true you want to be a parenting leader for your human/canine family, physical force or punishment or the threat of force or punishment are not necessary. The definition of dominance is "who's in control" such as controlling access to stuff, not physically forcing a dog into submission.

The Dominance Myth

For many years, concepts about hierarchy within the canine world led to the idea that one dog in the pack is the top ranking "alpha dog" and that that dog is dominant in all situations. In recent years this concept has been researched extensively by leading animal behaviorists who now consider it to be outmoded and simplistic. Still, the perception that dogs look up to the alpha in the pack as some sort of tyrannical dictator and that humans should take on this role has been perpetuated by the authors of many mainstream dog training books and trainers on television. They use this theory to teach you to mandate your authority as the physical-force leader of your dog's pack—the boss, the head honcho, the big cheese, the numero uno. Woe to him if he doesn't obey. Unfortunately, this outmoded idea has some trainers perpetuating the myth that humans should use physical displays with the family dog, including physically forcing dogs to walk behind them, standing over them, pinning them to the ground, always entering a room first, and so on, supposedly to mimic the behaviors of packs in the wild. Well, none of these things actually exist in the wild except around food or procreation issues.

The most frequently repeated phrase by trainers who endorse this outdated "dominance" theory is. "You must always win when training your dog." If you think about it, the phrase "you must always win" conveys that there is a competition going on. And a competition means there is a "win-lose" mentality. How can you and your dog become a behavioral team when you are caught up in an environment of having to compete and win at all costs?

Dogs are social animals. When they were domesticated way back when, we became part of their social order and along the way we also became their guardians, caregivers, protectors, and guides. There is no "one dog rules all" pack mentality. The best way to view your role in your dog's life is as a member of his family—and the dog as a member of your family. Just as parents and children have different roles in the family, so, too, humans and dogs have different roles. But we're all part of the same family. In nonviolent dog training, you are not out to compete or "win" anything. There are no "commands" and no threats. Instead, you give your dog "signals" and reinforce his correct "responses." You are learning from each other how to work together.

Although not a perfect mirror, some similarities exist in the social orders between wolves and dogs. L. David Mech, one of the world's leading experts on the pack behavior of wild wolves, prefers to associate the term alpha with parenting. He says, "In natural wolf packs, the alpha male or female are merely the breeding animals, the parents of the pack, and dominance contests with other wolves are rare, if they exist at all." Mech continues, "Breeding wolves [only] provide leadership because offspring tend to follow their parents' initiative . . . The point here is not so much the terminology but what the terminology falsely implies: a rigid, *force-based* dominance hierarchy." Mech's research shows that, while breeding wolves provided the most leadership, wolves who had subordinate roles also provided leadership during travel. He says, "No 'alpha' [emphasis mine] would suddenly run to the front of the pack and force the subordinate to get behind him."

According to Dr. Karen Overall, many animal behaviorists believe that although each member of a group works in his own self-interest, that self-interest manifests in shared responsibilities. It would be abnormal for one animal to constantly *have to* demonstrate through force that he was dominant. In reality, each situation in the group dynamic entails a collaborative effort. In the wild, these social interactions are dependent on what's going on in the environment because success for the group is dependent on working together. Wolves have a complex communication system; we are still trying to translate their subtle language. We do know, however, that studies suggest the only situations that trigger an absolute rank hierarchy are around disasters or stressful situations relating to resources like food and sex (procreation).

So the question arises, why do some trainers seem to elicit almost miraculous results in getting dogs to do what they want through what they call "dominance" training? The truth is, it isn't miraculous, nor is it related to dominance. The results are due to using physical force in order to suppress behaviors, which is done by using positive punishment and physically forcing fearful dogs into overwhelming situations until they "shut down," which is called flooding. Calling this dominance training is simply incorrect and its practice can be dangerous for both dogs and humans, especially when aggression is involved. It's pure abuse when used with fearful dogs.

Animals defer to one another to keep their group safe, strong, and healthy. If one individual threatens the group's collaborative efforts by asserting himself in ways contrary to the group's well being, he is thrown out. There are many examples of animal packs ousting members who tried to rule by brute force. Wolves have banished individuals who constantly used undue physical force to exert their authority. Monkeys also have been shown to attack and oust brutish members who used their strength and size against other members of the group.

Behavioral scientists are helping us better understand ourselves and our world by their study of collaborative efforts within various species. The following story is a terrific example of how we humans can learn from nature—in this case, from geese:

The Goose Story
Author Unknown

Next fall, when you see geese heading south for the winter, flying along in "V" formation, you might consider what science has discovered about why they fly that way.

As each bird flaps its wings, it creates an uplift for the bird immediately following.

By flying in a "V" formation, the whole flock adds at least 71 percent more flying range than possible if each bird flew on its own.

People who share a common direction and sense of community can get where they are going more quickly and easily because they are traveling on the thrust of one another.

When a goose falls out of formation, it suddenly feels the drag and resistance of trying to go it alone . . . and quickly gets back into formation to take advantage of the lifting power of the bird in front.

If we have as much sense as the goose, we will stay in formation with those who are headed the same way.

When the head goose gets tired, it rotates back in the wing and another goose flies point.

It is sensible to take turns doing demanding jobs, whether with people or with geese flying south.

Geese honk from behind to encourage those up front to keep up their speed.

What do we say when we honk from behind?

Finally—and this is important—when a goose gets sick or is wounded by gunshot or falls out of formation, two other geese fall out with that goose and follow it down to lend help and protection. They stay with the fallen goose until it is able to fly or until it dies. Only then do they launch out on their own or with another formation to catch up with their group.

If we have the sense of a goose, we will stand by each other like that.

Parents understand the importance of protecting and educating their children. After all, the parenting role requires not just providing food, shelter, and clothing, but also setting boundaries. What you want the dog to do and the child to do is to take their cues about the appropriateness of their behavior from you and that is the context within which you guide and protect them. A child can't just run out into the middle of the street or steal a toy from another child in the schoolyard without consequences. In the best of circumstances, the parent acts as a loving, nonviolent guardian; he is the source and provider of safety and comfort, and he educates the child through the use of examples, boundaries, and limits. In the same way, you must educate and act as a loving, nonviolent, benevolent guardian in your dog's life.

If a three-year-old child has her hand on the doorknob, she is dominant because she controls whether the dog goes in or out. If she is holding a ball, in the dog's eyes, she is dominant because she controls access to the ball. So dominance doesn't mean who is bigger or stronger . . . although that sometimes plays a part. It simply means setting up your environment so that you control access to things your dog wants and he has to look to you to get what he wants. You control the food, affection, toys, social freedom, climate control, and everything else in his universe. There is no negotiation. In effect, you are saying, "I'll give you the world, but you've got to do something for me first." When the dog figures this out, you simply ask the dog to do something before providing the reward, whether it be food, chasing a ball, going outside, and so on.

Asking your dog to lie down before releasing him to go up the steps or out the door presents terrific everyday training opportunities. So does asking him to sit before being fed, or asking him to jump off the couch so he can be rewarded by getting back on the couch to sit with you. But asking for these behaviors and rewarding your dog is much different than "showing him who's boss" and forcing him to sit, lie down, and obey you in all things under the threat of punishment.

So ask yourself why you are teaching your dog to sit, lie down, and come when called. For safety purposes? Ideally, we train our dogs to respond to our signals so we can help them and ourselves be all that we can be. Training stimulates growth and forms a bond between us because it involves communication and interaction. A synergy emerges allowing both our dogs and ourselves to grow and learn in ways that are unique and might otherwise be impossible. I have learned as much, if not more, about patience, honesty, compassion, and congruity—matching my words to my actions, thoughts, and emotions—in the companionship of dogs as I have in any other endeavor. In addition, I believe my dogs have also benefited in ways I can't even imagine.

So when you read about or hear about how important it is to control your dog by showing him who's boss by physically pinning him to the ground, jerking him on a leash, or grabbing his muzzle and yelling "No," I ask that you reconsider. Don't compete; instead educate. Show him how the world provides his food, affection, and freedom—and ignores him when he behaves inappropriately. (Of course, use common sense here—don't ignore him when doing so would cause harm to him, to others, or to the environment.) Educate your dog about the appropriateness of his behavior. Create an environment in which you can guide and protect him, yourself, and the environment.

Dr. Karen Overall, director of the Behavior Clinic of the School of Veterinary Medicine at the University of Pennsylvania, sums up the path to a great relationship with our dogs with the following overview:

- Practice deferential behaviors.
- Do not use physical punishment.
- Teach the dog that you are not a threat.
- Reward good behaviors, even when they are spontaneous.
- Don't worry about minor details—none of us are perfect.
- Always let the dog know he can have treats, love, or toys if he sits quietly first.
- Never do something just because you can.
- Talk to your dog. Use his or her name. Signal clearly.
- Be reliable and trustworthy.

Classical Conditioning, Counter-Conditioning, and Operant Conditioning

There's a story about an elderly woman who, around seven one night, reached for her walking cane and called her two dogs to go for a walk. As the dogs raced in from the yard, they both spied the cane. One dog jumped up, wagged his tail, and couldn't wait to go outside. The other dog, recently obtained from the local shelter, became distressed. His ears lay flat, his shoulders went down, his tail dropped between his legs, he began to lick his lips and pant, and finally urinated as the woman started to walk toward him with the cane. "What's the matter, Sparky?" the woman gently asked. "We're just going for a walk."

Here we have one cane and two very different reactions. This cane, a simple piece of wood, meant something completely different to each dog. Why? Association. The first dog had a history of pleasant experiences with the cane; it meant that he got to go for a walk, visit his friends, say hello to the neighborhood. The second dog had a history too. He had previously lived with a family that would whack him with a stick whenever they felt like it—mostly for urinating on the carpet. To this dog, a cane meant trouble.

Back in the 1930s, the famous behaviorist Ivan Pavlov discovered that when dogs learned to associate the sound of a bell with food, they would salivate every time a bell rang. After a while, whether food was present or not, the dogs would still salivate whenever the bell was rung. This kind of learning is called classical conditioning, also known as associative conditioning. The word "conditioning" simply means learning. In the story above, both dogs learned associations but one was negative and the other was positive. In classical conditioning the dog learns to associate or link things together. He learns that if "A" happens, then "B" will likely happen, like the bell ringing signaled the food was about to appear. But the results are not contingent upon what he does. In other words, some event will likely happen one way or another, no matter how he responds. As a result, he will start to respond automatically. The bell rings, food appears, and the dog's resultant behavior (or conditioned response) is salivation. This type of conditioning happens in our own lives, too. For instance, when you see the lights of a police car flashing in your rear-view mirror, you most likely will get a ticket. The result is that every time you see a police car you have heart palpitations and sweaty palms. Classical conditioning mostly deals with instinctive bodily responses, such as salivation, racing heart, blinking, fight or fight responses, and the like.

Classical conditioning can be used to empower your dog training clicker (which I'll discuss in Chapter 11) so it becomes almost as valuable as a food reward. So too, if you link or associate food with praise, you likely will increase the value of your praise. So if you say "good" whenever you give your dog a piece of turkey, over time the word "good" will become almost as good as the turkey itself.

Here are a few other examples of classical conditioning:

- 🦴 A ball being thrown becomes associated with play.
- 🦴 The sound of the treat bag opening becomes associated with treats.
- 🦴 The sight of the leash appearing becomes associated with walks, etc.

So with classical, or "associative," conditioning, the dog learns to predict good stuff is about to happen whenever something else happens, and he has nothing to do with the outcome.

Counter-conditioning differs from classical conditioning in one major regard. Classical conditioning deals with making an association with something that has no value (known as a "neutral") and, by so doing, increasing its value. Associate something great, such as a food treat with something the dog doesn't have any feelings about, in other words, something neutral. For example, when a dog training clicker is used for the first time, the dog has no experience with it and thus has no feelings about it other than initial curiosity. However, when the appearance (or sound) of the clicker is linked with food, eventually the dog associates the great thing (food) with the neutral thing (clicker). Counter-conditioning *changes* the way a dog feels about something he has already come to dislike. If the dog already hates the vacuum cleaner, you would use counter-conditioning to change his dis-like of the vacuum 180 degrees to "I *like* the vacuum." We also use counter-conditioning to change the way our dogs feel about dogs, cats, the mail carrier, objects that frighten him, and anything else he dislikes. By linking food with the disliked thing, we've changed or countered the dog's feelings. For example, if your dog is aggressive to the mail carrier or frightened by him, you might give the dog a treat every time the mail carrier approaches your house until eventually the dog loves the previously hated mail carrier. The mail carrier is now a predictor of yummy stuff and, as a result, the dog likes him.

Operant conditioning differs from classical and counter-conditioning because the dog can actually influence what happens. Operant conditioning or learning means the consequence *is* contingent upon the behavior. In other words, the dog learns that if he does something, he can produce a consequence. To make it simple, operant conditioning follows the ABC principle.

Each of the behaviors in the chart below is learned by the principles of operant conditioning.

The ABCs of Operant Conditioning

A. The **A**ntecedent (any sensory stimulation) that signals ➡	**B.** The **B**ehavior (anything your dog does) in anticipation of ➡	**C.** The **C**onsequence (something the dog receives after performing the behavior)
A *sound*, such as: The word "sit" signals ➡	Putting the behind on the floor in anticipation of ➡	Receiving a food treat.
A ringing bell signals ➡	Running to the mat in anticipation of ➡	Getting to go outside.
The footsteps of a person approaching the house signals ➡	Running to the door and barking in anticipation of ➡	Receiving praise.

A *touch,* such as: Being touched on the paw signals →	Raising the paw as in "let's shake hands" in anticipation of →	Getting to chase a ball.
Being petted on the head signals →	Jumping on the couch in anticipation of →	Getting to be with you.
A *smell,* such as: Dog food signals →	Running to the kitchen and lying down in anticipation of →	Dinner being served.
Cologne signals →	Running to the door to greet a favorite person in anticipation of →	Receiving praise and petting from the visitor
Illegal drugs signal →	Barking to announce the presence of drugs in anticipation of →	Receiving praise and more food.

PART 2

Training Essentials

Chapter 9

Motivation and Rewards

Several factors influence learning. At the simplest level, though, we can say that dogs do stuff either because they want to avoid something or because there's something in it for them, as in "Show me the money!" Getting a dog to do what we ask can seem difficult at times because a dog comes with predisposed motivations provided by Mother Nature that compete with our requests. Mother Nature can be worth a lot of money to a dog. Chasing squirrels: $20,000; affection from you, a couple of bucks. If you are competing with Mother Nature (squirrels, et al.) you'll need some motivation of your own. That means great food treats.

Motivating Your Dog

When you first start training your dog, what happens when you yell "Sit!" just as a squirrel runs through the yard? Who's worth more? The $20,000 squirrel or you? At that moment in time, chasing the squirrel is a huge payoff and your shout of "Sit!" is worthless. And if you keep repeating the word "sit," the word loses its power. If the next-door neighbor's female dog is in heat and your intact male hears you yelling, "Come!" where's the $20,000? It's the female, of course.

Chasing squirrels, greeting mail carriers, meeting other dogs, and smelling road kill are all powerful motivators that distract your dog's attention from what you are asking him to do. In these situations, you, the erstwhile provider of all things good in your dog's universe, have taken a back seat. Therefore, in order to get your dog to do what *you* want, you need to become worth more than the distractions. You want to elevate yourself in your dog's eyes to the position of prime motivator so no matter what, you're *it*. You do this by controlling access to everything your dog wants. That means that your dog must earn everything he wants, including food, toys, and freedom.

The Hierarchy of Rewards

Dogs have different likes and dislikes. In human terms, think of a Las Vegas slot machine, the lottery, or horse racing. In all of these cases there are great rewards, good rewards, and average rewards. In the dog's Las Vegas mentality, one dog might consider a piece of raw liver as a $10,000 reward, while another dog, at times, might consider a squeaky toy the highest reward possible.

Carrying Treats with You

One of the easiest and cleanest methods to keep food treats at the ready is to carry them in a treat pouch (sold at pet stores) or a hip pack (also known as a fanny pack), which is sold in department stores and sporting good stores. Just remember to clean your treat pouch or pack at the end of the day!

You first need to identify what your dog values most. It's a pretty good bet that chicken, turkey, and cheese will do nicely. Use whatever works for your dog.

Primary ($10,000) Rewards

- Special food treats
- Play (in some instances)

Secondary Rewards

- Affection through praise and touching
- Play, including toys
- Social interaction, including allowing your dog to go places with you (such as a ride in the car), walking up

and down the stairs, going in and out of doors, or being allowed on the bed or other furniture.

Lures, Bribes, and Rewards

A *lure* is a promise of a reward. It is a piece of food or other item that entices your dog to do what you want. For instance, if your dog is hungry and you put a piece of turkey in front of his nose, you can use it to lure him to follow you. Squeaky toys can be lures, opening a can of dog food can be a lure, and opening the front door can also be a lure.

A *bribe*, on the other hand, is a lure gone astray. If you have to show your dog a piece of turkey every time you want her to do something, you're bribing her. A lure is used only to get her interested, and then only if it's necessary. If you find yourself dependent upon food or toys in order to get your dog to do something, you can bet that you are using these things as bribes.

A *reward*, as the term is used in this book, is a positive reinforcement. A reinforcement is a reward for desired behavior. Unlike a lure, which is used to get your dog interested in doing something, a reward is something you give him after he has performed the desired behavior. When you give your dog a piece of turkey as soon as his behind hits the floor, you are rewarding him. Never bribe a dog. Once your dog knows something good is associated with his behavior, he will work to get what he wants.

As I mentioned, rewards have a pecking order. Some are great, some good, and some just okay. To keep your dog highly motivated, especially when teaching a new exercise or behavior, always use a great reward—one that's worth $10,000 in human terms. But there's a caution involved here. Rewards have to *keep* their value. If the same great reward is given over and over again, it will lose its value. Also, if you give too much of the same reward at any one time, it can lose its value. The classic example of this point is the story of the trainer who guaranteed she could get a dog to ignore a freshly cooked steak without resorting to any negative training. How? Shortly before the demonstration she simply gave the dog more steak than he could possibly eat. Then, when it came time for the demonstration, she offered him yet another piece and he ignored it. The steak had lost its value because the dog couldn't eat another bite.

Other rewards, such as praise, can also be misused and lose their power. Of course, you want to praise your dog consistently for doing what you've asked. But if you give him praise for doing nothing, he may begin to ignore you. The same goes for your dog's favorite toys. They, too, should be rewards for doing what you've asked, rather than always being available. Rewards—to be rewards—have to keep their value. Of course, you can cheat a little and occasionally give a $10,000 treat just for the heck of it, because she's such a great dog and you're a wonderful person.

Weaning a Dog Off Treats

When I started training in 1974, I was adamant that I would never use treats to reward my dog. I used praise and petting and "life rewards" but never treats. Of course the only method I had to ensure my dog responded was to use physical punishment if she didn't do what I asked. When I switched to training exclusively with nonviolent methods, one of the first things I focused on was learning how to wean my dogs off food treats. Obviously you don't want to have to carry treats around with you for the rest of your life. Therefore, you should wean him off treats as soon as possible. This is done in three ways:

1. Consistently use life rewards throughout the day. It is important that your dog cannot obtain anything she wants on her own for this to work, hence the need to keep her on leashes (supervised!), behind baby gates, or in a kennel or dog run (taught with positive methods).
2. Form behavioral chains. This means adding one behavior after another before rewarding, such as: sit, down, stay, come, and then a food reward. Vary these behavioral chains by asking for different behaviors.
3. Use intermittent food reinforcement. Always praise your dog, but gradually get to a point where the food reward treats are far and few between.

If you are consistent in following these three suggestions, your dog will be weaned off treats while becoming more and more reliable. The reason this works is that all of these suggestions reinforce you as being in control of everything your dog wants.

Chapter 10

The Secrets of Professional Dog Trainers

If you've ever said, "My dog knows this; he's just being stubborn," you've not been introduced to the concepts of context learning, shaping behaviors, the ways to use repetition in training, or the influence of your dog's biorhythms and learning curves. These are the secrets of professional dog trainers. They're not really secrets, of course, it's just that most people don't consider these factors in training their dogs. Professionals consider them of utmost importance.

Context Learning

Have you ever found yourself in that embarrassing situation where someone came up to you and greeted you and you were totally stumped about who they were? You know that you know the person but you can't associate the face with how or where you met. We've all had this kind of experience. You know someone from work or church or the PTA, but when you run into him at the supermarket or on the street, you just can't quite put your finger on who he is or how you know him.

What you're experiencing is a situational or contextual conundrum. You know the person from one context or situation in your life and he's suddenly appeared in another context. And your mind goes blank trying to make a connection. The same thing happens in dog training.

Mike, who believed that his golden retriever, Sunny, was the smartest dog in the Western world, taught him all sorts of tricks. He taught Sunny to sit, play dead, crawl, shake hands, roll over, and balance a biscuit on his nose. One night, while watching *Buffy, the Vampire Slayer,* Mike saw a commercial where a dog opened a refrigerator, grabbed a can of beer, and brought it to his handler. Mike decided that Sunny could do that. So, he taught him to open the refrigerator, get a can of beer, bring it to him, sit quietly by while he drank it, and then take the empty can and ceremoniously deposit it in the wastebasket.

It took several weeks, but finally Sunny had the trick down pat. Mike couldn't wait to have his friends over for Super Bowl Sunday so he could show off Sunny performing this amazing feat. With the masses gathered and in high anticipation, Mike confidently instructed Sunny to "get me a beer." Sunny jumped up and down, wagged his tail, barked excitedly, and did every trick in the book except going to get the beer. You can imagine the heckling from Mike's buddies. What Mike didn't understand was that Sunny had no idea what Mike was asking of him because he had been trained to do this behavioral sequence in an environment with no distractions. Mike never trained him with ten people hanging around. That new context formed a kind of "excitement wall"—blocking his memory.

Mike's experience illustrates the idea of contextual learning. When you teach a dog to sit in the living room with no one else around, that doesn't mean he'll do it when you ask him to sit outside in the yard. Not only are there more distractions outside, which is part of the "context," but the grass—where he's being asked to put his behind—is also a new factor. Then when you add friends, other animals, and other sundry distractions, your dog needs time to regroup and assimilate each change. Every time you change the context, you must start training the behavior from the beginning again as if he never learned it at all. He's not being stubborn, defiant or spiteful; instead, he really doesn't know the behavior in that context!

Eventually he'll "generalize" and perform the expected behavior wherever and whenever you request it. When a dog generalizes, he's saying, "I got it—you don't have to start over every time we go someplace new. Now I know that 'sit' means 'sit' in any place or situation."

Shaping a Behavior

Shaping a behavior means rewarding one baby step after another baby step until you have achieved the final behavior you want. This is done through the use of "successive approximations." In other words, each rewarded baby movement is a part of—or an approximation of—the final goal. Reward all successive behaviors that lead to the final behavioral goal. Confused? Hang on.

Shaping a dog's behavior is like the game of "hot and cold," in which the person who is "it" tries to determine which object in the room the other players have selected for her to find. She moves around the room while the other players say, "You're getting warm" and "Now you're getting colder" until finally the person gets close to the object she's supposed to find and is told, "You're red-hot!"

It's just the same with a dog. Each time your dog gets closer to doing what you want, reward his efforts with praise and treats. When he gets further away from the behavior you want, ignore the behavior—which is the same as saying "You're getting cold." Then, when he finally "gets it," he receives a jackpot—several $10,000 rewards.

You can shape virtually any behavior you want from your dog, including wagging his tail at various speeds, a very fast or a very slow sit, sneezing three times in a row, or nodding his head yes and no. All of these behaviors are simply shaped and molded one step at a time.

For example, to shape your dog's behavior to sit up in the begging position, first reward her for sitting. Then, hold the treat a little higher and reward her for stretching up or craning her neck to get the treat. Then reward her again when she lifts one paw off the ground, again when she lifts two paws off the ground, and finally only when she holds the finished balanced pose.

In nonviolent training, we use three ways to shape behavior: positive reinforcement, negative reinforcement, and negative punishment. Scientifically speaking, a reinforcement, whether positive or negative, increases the likelihood of a behavior being repeated, and punishment decreases the likelihood. Occasionally some negatives are used in nonviolent training, but only when they do not harm the dog or the human physically, emotionally, or mentally.

Positive reinforcement means rewarding behaviors you want your dog to repeat. When your dog performs the sit behavior, reward him for it. Give him a treat every time he puts his behind on the floor, and there's a good chance he'll keep putting his behind on the floor. Give a child $10 every time she gets an "A" on her report card, and there's a good chance she'll continue getting good grades. Again, this is one of the primary ways to shape your dog's behavior in positive dog training.

Negative reinforcement means taking something bad away in order to get her to do something. For us, the seat belt alarm in a car is a form of negative reinforcement. Unless you snap the seat belt together, the irritating buzzer continues to sound. The age-old silent treatment is also a form of negative reinforcement. Your significant other's refusal to speak to you is a negative (well, in this case) and until you apologize, you're in the doghouse. In this book we occasionally present negative reinforcement methods, but only when it does not harm the dog. While it is possible to use negative reinforcement nonviolently, some people use aversive methods including shocking, shaking, ear pinching, and continual jerking. If you use any of these methods, you are saying to your dog, "I'm only going to stop hurting you when you pick up that ball."

Punishment means doing something to decrease the likelihood your dog will ever repeat a particular behavior again. Punishment can be either positive or negative. That may sound confusing but bear with me. *Positive punishment* includes physical methods such as hitting, kicking, shocking, shaking, swatting with newspapers, and so on to try to stop behaviors like jumping, pulling on a leash, stealing food, mouthing, and so on. *Negative punishment* means taking something good away from your dog to get him to stop doing a behavior. If your puppy bites you, for example, you withdraw your attention by walking away. If you ask your dog to sit but he barks instead, you eat the treat that was intended for him. The human equivalent would be taking away your child's computer or phone privileges to stop him from coming home late. This is called negative punishment because you are taking something away from your dog. In this case, the word "negative" means removing. To clarify what this book's training is all about, we use negative punishment but do not use positive physical punishment.

The Repetition Factor

The only way your dog will learn to do something reliably is to have him repeat the behavior over and over. There are no shortcuts. Depending on things like the dog's age, genetic predisposition, history, motivation level, ability, and lifestyle, the repetition factor can range from several hundred to over 10,000 repetitions of any one behavior over a period of months or years. The degree of reliability is directly related to the number of successful responses in various environments. Professional trainers view the age between one and a half and four years as the period when reliability sets in.

Biorhythms and Learning Curves

Common sense dictates that dogs have good days and bad days, just as we do. Emotionally and physically they just might be feeling a little low or anxious one day and really motivated the next. What works in the morning might not work in the evening. What works in a low distraction environment won't work in a busy environment. What works when a dog is feeling well might not work if she is suffering from a digestive upset or if an arthritic condition is acting up.

Just like humans, dogs have their own biorhythm cycles. Physically, emotionally, and mentally, they learn on a roller coaster curve—integrating more and more information, gradually reaching higher, then going down a little, then reaching higher than before. One day she enthusiastically sits every time you request it, and the next day she acts as if she never heard the word. The trick to being a really great instructor is learning when your dog is "up" and when it's time to back off in training, so you will be nurturing and challenging her at her own learning rate.

In a strictly controlled environment, like a laboratory or a marine mammal water park, learning curves are plotted and vigilantly followed for optimum results. But in an everyday, typical harried home, who has the time? Most people feel it's the dog's job to fit into the human's schedule and lifestyle. I agree with this notion—but not at the expense of the health and welfare of the dog, which means taking into account how the dog is feeling physically, mentally, and emotionally. After all, how your dog is feeling directly relates to the success of your training program. Developing your observational skills and intuition plays a big part in helping this process along.

Remember that dogs are on dog time—they live in the present. Their attention can be diverted in a split second. It may be riveted on you one second, and in the next, distracted by the slightest sight, sound, touch, or smell. Taking this as well as your own busy lifestyle into consideration, all you need to do is take ninety seconds to tune into your dog both mentally and physically before you begin a training session. You can do this by practicing the communication exercise on page 85.

Chapter 11

Ways to Fast-Track Your Training

In this chapter, you'll learn some nifty ways to communicate with your dog and, in the process, learn how to quickly shape reliable behavior.

Markers—Clickers and Words

Dogs have only a short window of time in which they associate what they're doing with a consequence—whether it is a reward or a punishment. Let's say you are teaching your dog to sit. When your dog puts his behind on the floor you've got up to one second to let him know, "That's it. That's the behavior I'm looking for!" In other words, in order to get the message across to him, you have to give him your signal of approval virtually the exact moment he sits. If you walk into a room three seconds after your dog has eliminated on the carpet, there's no use even commenting on it. Your dog simply won't associate his urination three seconds before with your yelling. As far as he's concerned, you're yelling because of what he's doing at that exact moment—lying quietly on the floor. (See more on how to deal with elimination problems on page 257.)

So how can you develop the split-second speed required to communicate how pleased you are with your dog for sitting when you ask him to? How do we get information to our dogs so quickly? It can be pretty difficult to consistently deliver a food treat in a split second to reward your dog every time you see a behavior you're looking for. So do what the famous behaviorist Pavlov did—turn a sound into a predictable reward.

The tools we use to give this sound reward are words and clickers. A clicker is a cricket-sounding toy used by many dog trainers to clearly and crisply mark a dog's behavior. These inexpensive tools are small plastic boxes about the size of a matchbox. A clicker gives your dog information very fast, usually much faster than saying any particular word. Remember, you need to communicate to your dog that what she just did was exactly what you were looking for and this communication has to happen at virtually the same moment she performed the desired behavior. Normally our ability to respond verbally is simply not that fast or consistent—that's why I recommend the use of a click to mark the behavior. A clicker is a quick, accurate, novel tool that can mark your dog's behavior as good, something you want her to do again. But, once again, a clicker is an optional tool.

Eventually you'll stop using the clicker and just use words of praise as a reward. (Clickers are difficult to find in stores, but they can be ordered at *www.dogwhisererdvd.com* or by calling 1-800-955-5440.)

How to Use a Clicker

Initially a clicker has no value to your dog. It's neutral. To give it value or empower it, do this: Put it in your hand and *immediately* after clicking, throw your dog a great food treat. Click and treat like this ten to fifteen times. Do two or three of these sessions during the day. You'll know your dog has "got it" when she starts looking around for the treat after hearing the click. Now that the clicker has meaning, you're ready to "mark" the exact behavior you're looking for. For example, when teaching your dog to sit, move your hand an inch or so over her head. If she sits, click and reward the moment her behind hits the floor.

Some dogs are a bit sound sensitive, so be cautious and sensitive when introducing the clicker.

Tips for Using a Clicker

If your dog is shy or sensitive to sounds, it helps to do a little planning when introducing the use of a clicker. Here are some tips:

- Make sure you use your dog's absolute favorite food as a treat in conjunction with the use of the clicker.
- Muffle the clicker by putting it in your pocket or wrapping a towel around it and increase your distance from your dog.
- Instead of doing a complete click, which consists of two clicking sounds—one when you press the clicker and another when you release it—press for one click only. Then, the next time your dog does a desired behavior, release your thumb to make another clicking sound.
- Single click and treat three to five times and then stop. Remember, the treat is given a split second after the click. Repeat the process later.
- Once your dog associates the muffled single click with the treat, you can try a muffled double click. Then graduate to an unmuffled double click.
- As soon as you click, throw the treat or have someone who is standing next to your dog immediately drop the treat.
- Gradually close the distance to your dog. For especially sensitive dogs this may take a couple of days.
- Make sure your demeanor is happy and fun.

Trainers at marine mammal water parks use whistles as "markers" instead of clickers when they train whales and dolphins. A clicker doesn't work for them because they need their hands free to give two-handed signals. Although a whistle can work in training your dog, I prefer a clicker because when you use a whistle, you can't simultaneously give verbal praise to your dog.

Deaf people use flashes of light from a flashlight or a light in the room as markers. They also use other methods to mark a behavior, such as touching the dog or giving a hand signal.

Clickers are optional. If you don't have a clicker, you can use words to mark a desired behavior. For instance, say "good dog" or "yes" or "that'll do" or "hooray," etc. every time your dog does the behavior you're asking for and he'll get the idea. In the beginning try to use the same word or phrase consistently.

While not absolutely necessary, clickers are valuable training tools because

1. They're novel for both human and dog.
2. Once you get used to using a clicker, it's a much more reliable marker because it's difficult to consistently say the word "good" as quickly as you can click.
3. A clicker can be used as an "occasion setter."

An occasion setter is any stimulus that triggers a dog's anticipation that something good or bad is going to happen. For instance, when you open a can of food, he anticipates that he is going to eat. When you grab the leash, he anticipates going for a walk. Just like these examples of positive anticipation, when you grab the clicker it can mean that fun times are ahead. It's as if you flip on a switch in your dog's head and he's suddenly ready to work. He'll immediately recognize the clicker and say to himself, "Oh boy, something good is about to happen." This is an important concept because no dog is "on" all the time. An occasion setter can flip on a switch in your dog's head that helps him tune in to you and pay attention.

Remember to click immediately when your dog does the desired behavior and reward with a treat. Otherwise, he won't associate the click and treat with the behavior.

"No-Reward" Markers

Just as a clicker or the word "good" can mark a correct response, you can help your dog learn by letting him know when he makes an incorrect response. You do this by using a no-reward marker such as the word "oops," "ah-ah," or "uh-oh." Let's say you ask your dog to sit. You give her two seconds. If she doesn't sit, say "oops" and remove the chance of getting a reward. Another example is asking her to stay. If she gets up right away, say "oops" and turn away.

Two things are happening here:

1. If your dog doesn't do what you've asked, you've gone too far too fast. So you have to go back to the point where she was successful and build from there; but . . .
2. She's also learned that she's really in control of getting a reward because you've identified not only what behavior gets her the reward—the sound of the clicker—she's also learned what not to do by your signal of "oops."

The 80 Percent Rule—How to Make Your Words Mean Something

There were two sets of twins, and five children in all, in my home when I was growing up. As typical kids we'd be upstairs at bedtime jumping up and down on the beds, giggling, and making all sorts of racket when we were supposed to be going to sleep. My parents would yell from downstairs, "If I have to come upstairs . . ." But we'd go on giggling and romping.

Eventually my father would take the threat even further. He'd pretend he was coming upstairs by standing at the bottom of the stairs and making stomping noises. That didn't get us to quiet down either. We had learned that our parents' threats were irrelevant. They didn't have any power because they were all empty threats. It would take nine or ten threats before there would be any serious action on my parents' part to stop our inappropriate behavior. Finally, my dad would actually come up the stairs. Then we'd really shut up, dive under the covers, and pretend we were asleep, hoping he couldn't hear the pounding of our hearts.

Dogs learn the same way as humans do. Words are irrelevant unless they have power behind them and really mean something. Words will have power if you link them with consequences, like receiving a reward, and that introduces us to the 80 percent rule. That is, when to label a behavior to make it mean something and when to add duration, distance, and distractions to your training.

Throughout the lessons in Part 3, we will refer to the 80 percent rule: When you are 80 percent sure your dog will do such and such, move on to the next level. The way to know when your dog is ready to go on to something else is based on your judgment. You know your dog better than anybody. The rule of thumb, however, is this: If your dog does what you're asking eight out of ten times in any particular situation, move on.

Some behaviors, such as sit and lie down, must be established before you can label them. In other words don't say "sit" unless you're sure she'll sit. These behaviors are first taught using lures, hand motions, clickers, and rewards. When do you start saying the word "sit," for example? When she sits eight out of ten times, it is time to label the behavior by saying "sit" immediately preceding the hand motion.

Other behaviors, however, can be labeled immediately because you're already 80 percent sure your dog will respond. Examples of this are stay, come when called, go to your spot, and asking your dog to touch either a stick or your hand. In these behaviors, your dog figures out what you want very quickly. For example, when you want your dog to stay, your hand blocks her from moving forward and the reward comes in split seconds, so she is immediately successful. The same holds true for "go to your spot." She follows the treat to the spot, so she's already doing the behavior.

When you begin teaching any new behavior, you must be in a nondistracting environment AND you must have your dog's attention, which is where the $10,000 lure comes in. Motivation is the key. *Only* use a signal when you're 80 percent sure your dog will respond. You may be able to get your dog to come when called inside the house, but outdoors with a raccoon nearby is another story. You must gradually progress in each behavior to make your dog more and more reliable.

There is no such thing as 100 percent reliability. Factors such as illness, injury, accumulated stress, age, what you have trained for, and so on affect your dog's reliability. If your dog responds 80 percent of the time on any one behavior, you should consider it reliable behavior. If your dog gives you the behavior you are asking for 90 percent of the time, in different environments, that is considered very reliable. I refer to this degree of reliability as being under "stimulus control," or in simpler terms, you've got an obedience trained dog.

Giving Your Words Power

Labeling a behavior *after* your dog has learned it is extremely important insofar as giving your signal word power. This is where many handlers get confused. They repeat "sit," "sit," "sit" over and over with no results. Their words simply have no power. Repeating a word over and over eventually results in the signal becoming totally irrelevant to the dog. Other people make the mistake of saying "sit *after* the dog has already sat. They say, "Good, sit." They should say, "Good dog." The word "sit" should be the signal to sit, not something you say *after* the dog is already in position.

Here are the rules:

- Don't say "sit" or "down" until the behavior is already established and you are 80 percent sure your dog will sit or lie down.
- Don't repeat the word more than once in a 45-second period.
- Keep the words one or two syllables long.
- Make sure every behavior has a beginning and an end. Don't say sit and then forget to release your dog.
- Don't say "sit" if you mean "down."

The 45-Second Game

Over many years of training, I've noticed that as dogs are trying to figure things out, they do the same things we humans do . . . fidget. For example, let's say I really can't decide what I want to do tonight: go to the movies, stay home and watch the Lakers, order a pizza and rent a video, etc. While I'm deciding, I might drum my fingers, scratch my beard, tap my foot, hum to myself, walk back and forth, play with my hair (the little I have left), etc. In other words, there are a host of things I might do while I'm in the process of pondering. Dogs do the same thing. One might sniff the ground and walk in a circle. Another might back up, jump and then nudge you. Most will blink, cock their head, yawn or lick their lips. Some dogs have that lower jaw thing going on where it goes up and down as if they're talking to you. As long as there are no other distractions, dogs will do one or more of these things until they figure out what behavior will get them a reward. The average length of time it takes a dog to figure out what you are asking for is 45 seconds. Then, all of a sudden, he will sit or lay down or do whatever you have asked. It's a wonder to behold—watching a dog processing and figuring out what you're asking for. Most people have a real bonding moment with their dog when they see this happen because it is such a wonderful indication of interspecies communication and understanding. It works for puppies as well as older dogs. It works for rescues as well as pure bred dogs, male or females. If you would like to see the 45-Second Game demonstrated, pick up a copy of The Dog Whisperer DVD and check out "Teaching Go to Your Spot," "Down," and "Come."

Here's how to play the 45-Second Game. I'm illustrating the "down" behavior because it demonstrates the process so vividly, but this works for every behavior in this book.

Follow the instruction for Down (page 167). Repeat Step Two, voice with hand signal approximately ten to fifteen times. Be ready because on one of these attempts your dog will hesitate and stay down for an extra moment before getting up. When that happens, be ready to jackpot your dog, which means giving ten treats as quickly as possible before he has a chance to get up.

Now immediately go to Step Three, *Word Only* (no hand signal). Say the word "down" one time and wait. As long as your dog is processing . . . wait. Some dogs will lie down within seconds, others might take up to 90 seconds . . . but the average length of time is 45 seconds. So wait. Do not repeat the word. Your dog will lie down . . . at least 90 percent of dogs do. At that point you'll make a huge fuss and *really* jackpot him. If your dog is one of the ten percent who looks blankly at you and you can tell there is nothing going on in his brain, repeat the process by going back to Step Two and repeat "down" using the hand signal and vocal signal and do five repetitions. Then say down without the hand signal and once again wait. Barring a distraction that breaks the waiting-while-processing interval, or physical or mental problems, all dogs will lie down. And this process works for all behaviors.

How do you know when the dog has really understood? While a dog first starts processing, the tail does not move. (This is true of most dogs anyway . . . all bets are off for a wound-up Jack Russell terrier.) Once the information begins to make its way from point A to point B in your dog's head, you'll see the tail begin to flicker back and forth. This means he's almost got it. The neat thing is that the dog's body becomes aware of what's going on before the dog himself becomes aware of it. When the light bulb goes off in your dog's head, you'll see the tail begin to really wag.

When that happens the length of time between your signal (the word "down") and the dog actually doing it (this is called the "latency") begins to decrease. Occasionally you'll see a spike of increased delay, especially with older dogs. I think it's because they have more life experiences in their memory banks so it takes a little longer. Within two days of several short sessions, the latency will drop to three seconds or less. Your dog will lie down immediately upon hearing the word.

Now that I've explained all this, let me say it really isn't necssary to play the 45-Second Game. No matter what you do, your dog will eventually figure out what you want if you follow the training guidelines outlined in this book. However, I enjoy watching the process and it's a real "ooh-ahh" moment when clients see the proverbial light bulb go off in their dog's head.

Immediate Behavioral Responses—How to Get "Quick Sits"

Obviously you don't want to wait 45 seconds every time you ask your dog to do something. To get quick responses, professional trainers shape a dog's behavior to a zero-second latency. This means your dog will do whatever you're asking immediately. In the course of training, sometimes your dog doesn't do what you ask quite as quickly as before. He might start getting a little lazy . . . like sitting five to ten seconds after you've asked. That's normally due to lack of motivation. Maybe he doesn't like the food treat you're offering. Maybe he's already full. Maybe he feels like he's going to get the treat anyway, so why bother rushing.

In order to shape a quick response, three things are necessary:

Make your dog's world smaller. This means you'll need to restrict him through the use of supervised tethering and baby gates so he doesn't have as much free time or access to roam around the house or yard. This refocuses his attention on you as the one who controls everything he wants. I suggest doing this for three weeks.

Pick a simple behavior and train for only that behavior for a period of time. Choose a specific behavior such as sit, down, or having your dog touch your hand (targeting). You won't be giving food treats for any other behavior during this period of time.

Make sure the food treat is highly valued.

Once you are ready to proceed, follow these steps:

1. Let's say your dog usually sits five seconds after you've asked. Your goal is to get him to sit within one second.

You begin by clicking, praising, and rewarding every time he sits at the five-second timeframe. If your dog doesn't sit within five seconds, walk away and end the session. Wait ten seconds, return to your dog, and resume the session. As long as he responds at the five-second timeframe, you'll stay and work with him. If he doesn't, walk away. Do several short sessions throughout the day.

2. Once your dog is reliable with the five-second timeframe, you are ready to ask your dog to sit even more quickly. If he sits four seconds after you ask, this becomes the new success point. From now on, only click praise and treat the four-second mark. This change of response speed may happen in one session, one day, or two days.

3. Use this same process to continue to shorten the timeframe until your dog sits within one second of being asked. From that point on, you will only reward your dog if he sits immediately. Also integrate different contexts and life rewards. For example, if your dog wants to go outside, say sit. If he sits one second after you've asked, open the door. If he doesn't, walk away and try again a few seconds later. Here's another example: ask him to sit before you throw a ball. If he sits one second after you've asked, throw the ball. If he doesn't, game over.

Once your dog is reliably sitting immediately whenever you ask, you are ready to install the variable and intermittent reinforcement schedules (see page 134).

Important: Your dog must know the behavior well before using this process.

The 3 Ds—Adding Duration, Distance, and Distractions to the Training Process

Once your dog has learned to do a basic behavior, such as "sit," in a low distraction environment and she sits when you ask her at least 80 percent of the time, she is ready to move on to new levels of "sit." It's time to gradually add the three Ds: duration, distance, and distractions.

1. Duration is added first by asking her to sit for longer and longer periods of time.
2. Next, add distance by asking her to sit from a greater and greater distance.
3. Finally, add an increasing number of distractions. For example, train your dog to sit outdoors, then with other people around, then with other dogs around, etc.

You always begin with duration and then add the other variables separately. If you're asking your dog to sit for longer periods of time, don't simultaneously introduce distance and start walking away. Duration is one thing, distance is another. And, if you're working on distance and asking your dog to sit while you walk away, don't add duration at the same time by asking him to stay in that position for a longer period of time.

Whenever you add another factor to the training process, whether it is the length of time she is asked to do the behavior, your distance from her while she's doing it, or distractions while she's doing it, always add them individually, one at a time.

In the lessons in Part 3 of this book, most behaviors are taught in four different levels. Each behavior starts at the grade school level. Then you gradually add duration, distance, and distractions as you proceed through the more advanced levels.

Reinforcement Schedules

Professional trainers and behaviorists use training schedules that dictate when and how often to reward your dog. These reinforcement schedules, as they are called, can be quite complex—and they are strictly adhered to. This book introduces only a general application of these rules:

Continuous reinforcement: When you begin training for any behavior, it's important to reward your dog each and every time he responds to your signal, for example, sit, treat, sit, treat, sit, treat, etc. For simple behaviors in a nondistracting environment, a few hundred repetitions spread out over several days or weeks may be all that's necessary for your dog to grasp what's going on. You'll also revert to this schedule whenever you add duration, distance, or distractions to each behavior.

Variable reinforcement: At the next stage of training, instead of rewarding the dog after every response, he is rewarded on a predetermined schedule, such as after every second, third, or fourth response (sit, sit, treat—or sit, sit, sit, sit, treat), or after two, three, or more different behaviors, for example, sit, down, sit, treat, etc.

Intermittent or random reinforcement: In this stage, you progress to rewarding every so often, like the occasional win in Las Vegas. Once the dog knows that a payoff is coming sooner or later, he will remain motivated.

Following these progressions will take you a long way toward your goal of obtaining reliable behavior with your dog. Learning when to go from one reinforcement schedule to another is what makes a good trainer. Some dogs learn more quickly than others; go too slowly with those dogs and they quickly become bored. Other dogs need to remain on one schedule for a longer period of time; if you go too fast, they become stressed and you end up having to retrace your steps. The trick is learning how to use these schedules in order to challenge your dog and progress at a pace that works for him. And this is all influenced by the individual dog, the particular behavior you are teaching, the reward you are using, and, in the end, your skill.

I strongly suggest enrolling in a class with a competent trainer versed not only in nonviolent training principles, but also in the correct use of reinforcement schedules. Hopefully you will find a trainer who is able to make these principles understandable to you. It's like learning to play a musical instrument. You can learn to read music from a book, but until you hear it played by a professional, you really don't know how it's supposed to sound. Also, visual learners, like myself, need to see someone in action in order to understand or "grok" it and then polish their skills. The following books are also helpful if you want to pursue a deeper study of the use of reinforcement schedules: *The Culture Clash* by Jean Donaldson, *Clicker Training for Obedience* by Morgan Spector, *Excel-erated Learning* by Dr. Pam Reid, and *Don't Shoot the Dog* by Karen Pryor.

Remember, timing is everything in dog training. Seeing a qualified professional apply these principles skillfully is worth its weight in squeaky toys!

Chapter 12

Six Training Tools to Modify a Dog's Behavior

These tools represent the six different ways you can modify your dog's behavior; that is, get what you want from your dog and thereby eliminate what you don't want. Note that each of the six tools relies on the use of positives. Negatives can also be used in training, when used appropriately. Later in this chapter, you'll find a section on the appropriate use of what would be termed "negative" training, but you'll note that the negative training does not include using physical punishment or anything else that's harmful to the dog.

> Health problems can lead to problems with your dog's ability to learn. Before beginning your training program, have your dog's health checked by your veterinarian.

Dogs do what they do because of consequences. They do stuff to get rewards and avoid stuff that doesn't pay them anything or that they perceive as harmful. Most behaviors that are problems for humans can be resolved by using one of the six training tools below or a combination of several of them. When you begin to work with them, they will soon make total sense to you and using them will eventually become second nature.

The following sections describe the six training tools. The suggestions offered are examples for shaping general behaviors. Part 4 of this book deals with problem behaviors in more detail.

Tool #1: Substitute Another Behavior

With this tool, you simply substitute a desirable behavior for an undesirable one. When you use the tool of substitution, you are diverting your dog's attention and asking him to do another behavior that is incompatible with or replaces the behavior that is unacceptable.

The process is simple. Instead of asking, "How do I stop my dog from doing such and such?" start asking, "What do I want my dog to do in this situation?" For instance, instead of, "How do I get my dog to stop jumping on me when I walk in the door?" ask yourself, "What do I want my dog to do to get my attention and affection when I come home?" One way to do this would be to teach your dog to sit or lie down when you walk in the door and then spend a minute or two giving attention and affection by praising her, scratching her behind the ears, and so on. Another example of substitution is to throw a tennis ball to a barking dog and teach her to hold it in her mouth. Once she's got the tennis ball in her mouth, she can't bark. (Well, she can still make noise—but she won't be barking.)

Tool #2: Put the Behavior on Cue

If you're dealing with a problem behavior, this particular tool of dog training is a bit like reverse psychology. Let's say your dog is barking at virtually everything that exists: doorbells, people who move quickly, other dogs barking or coming into the yard, the phone, and so on.

When you put the desired behavior on cue, you are telling the dog that barking is the exact behavior you're looking for. When the dog barks, click and reward the barking. (Review the instructions for how to use a clicker on page 124.) Then encourage her to bark again. Click and reward. Associate a word and/or a hand signal with the barking and use it whenever your dog barks. I use the word "Sing" and move my hands like I'm conducting an orchestra. Within no time, your dog will start barking on cue.

The next step is to reward the silence. Say "quiet" in a voice that is startling but not scary. (You're trying to interrupt the dog, not frighten her.) As soon as she quiets down, click and reward. Now you've got barking when you ask and quiet when you ask. Nifty, huh?

Tool #3: Change the Association from Negative to Positive

With this tool, which is also called counter-conditioning, you are changing the way your dog perceives the situation—that is, you are altering his associations with objects, situations, people, and so on.

For instance, if your dog barks at the mail carrier, the next-door neighbor with a beard, or the vacuum cleaner, it's obvious that, for whatever reason, he's not too comfortable with that person or object. Other dislikes might include hair dryers, nail clippers, and police sirens. Counter-conditioning means teaching your dog to look at these things as positive. This method takes time but works really well with many problem behaviors.

Just as soon as the mail carrier shows up, give your dog a $10,000 treat. Do the same thing over and over again—associate the mail carrier with a great treat. Eventually, you can enroll the mail carrier in your effort, asking him to come closer and closer to the dog on each visit. Finally, he can give the dog a treat himself.

As for dealing with clippers, vacuums, and so on, you can combine this tool with the previous one and put the desired behavior on cue.

Tool #4: Withdraw the Reward and Ignore the Undesirable Behavior

Also known as extinction, this training tool goes back to the principle that a dog stops what he's doing if he doesn't get "paid" in some way, shape, or form. In other words, when there is no longer a reward attached to a certain behavior, the behavior generally ceases. In psychology this is known as extinction. You can think of it as extinguishing a fire; after all, if you don't feed a fire, it goes out.

Think about what your dog gets out of the barking, jumping, chewing, digging, or begging. How is he being rewarded for the behavior? Dogs are, after all, pretty smart. In many cases, the dog's reward for the undesirable behavior is your attention. When you withdraw your attention, the undesirable behavior usually stops. If you stop giving your dog attention for barking, he has no incentive to continue. If you stop giving treats when he begs at the table, there's a good chance he'll eventually stop because there's simply no longer any reason to continue.

Jumping is another great example of how well it works to ignore a behavior. Dogs generally get attention when they jump. Sometimes the attention comes in the form of being petted; other times they get yelled at. When you stop petting and stop yelling, the jumping usually stops.

There are cases, however, in which withdrawing the reward and ignoring the undesirable behavior results in the dog resorting to another type of undesirable behavior. For instance, when he stops begging for treats at the table, he may try something else—like barking. When this happens, you have to go through the process again; this time ignoring the barking. This training tool works well when combined with another of the training tools, positive reinforcement.

Tool #5: Remove the Cause of the Behavior

This training tool is also called the causative approach. Determine what is causing the behavior, and then simply remove it from the dog's environment. If your dog is experiencing pain from a burr in his behind, he may not be willing to sit. If you remove the burr, he'll sit again. If your dog is barking at another dog, block his view or take the other dog away. Or remove the noisy vacuum cleaner and he'll stop urinating. Remove the boredom and replace it with exercise, training, and smart toys (see page 39), and he'll stop barking, chewing up the furniture, and destroying the house.

Tool #6: Get Your Dog Used to It

In some situations, the only way to get your dog to accept a person, animal, or object he objects to, such as the mail carrier, the neighbor's dog, or a vacuum cleaner, is to get him used to it. There are three ways to get a dog used to something:

Systematic desensitization: Introduce the scary person, animal, or object a little at a time. Over a gradually extended period of time, present the sight, sound, or touch of this person, animal, or object over and over again. Gradually increase the intensity of the contact. For an object like a bell, this is done by ringing it softly, then louder and louder. With an animal or person, start at a comfortable distance and slowly bring the animal or person closer and closer. For example, if your dog barks at another dog, start training at a distance far enough away from the other dog that your dog will no longer be distracted and will pay more attention to you. Then gradually bring the dogs closer together. Repeat this gradual process until the second dog no longer represents a threat to your dog. Desensitization can be used with a dog that is afraid of firecrackers, thunderstorms, and other loud noises, or that is sensitive to movement, like a person getting out of a chair quickly.

Habituation: If your dog doesn't like the sound of the doorbell, continue ringing it over and over until your dog gets bored with the sound. In other words, it will become "ho-hum" because it is no longer relevant.

Flooding: With this method, you flood the dog with the sights, sounds, and touches of the person, animal, or object that causes him problems. For instance, if he doesn't like other people, take him into a crowded room. Of all of the tools of dog training, this one is the trickiest.

Since it can be difficult to know which of these three methods is preferable, you may have to consult a professional dog trainer to know which one is best for your dog's unique situation. If you do the wrong thing, you could make matters worse. Obviously, all of these methods must be used with compassion, skill, and understanding.

Behavioral Building Blocks

So, how to do you know which of the six tools to use to handle a problem behavior? Here's a bird's-eye view of the process to determine the best tool.

The following chart will help you determine how to deal with a "problem" behavior. For illustration purposes, I'm using barking as an example.

A. When and where does the barking happen?

When the doorbell rings or other sounds occur?
When my dog looks out the window and sees people or animals?
When my dog is at the door?
When I'm on the phone?
When I'm in the kitchen?
When my dog is in the car?
When certain people are around?
In the morning? Afternoon? Evening?
Other?

B. Review the nine ingredients for optimum health and growth and select the ones that contribute to your dog's "problem" behavior. The examples that follow are just a sampling of the ways an imbalance in the nine ingredients can impact training. (See Chapter 2 to review the nine ingredients.)

Food: Is your dog stressed because she's hungry, or is she suffering from indigestion or a food allergy?

Play: Is your dog bored and understimulated?

Socialization: Does your dog get to mingle with other dogs, other animals, and other humans, and is she given a chance to adapt to the sights, sounds, smells, and touches of her environment?

Quiet time: Is your dog given time to get away from it all, or is she over her stress management threshold?

Exercise: Does your dog get a chance to run and express her energy? Are her muscles weak or tight? Is she in pain?

Employment: Does your dog have a job to do? Has she lost confidence because she doesn't know what is expected of her?

Rest: Is your dog exhausted? Does she just want to be left alone?

Training: Is your dog confused because she was never taught what to do? Is she in a learning dip? Have you unintentionally trained her to do the problem behavior? (See the discussion of unintentional training on page 251.)

Health care: Have you checked for allergies or physical problems such as a thorn in the paw, parasites, matted hair, fleas, or arthritis? Is your dog too young or too old to do what you are asking of her?

C. Set your goal. Decide on the specific behavior you want from your dog:

Bark three times and then stop.
Bark only when asked and ignore everything else.
Bark only at people who are carrying monkeys on their backs.
Other.

D. Select one or more of the six tools of training to change your dog's behavior:

Withdraw the reward and ignore the undesirable behavior.
Remove the cause of the behavior.
Substitute another behavior.
Change the association from negative to positive.
Put the behavior on cue.
Get your dog used to it.

Using Negatives in Training

How can someone talk about using negatives in a book about positive dog training? It all has to do with the definition of "negative training." Negative training methods can range all the way from harmless and beneficial to the extreme of harmful and abusive. In any event, negatives are a part of the training process because, in essence, the dog perceives any unfulfilled desire as frustrating or stressful—hence, negative.

You should never do anything to your dog that you wouldn't do to yourself, your child, or your grandparent. So once again, let me emphasize that positive training does not include hitting, kicking, shocking, shaking, pinning a dog, rolling him over on his back, or jerking. It does not include the even more extreme and abusive act of biting (hard to believe, but some trainers actually advocate this because "that's how dogs correct"), almost drowning a dog, hanging a dog from his collar, or pinching a dog's ear.

So what negatives are used in the positive training process? To illustrate, let's briefly review an example of positive reinforcement. Let's say you're on the couch watching your favorite television show and you notice your dog lie down. This is a behavior that you are striving to reinforce, so you get up to pet him. But when you get halfway there, your dog gets up. Since the behavior you want to reward is the dog lying down, the dog getting up causes you stop in your tracks and head back to the couch. Seeing you go the other way is a negative to your dog because he wants to be with you. He will very quickly learn that lying down and staying in the down position will bring you close and keep you close. Getting up, he will soon realize, pushes you away.

Here's another example. My dog Molly used to bark at strangers while she sat in the car waiting for me to return. In order to change this behavior, I engaged the help of a friend who was a stranger to Molly. We walked toward the car together and, as Molly began to bark, the stranger and I both stopped in our tracks and backed up. She would bark and we'd back up. She'd be quiet and we would approach. Then she'd bark again and we'd back up farther. Now she was confused. She wanted the stranger to go away but she wanted me to approach. When she stopped barking, we moved forward and I praised her, which was her reward. When she started to bark again, we delivered a negative by immediately backing away again.

After several repetitions of this lesson, Molly got the point. She learned that when she was quiet she would be rewarded and when she barked, her rewards would be removed. As a result, she stopped barking while waiting in the car for me. This is another classic example of the magnet game, which is taught on page 159.

You can use another type of negative for a problem such as chewing by putting something that tastes bad on the leash or other object that your dog wants to chew. Listerine or Binaca mouthwash usually works. There are many other products you can use, but stay away from those that burn like Tabasco and hot chilies. But the better way to handle a dog who chews things is to remove the temptation (prevention), teach the dog to chew on appropriate objects (the "find it" game) and also teach your dog not to touch inappropriate objects (as described in the "Leave it" and "Drop it" behaviors on pages 220 and 233).

Interrupters and Time Outs

Interrupters and time outs are training tools that I occasionally use for problems such as barking and jumping. Clapping, whistling, clearing your throat, saying "ah-ah," or dropping a book on the floor can interrupt inappropriate behaviors, such as stealing food off the kitchen counter. However, these same interrupters can be traumatic if your dog is sensitive. The key is to use the proper intensity to match the sensitivity of the dog so the sound will get his attention and interrupt him but not scare him.

One of my clients, a seventy-six-year-old woman, simply could not grasp the idea of using any kind of prevention and management despite my best efforts. She was adamant that her dog should never be tethered in the house, even though the dog's jumping had become dangerous. As a sixty-five-pound adult, her Labradoodle had actually knocked her down and, on one occasion, broken her arm. Nevertheless, my attempts to have her implement the appropriate training tools (of the six described on pages 138–142) were simply beyond her grasp. Because of the situation and because this dog was not overly sensitive, I suggested the use of a whistle as an interrupter.

I taught the woman to keep the whistle right outside the front door and put it in her mouth before she entered the house. Then, before her dog jumped, she could blow the whistle to interrupt him. That would allow her to redirect him to his bed or to lie down and stay. (If you're wondering why I didn't simply instruct the woman to throw treats on the floor to distract her dog instead of a whistle, good for you! The fact is the woman didn't have the dexterity or the timing necessary to throw treats before the dog jumped.)

The time out is a training tool that involves removing your dog from a situation as a consequence for inappropriate behavior. He is confined behind a gate or in a kennel, or he is tethered. Time outs are normally used for jumping, mouthing, and barking.

Let's say you've been practicing bite inhibition exercises with Atticus, your sweet four-month-old puggle, by teaching the puppy substitute behaviors such as chewing on appropriate toys, licking instead of biting, taking things gently, "drop it," and so on. Being the puppy he is, Atticus makes a mistake and grabs your hand instead of the toy you're holding. You yell "Ow!" which is the signal you've chosen that Atticus's behavior is inappropriate.

Instead of backing off, he gets even more excited and really goes for your hand. At this point, you give the time-out signal—something like "Uh oh" or "Too bad," delivered immediately and in a calm voice—and place him in his playpen or tether him in a safe place (as described on page 90). There Atticus remains for two to five minutes, or as long as it takes for him to settle down and relax. When the time is up, you pretend nothing has happened and you happily release him.

After a few time outs, he learns that inappropriate mouth exuberance produces temporary detachment from you. He also learns that when he relaxes it means freedom and socialization. The idea with time outs is that you are addressing a specific behavior—in this case, inappropriate use of teeth. However, you are still able to convey love for your dog. You correct the behavior, not the dog.

Your attitude is extremely important, so never yell, "Okay, that's it, you mutt. Here's your punishment!" Stay upbeat and matter of fact. In essence, you're saying to your dog, "This behavior produces this result; while this other behavior produces this result." If you do this correctly, your dog will actually put himself in a time out. If my dog Grady doesn't do what I ask or is acting out of control and I say "uh oh," he gets in the van or goes into the kitchen.

Before you use any training method, including an interrupter, consider your dog's physical and emotional health in terms of the impression the interrupter will leave. It's imperative that you avoid traumatizing your dog! Interrupters are examples of negative training methods. A negative must be of sufficient intensity so as to decrease the probability a particular behavior will be repeated. But the proper level of intensity varies from dog to dog. Too much intensity, and the dog can be harmed physically and emotionally. Too little and you can actually increase the behavior. Every dog is different. This is the great thing about using positive training whenever possible. Even if you make a mistake, the dog doesn't suffer, and everything remains a game.

PART 3

The Lessons

Chapter 13

The Big Picture—How to Work with These Lessons

It's easy to get your dog to do what you want him to do when you understand the scientific principles behind the canine learning process and apply them consistently. Consistency means that everyone who interacts with the dog uses the same methods on a regular basis. The more we reinforce a dog's behaviors, the more deeply ingrained that behavior becomes and the more we increase the probability that the dog will repeat those behaviors in the future.

The positive methods presented in this book consist of two elements that reinforce each other. One element, which I call the magnet game (described on page 159), consists of rewarding behaviors that your dog does without having been asked; the other element consists of rewarding "asked-for behaviors." The synergy of both training elements makes learning fun, quicker, and more effective.

1. **The Magnet Game—Rewarding "Unasked-for" Behaviors:** You can think of The Magnet Game as unscheduled training. With this method, you simply wait for the behavior to occur, then let the dog know that what he just did thrilled you to no end by rewarding him with praise, a scratch behind the ear, and treats. The magnet game should be at least 50 percent of your training and will speed the entire process along. (You'll learn the magnet game later in Chapter 14.)

2. **Structured Training Sessions—Rewarding "Asked-For" Behaviors:** The rest of your training is rooted in more structured training sessions which are best done in short sessions throughout the day. For the basic behaviors, such as sit, lie down, and so on, you will learn a simple three-step training process. Once you've got that down, all the other behaviors are easy.

The Learning Baseline

Because every dog is unique, it is necessary to determine at what point your dog can be successful doing what you ask, which is referred to as his learning baseline or starting point. Depending on factors like age, training history, personality, health, and so on, the learning baseline varies from dog to dog.

Dogs learn quickly when they build on their successes. But at what point do you start training a particular behavior, and when do you begin to make a behavior more challenging? It's not only important to start at the point where your dog can succeed, it's also critical to keep her interested and mentally stimulated. It's up to you to watch for those moments your dog says, "Got it! This is exciting. What else is there?" That's when you take her to the next level of training for that particular behavior.

Developing an awareness of when to challenge and when to hold back distinguishes a really talented trainer. This awareness keeps the training fresh and motivating, something your dog looks forward to. Your awareness will also grow, and you will intuitively know when to "reset" your dog's training regimen. *Sometimes this happens several times in one session; sometimes it happens over several sessions.* This increasing awareness is directly linked to greater training skills, which in turn will lead to you and your dog becoming a behavioral team.

The Triangle for Success

This book is structured upon on the three training principles I call the triangle for success (illustrated in Figure 13.1):

1. **Environment:** Set up a safe environment where the dog can learn to be successful.
2. **Positive associations:** Use classical conditioning to associate a dog's life experiences with things he likes, such as food treats and fun.
3. **Positive reinforcement:** Use operant conditioning by using positive reinforcement to teach your dog what you want him to do until he realizes there are consequences to his behaviors. In other words, he learns that he gets what he wants based on what he does.

Figure 13.1

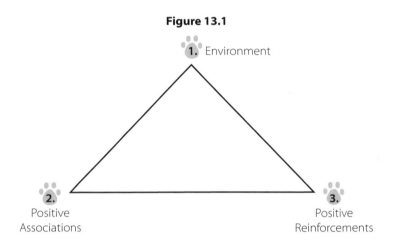

Begin each training session with the first point of the triangle so your dog can be successful. In other words, begin training in a distraction-free environment, and make your expectations realistic. It's important that your dog be able to do what you're asking, both physically and emotionally. If she can't, she'll get frustrated and stop trying. In turn, you'll get frustrated and angry and might think your dog is being stubborn, stupid, or just plain lazy. You have the power to make learning fun by creating positive associations (the second point on the triangle) and to teach your dog what you want him to do (the third point on the triangle).

Preparation Is Key—Get Focused Before Each Training Session

Before each training session, take a minute or two to collect yourself. If your focus is scattered, your signals to your dog will be imprecise and confusing.

1. Tense all the muscles in your body at once. Hold for three seconds and then relax and let your body go limp. Make fists with your hands and make a fist with your face and then relax (see the total relaxation exercise on page 70).
2. Do one complete round of the complete breath exercise (described on page 72).
3. Think about each of the behaviors you are going to work on in the upcoming session. With your eyes closed, spend ten seconds picturing your dog in the final position of each behavior (as described for the communication exercise on page 85).

Rewards

Have $10,000 rewards on hand. For some dogs, a favorite toy is as valuable as a $10,000 food treat. If that's the case, use the toy as a reward in the same way that you'd use the food treat.

"Starting Position"

For most behaviors, you will place your hands on your chest in "starting position" and keep them there until giving a hand signal. By holding your hands close to your chest, you help your dog stay more attentive and focused on what you are doing. Because dogs have an oral-eye reflex, when you move your hands around, a dog's tendency is to follow the movement and then catch whatever is moving with their mouth. These instructions may sound a bit formal and a little robotic; however, they are just suggestions. Our intent is to simply remind you to move less and focus more.

A Note About Using Clickers

As you work with these lessons, you'll notice that every successful behavior is acknowledged with "click, praise, and treat."

If you don't have a clicker, you can use words to mark a desired behavior. For instance, say "good dog" or "yes" or "that'll do" or "hooray," every time your dog does the behavior you're asking for and he'll get the idea. In the beginning try to use the same word or phrase consistently.

Putting It All Together

Dog training is a fluid process. Your dog's success depends on her learning baseline on the specific behavior you are teaching. If you are teaching a puppy or an untrained, poorly socialized older dog, you will likely begin at step one for all behaviors. If your dog already has some training, you may begin at step two or three for behaviors she's familiar with but at step one for new behaviors.

Once you have successfully gotten the behavior—meaning your dog does the behavior eight out of ten times—you are ready for more advanced training for that behavior. Gradually, one by one, add challenges, such as more time to the behavior, more distance, and distractions of sounds (auditory), touches (tactual), and movement (visual). (If needed, review the 3 Ds on page 133.)

The following example outlines the three steps as they relate to teaching your dog to sit.

Prepare: Put your hands in "starting position," holding them close to your chest.

Step 1: Get the behavior using a treat (lure) and a hand signal. Facing your dog, move a food treat (lure) over her head. The hand moving over your dog's head becomes the hand signal for "sit." As your hand with the lure moves over your dog's head, she will look up and her behind will automatically lower to the floor. Click, praise, and treat. Repeat ten to fifteen times. Do several sessions per day or over the course of a few days until your dog reaches the 80-percent success rate—that is, she'll sit eight out of ten times. (Most dogs are successful learning how to sit in one session.) At that point, you are ready to proceed to step two.

THE 3 EASY STEPS TO SHAPE RELIABLE BEHAVIOR

Warm Up

Make sure there are no distractions.

Remain positive and remember to BREATHE!

Rev up your clicker (if you're using one) and gather $10,000 rewards

1. Get the behavior

Encourage your dog and get her attention by using vocal sounds such as "tch-tch," whistling, using her name, clapping, patting your leg, etc. Use a food lure in almost all cases when you begin to teach a new behavior.

Use your hand signal. Start with simple parts of the behavior and continuously reinforce baby steps. Do 10 to 15 repetitions of each behavior in each session.

Now increase the distance: If you're 80 percent sure your dog will do the behavior without using food as the lure, put the treat in your other hand, make the hand signal with the hand that's not holding the treat, click and praise the behavior, and then reward with the treat that you're holding in the other hand.

2. Attach a word along with the hand signal

When you're 80 percent sure your dog will sit each time you make the hand signal, begin to use the word "sit" immediately before making the hand signal.

3. Use the word only.

Then begin adding other criteria (duration, distance, distractions)—one at a time. Go back to the point your dog was successful (including using a lure if necessary) each time you add something new. Reward each behavior every time. Then, when your dog is successful 80 percent of the time, ask for more by having your dog do the behavior two or three times in a row and then giving a treat. Finally, progress to a "Las Vegas style," intermittent reward schedule—reward your dog every once in a while so she never knows when the treat is coming. Vary the rewards as you go along (turkey, cheese, freeze-dried liver, etc). Gradually progress to rewarding only the best behavior...such as speed. Eventually you'll progress to a point where one behavior will actually become a reward for another behavior. This is called forming a behavioral chain. Also, remember to use "life rewards," such as going for rides, playing Frisbee, getting to go in and out of doors, etc.

Step 2: Attach a word to the behavior along with the hand signal. Say the word "Sit" as your hand with the lure moves over her head. Click, praise, and treat. When your dog is successful eight out of ten times, put the treat in your other hand and repeat the process, giving the signal with your empty hand. This is to ensure that your dog is following the signal, rather than being bribed by the food. When your dog is successful eight out of ten times, go to Step 3.

Step 3: Use the word without the hand signal. Put your hands in starting position on your chest and say "sit" without using the hand signal. Then click, praise, and treat.

Once you've mastered the grade school level of a behavior, you're ready to add some challenges and lead your dog through high school and college levels. College level reliable behavior means that your dog will respond to your signal at least 90 percent of the time, anywhere, anytime. This more advanced level is further than most people go in their training but it's up to you— you can take your dog to the level of reliability you choose.

You always begin with duration and then add the other variables separately. If you're asking your dog to sit for longer periods of time, don't simultaneously introduce distance and start walking away. Duration is one thing, and distance is another. If you're working on distance and asking your dog to sit while you walk away, don't add duration at the same time by asking him to stay in that position for a longer period of time.

Similarly, when you are teaching a behavioral sequence like getting a soda from the refrigerator, each behavior in the sequence is taught individually in an environment without distractions. Then the entire package or series of behaviors making up the trick must be practiced and linked together with more and more distractions, for shorter or longer periods of time, and/or at greater distances.

Whenever you add another factor to the training process, whether it is the length of time your dog is asked to do the behavior, your distance from him while he's doing it, or distractions while he's doing it, always add them individually, one at a time. You can add more challenges whenever you and your dog feel ready for it. If your dog seems bored, you're going too slowly. Kick it up a level.

It is important to remember that dogs learn on a curve. They have good days and bad days, just as we do. They need time to integrate what they've learned. Each day, begin each exercise at your dog's learning baseline. Build on success. Here are the trainer's two golden rules:

1. If your dog won't do what you want him to do, just go back to the last step that he did successfully.
2. Whenever you change the training context (situation), always start teaching the behavior from scratch. That is, return to step one for each and every behavior.

If your dog does something other than what you're asking for, you've gone too far, too fast. Return to simpler forms of the behavior, increase your dog's successful responses, and then ask for more.

How Much Training Is Required?

An effective training session can be quite short—you can do a lot in as little as thirty to sixty seconds. For example, you might do five to ten repetitions of a single behavior, such as "Down," or a combination of behaviors, such as ten repetitions of "Down," ten of "Stay," and ten of "Come." Short sessions throughout the day, each of up to five minutes, are much better than one or two twenty- to forty-minute sessions.

You may find that your daily schedule allows you to include three or four behaviors in each of several different training sessions throughout the day. (See the suggested daily routine on page 54.) If so, start with those three or four and then gradually add more behaviors as your schedule permits. In each subsequent training session, you will make the behaviors you've already taught more and more challenging, while also adding new behaviors. Keep it easy, fun and simple.

Troubleshooting

Here are a few general tips in case you have problems training any of the behaviors:

- Keep the sessions short. Several one-, two-, or three-minute sessions sprinkled throughout the day are much more effective than one or two thirty-minute sessions.
- If your dog is confused, use approximations, or simpler forms of the behavior you desire. For instance, if you're training a puppy to sit, you can click and treat the first approximation, represented by her behind lowering an eighth of an inch. Then you can click and treat her when she lowers her behind a little bit more, and so on. Then you can click, praise, and jackpot the final behavior, which is her behind actually touching the floor.
- Use the magnet game (as described on page 159). Throughout the day, whenever you happen to see your dog do something that you like, "capture" it by giving praise and throwing her a treat.
- Check with your veterinarian. Make sure that there are no physical problems that keep your dog from being able to perform a given behavior.
- Relax your expectations. It isn't necessary for your dog to master a behavior in one session. Go with the flow.
- Don't keep repeating the word for a behavior if you're looking for reliability. Say it once and wait. If your dog can't figure it out, go back to the point where she was successful.
- Have fun. If your dog stands around or seems bored, get happy! Dance around and use different vocal sounds from kissy sounds to howls. Pretend to eat food and exaggerate with "Hmm, look what I have!" Drop to the ground and pretend you found something interesting. Use a tennis ball or another of your dog's favorite toys in order to generate interest.

Chapter 14

Teaching the Behaviors

In this chapter, instructions are presented for training the basic behaviors. Training for each behavior follows the same general progression of levels, from grade school to college level. At the grade school level, each behavior is taught in three steps. Once your dog has learned the basic behavior in grade school level, you no longer need the three-step process. At that point, additional challenges are introduced in the form of the three Ds: distraction, distance, and duration (see page 133).

> Throughout the training process, remember to adjust your dog's diet to account for all the treats he gets.

You'll know when it's time to progress to the next level of training when your dog has reached the 80 percent mark. This means that your dog does a behavior within three seconds of your asking, eight out of ten times.

The Magnet Game

Positive dog training is all about attraction. Your dog attracts your attention through his actions. Your job is to teach your dog which actions or behaviors will work. This is done in two ways that are practiced throughout the day: the magnet game and the lessons. The magnet game is so named because your dog's unasked-for behaviors attract you, your affection, and your treats—like a magnet. This is actually the easiest form of training because all you have to do is catch your dog doing something you want him to do and reward him for it. Let's say you're watching television or washing dishes or working on your computer. You happen to see your dog lie down on his bed. You didn't ask him to lie down, he just did it—so you throw him a treat.

I suggest that you use the magnet game as 50 percent of your training. It's incredibly easy and powerful tool. Basically, the magnet game presents your dog with opportunities to receive rewards based on appropriate behaviors.

On the other side of the coin, he also learns that when he does something other than behaviors that are acceptable to you, he no longer gets your attention. In other words, the "magnetic attraction" is broken. An example of this is your dog jumping on you. If you turn away, your dog eventually learns that jumping gets no attention.

Here's how to play the magnet game:

1. Several times during the day, tether your dog to the bottom of the couch or to a door in a social area where you can supervise her. (See page 90 for a discussion of the proper way to tether, along with illustrations.) Never tether a dog and leave her alone.

2. Whenever she does a particular behavior you want to reinforce, such as sitting or lying down, she becomes a magnet, drawing your attention. At this point you can (1) throw her a treat, (2) praise her, (3) get up and pet her, or (4) combine all three actions as a triple reward.

3. If she gets up from the sit or down position, immediately withdraw your attention. (At this point, she is no longer a magnet attracting your attention.) Let's say she sits, which is the behavior you are looking for, and you start to go over and pet her. When she sees you coming, she gets up. As sitting is the behavior you want, not standing, this breaks the magnetic attraction. You immediately turn around and go the other way. She sits down again, meaning the magnet is back in action, so you immediately walk toward her again.

This is a great exercise to do while you're watching television, talking on the phone, eating dinner, or working at your desk. We use it in group classes all the time. As long as a dog is sitting or lying down, the handler stays by her side. But if she gets up, the handler moves away. Dogs pick this up very quickly, and it really helps in the overall training process.

Figure 14.1

The magnet game consists of waiting for your dog to figure out what you want without your having to ask for it. In this photo, Orbit, a Chinese crested, is being ignored because she is standing up on her bed.

Figure 14.2

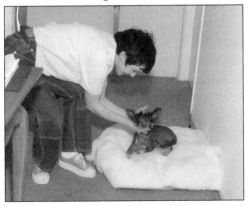

As soon as Orbit lies down without being told, she is immediately rewarded with praise, treats, and affection.

Pay Attention

A big reason your dog doesn't do what you ask, when you ask, is due to her lack of attention. To motivate a dog, you've got to get her attention first. This entire book is geared toward linking up with your dog. When you're linked, both you and your dog are paying attention to each other.

Every day, you inadvertently trigger your dog's attention when you do things like open a bag of dog food, open the door to go outside, pick up the leash, put your jacket on, and so on. Without formally training her to do so, you have established a "pay attention" behavior. You have turned a switch on in your dog's head that signals to her that something good is about to happen, and she looks to you for that event.

You can label the "pay attention" behavior with a vocal signal, such as "pay attention" or "watch." To get your dog to pay attention to you whenever you ask, follow these steps.

Prepare: Practice in a nondistracting environment. Put your hands in "starting position," holding them close to your chest.

Step 1: Get the behavior using a treat (lure) and a hand signal. Place a food treat in your hand and hold it in front of your dog's nose. (See Lures, Bribes, and Rewards on page 114.) Move your hand to your eyes in a smooth gesture. The movement of your hand moving from your dog's nose to your eyes will become the hand signal for "pay attention." As your dog's eyes follow your hand moving up to your face, click and reward by releasing the treat from your hand. Repeat five to ten times. When your dog reaches the 80 percent goal— that is, she'll follow your hand up to your eyes eight out of ten times, you are ready to proceed to Step 2.

Step 2: Attach a word to the behavior along with the hand signal. Say "watch" or "pay attention" or "look," followed a split second later with the hand signal (moving your hand from your dog's nose to your eyes in a smooth gesture). As your dog's eyes follow your hand going up to your face, click and reward by releasing the treat from your hand. Repeat five to ten times. When you are 80 percent sure your dog will follow your hand motion, you are ready to do the exercise with the treat in your other hand. (This is to ensure that your dog is following the signal, rather than being bribed by the food. The food should only be a reward, not a bribe.) Place your empty hand in front of your dog's nose and repeat as above, using the same marker word, such as "look," as you move your hand to your eyes. Click and give the treat from the other hand. Repeat five to ten times. When you are 80 percent sure your dog will follow the vocal cue only, you are ready for Step 3.

Step 3: Use the word without the hand signal. Keep your hands on your chest and say the word "watch" or "pay attention" or "look" without using the hand signal. If your dog looks to your face, click and reward.

Hints
- You can drop a treat from your mouth to help your dog learn the vocal cue without the hand signal. Say "look" and as your dog looks at your face, let the treat drop from your mouth. This will help her focus on your face because that's where the $10,000 reward is coming from.
- Face your dog. Put a treat in your hand and stretch your arm straight out from your side, perpendicular to the floor. Your dog will look at your hand. Now wait. Within 45 seconds, your dog will turn her attention away from your treat-filled hand and glance at your eyes. When she does, immediately praise her and give her the treat. Repeat this five to ten times. When your dog figures this out, she will look at you as soon as you extend your hand. You can now add the words, "pay attention."

Sit, Lie Down, and Stand
If your dog already knows how to sit, lie down, and/or stand due to previous training, you can immediately proceed to high school or even college level of each of these behaviors. As I mentioned

in the section on the Learning Baseline, it's important to determine the level at which your dog is already successful and start there. Remember, never bore your dog.

Sit—Grade School Level

Prepare: Begin in an environment that has few distractions or no distractions at all. Put a treat between your thumb and index finger. Hold the clicker in your other hand. Place your hands in the starting position on your chest.

Step 1: Get the behavior using a treat (lure) and a hand signal. Put your hand with the treat over the top of your dog's nose about two inches from his head. The hand moving over your dog's head becomes the hand signal for "sit." Go no farther back than the crown of his head. The idea is to get your dog to tilt his head and look up at your hand. As he looks up, his back end will tend to go down. (Figure 14.3) If you move your hand too far, he'll back up. If you move your hand too high, he might jump to get the treat. (Figure 14.4) If you move your hand too low, he won't do anything except nibble your hand. You can encourage him all the while with "gooooood dog," "you're the best," "way to go," or the phrase of your choosing in a friendly but not too exuberant voice. As soon as his behind hits the floor, click, praise, and treat! Repeat these steps ten to fifteen times in each training session. Most dogs are able to learn sit in one session. If necessary, do several sessions per day or over the course of a few days until he reaches the 80 percent success rate—that is, he'll do it eight out of ten times. At that point, you are ready to proceed to Step 2.

Step 2: Attach a word to the behavior along with the hand signal. Put a treat between your thumb and index finger. Hold the clicker in your other hand. Place your hands in the starting position on your chest. Say "sit" immediately preceding the hand signal of moving your hand over your dog's head. When your dog sits, click, praise, and treat. Repeat ten to fifteen times.

Figure 14.3

With a treat in one hand and a clicker in the other, introduce your dog to a sit by bringing your hand with the
treat over the top of your dog's nose. When your dog's
behind hits the ground, click, praise, and treat.

Figure 14.4
If your dog jumps out of her position, use a "no-reward"
marker such as "uh-oh" or "oops" to let her know that
isn't what you're looking for.

When you are 80 percent sure your dog will follow your hand motion, you are ready to do the exercise with the treat in your other hand. This is to ensure that your dog is following the signal, rather than being bribed by the food. Place your hands in the starting position on your chest. Say "sit" just before you move your empty hand over your dog's nose. Click, praise, and treat *from the other hand*. Repeat five to ten times. When your dog sits eight out of ten times, you are ready for Step 3.

Step 3: Use the word only without the hand signal. Keep your hands on your chest, say "sit," and wait. Remember the 45 second game. If your dog doesn't sit within 45 seconds and seems distracted, repeat step 2, then try again. When your dog sits within three seconds of hearing your voice (without the hand signal), he now knows the sit behavior in that particular context or situation.

Incorporate the sit behavior into your dog's daily routine by using life rewards. Have her sit before going indoors and outdoors, up and down the stairs, before being let out of her kennel, and so on. In these examples, the reward is the freedom to be with you. You don't have to use treats.

Having problems?

- If your dog jumps instead of sitting, use the no-reward marker. Say "oops" or "uh-oh" and very quickly pull the treat away. As soon as he is on all fours again, immediately begin the process over, moving your hand over his head and continuing to encourage him. (See "No-Reward" Markers on page 127.)
- If your dog is confused, use "approximations," or simpler forms of the sit behavior. For instance, if you're training a puppy, you can click and treat the first "approximation" represented by her behind lowering an eighth of an inch. Then you can click and treat her when she lowers her behind another eighth-inch lower, and so on. Then you can click, praise, and jackpot the final behavior, which is her behind actually touching the floor.

🦴 Use the Magnet Game. Throughout the daywhen your dog sits, praise and throw a treat.

🦴 Check with your veterinarian. Make sure that there are no physical problems that keep your dog from being able to sit.

Note: High school and college level sit are taught along with those levels of lie down and stand because the protocols are identical (see page 172).

Lie Down—Grade School Level

Prepare: Begin in an environment that has few distractions or no distractions at all. Put a treat in one hand and hold the clicker in your other hand. Place your hands in the starting position on your chest.

Step 1: Get the behavior using a treat (lure) and a hand signal. Start with your dog in a sit position. Imagine there's an invisible string attached to your hand and your dog's nose, as though you're pulling her nose to the ground. The hand moving to the ground becomes the hand signal for "lie down." (Figure 14.5) Verbally encourage her. At the moment she lies down, click, praise, and treat. Repeat five to ten times. When she is successful eight out of ten times, you are ready to proceed to Step 2.

Figure 14.5

In teaching your dog to lie down, use hand signals first, with lots of praise and $10,000 rewards.

Step 2: Attach a word to the behavior along with the hand signal. Present your hand with a treat just under her nose and move it straight to the ground. Say the word "down" *immediately before* the hand signal. When your dog lies down, click, praise, and treat. Repeat five to ten times. When you are 80 percent sure your dog will follow your hand motion, you are ready to do the exercise with the treat in your other hand. This is to ensure that your dog is following the signal, rather than being bribed by the food. Present your empty hand just under her nose and say "down" just before you move it to the ground. Click and treat *from the other hand.* Repeat five to ten times. When your dog lies down eight out of ten times, go to Step 3.

Step 3: Use the word only without the hand signal. With your dog in a sit position, say down without using the hand signal. (Keep your hands on your chest.) Wait up to 45 seconds. Even if your dog gets up, wait the 45 seconds. If your dog *doesn't* lie down, go back and do five repetitions of Step 2. When your dog does lie down, click, lavishly praise, and "jackpot" her (Illustration 14.6).

Figure 14.6

When your dog lies down eight of ten times when you say "down," add an additional long-distance signal for down—putting your hand over your head.

Additional Challenges:

Practice having your dog lie down from his standing position (instead of the sit position), using your voice signal only.

Teach your dog to sit from a down position. Imagine that an invisible string is attached from her nose to your hand. Begin with a treat in your hand and slowly move it straight up. Click and reward. Then practice "sit-ups": sit, down, sit, down. Click, praise, and reward.

Having Problems?
- ☞ Use "approximations," or simpler forms of the down behavior. For instance, if you're training a puppy, you can click and treat the first "approximation" represented by her head lowering a few inches. Then you can click and treat her when she lowers her head lower *and* moves a paw forward. Then you can click and treat the final behavior when she goes all the way down. If your dog gets up from the sit, quickly withdraw the treat, say "oops" and start again. But go a little slower because you want to build on success.
- ☞ Curl your hand around to your dog's side instead of straight down. That way, she has to turn her head and body to reach the treat. This sometimes help to facilitate the process.
- ☞ Practice on a slippery floor. Oftentimes the dog's behind will simply slide into position.
- ☞ Relax your expectations. It isn't necessary that your dog lies down in one session. Go with the flow.
- ☞ Don't keep repeating the word for the behavior. Say it once and wait. If your dog can't figure it out, go back to the point where he was successful.
- ☞ If it's fun for you, it's fun for your dog. So if your dog stands around or seems bored, get happy! Dance around and use different vocal sounds from kissy sounds to howls. Pretend to eat food and exaggerate with

"hmmmmmm . . . look what I have!" Drop to the ground and pretend you found something interesting. Use a tennis ball or another of your dog's favorite toys in order to generate interest.

🦴 The Magnet Game is the biggest help for the down exercise (see page 159).

Stand—Grade School Level

Teaching your dog to stand is really helpful for visits to the veterinarian, when wiping your dog's paws, and for grooming and washing.

Prepare: Begin in an environment that has few distractions or no distractions at all. Put a treat between your thumb and index finger. Hold the clicker in your other hand. Place your hands in the starting position on your chest.

Step 1: Get the behavior using a treat (lure) and a hand signal. Place your dog in a sit, facing you. Move the hand that's holding the treat from your chest to a position directly in front of and one inch away from your dog's nose, palm forward. The hand moving parallel to the ground, away from your dog, becomes the hand signal for "stand." As your dog lifts his behind the least little bit, click, praise, reward. Repeat this a few times, and with each subsequent attempt, click and reward your dog for lifting his behind a little more off the floor. Some dogs get this immediately and you don't have to go in baby steps (incrementally). Repeat ten to fifteen times. When your dog is successful eight out of ten times, you are ready to proceed to Step 2.

Step 2: Attach a word to the behavior along with the hand signal. Put a treat between your thumb and index finger. Hold the clicker in your other hand. Place your hands in the starting position on your chest. Say "stand" *immediately preceding* the hand signal of moving your hand away from your dog's nose as in Step 1. When your dog stands, click, praise, and treat. Repeat ten to fifteen times. When you are 80 percent sure your dog will follow your hand motion, you are ready to do the exercise with the treat in your other hand. This is to ensure that your dog is following the hand signal, rather than being bribed by the food. The food should only be a reward, not a bribe. Place your hands in the starting position on your chest. Say "stand" just before you move your empty hand away from your dog's nose. When your dog stands, click, praise, and treat *from the other hand*. Repeat five to ten times. When your dog stands eight out of ten times, you are ready for Step 3.

Step 3: Use the word only without the hand signal. Put your hands in starting position on your chest. Say stand without using the hand signal. Wait up to 45 seconds. Click, praise and jackpot if he does it. Repeat. If he doesn't do it, go back to Step 2.

Having Problems?

- Make sure the hand with the treat isn't more than an inch from his nose at any time.
- Reward incrementally (baby steps). Reward your dog for leaning forward. Then reward your dog for leaning a little bit more forward, then for slightly lifting his behind off the floor, and so on.
- Relax your expectations. It isn't necessary that your dog stands in one session. Go with the flow.
- Don't keep repeating the word if you're looking for reliability. Say it once and wait.

For this and all exercises, your attitude can help tremendously. If it's fun for you, it's fun for your dog. So if your dog seems bored, get happy! Dance around and use different vocal sounds from kissy sounds to howls. Pretend to eat food and exaggerate with "hmmmmmm, look what I have!" Drop to the ground and pretend you found something interesting. Use a tennis ball or another of your dog's favorite toys in order to generate interest.

Sit, Lie Down, and Stand—High School Level

The instructions for teaching the "Sit," "Lie down," and "Stand" behaviors at the high school level are identical. Therefore, the following instructions pertain to all three behaviors. You can teach the different behaviors in the same training session or teach them individually.

If your dog is successful doing one of these behaviors, it does not mean that he will be successful doing another behavior. For instance, he may be a star in sitting but not yet proficient at lie down or stand. Remember to start at your dog's learning baseline for each and every behavior, and do not ask for more than what your dog can do. Each individual behavior is built incrementally—that is, step-by-step.

Add Duration, Also Known As Stay

At high school level, the additional challenge for your dog is to stay in position for longer periods of time. (See the 3 D's—duration, distance and distraction.) Some trainers don't teach "stay" because they feel that once they've taught a dog to sit or lie down or stand, there is a built-in expectation that the dog will remain in that position until released. The theory is perfectly sound, but I find most people forget to release their dogs from a behavior and the dogs end up releasing themselves. There is no separate protocol for stay here because, in the advanced levels of sit, lie down, and stand, as you add duration, you are, in essence, teaching your dog to stay.

NOTE: Every behavior has a start and a finish. If you have asked your dog to stay in any position, you must remember to "end" the behavior and give a signal that releases your dog. If you forget to release your dog from a stay, she will eventually just release herself and leave. This makes for really unreliable stays. I use the word "okay" as a release word. Some trainers feel the word "okay" is used so often in our daily vocabulary that the dog might hear the word somewhere in the environment and take off. So, if you prefer, you can say "find it," "that'll do," "thank you," "you're free" or whatever words you like to end the behavior and release your dog.

Prepare: Put a treat in one hand and hold the clicker in your other hand. Place your hands in the starting position on your chest and stand facing your dog, one foot away.

1. Ask your dog to sit, lie down, or stand. Say "Stay" and position the palm of your hand facing toward your dog. Count one second ("one thousand one") and, if your dog stays, click, praise, and treat.

2. Ask your dog to stay and this time count two seconds ("one thousand one, one thousand two"). If your dog stays, click, praise, and treat. With each successful attempt, which means your dog isn't moving from her position, increase the length of time in five-second increments. Progress to a point where your dog will stay for up to three minutes. This can happen in one week or one month. If your dog is not successful at longer durations, return to the last duration at which she was successful and proceed from there.

Add Distance

The goal of this exercise is to teach your dog to sit, lie down, or stand from increasing distances. The instructions are the same for each of these three behaviors. You will start with your dog in one position and increase your distance a foot at a time and then ask your dog to do a different behavior. For instance, ask your dog to stand, move away two steps, and then ask your dog to sit. Or ask your dog to sit, move away two steps, and then ask her to lie down. Below is the protocol for teaching your dog to sit at increasing distances. To teach lie down or stand at a distance, you will follow the exact same protocol.

1. Face your dog from one foot away and ask him to lie down or stand. Say "stay." Back away 2 feet from your dog. Ask your dog to "sit," click, praise, and give him a treat and then return to your dog.

2. Ask your dog to lie down or stand. Say "stay" and back away 3 feet from your dog. Ask your dog to "sit" using only the vocal signal. Click, praise, and treat and then return to your dog.
3. Continue adding a distance of an additional foot for each successful attempt until your dog will sit from a down or a stand at a distance of 20 feet.

Now follow this same protocol for down or stand from increasing distances. For example, if you are teaching your dog to lie down, you would start by having her in a stand or a sit position. If you are teaching your dog to stand, you would start by having her in a sit or lie down position.

Hint: If your dog is confused, add the hand signal along with your vocal signal.

Add Distractions

I refer to this exercise as "walk around the clock." This exercise prepares your dog for the real world, that is, when people are passing by, coming and going from all directions. Dogs are also very sensitive to anything that comes up behind them and the "walk around the clock" exercise will help desensitize your dog to those surprises.

1. Have your dog sit, lie down, or stand in front of you. Imagine your dog is in the center of the face of a clock. Twelve o'clock is in front, three o'clock to the left side, six o'clock behind your dog and 9 o'clock on the right side. Ask her to stay. Step to the "one o'clock" position and back again to twelve o'clock. Click, praise, and treat. Repeat three to five times. When she is successful, go to Step 2.
2. Say "stay," move to the two o'clock position and return. Click, praise, and treat. Continue this progression until you're able to walk all the way around your dog. Each time you return to the start position, click, praise, and treat. Just go at your dog's own speed. Once you get all the way around, give her a jackpot, that is, reward with four or five

treats one after another, all the while telling her how great she is. Keep the sessions short.

3. When you can walk all the way around your dog while she is sitting, lying down, or standing in a stay add additional challenges by:

⌐⊸ Asking your dog to stay and walking *quickly* around her. If she is successful, click, praise, and treat.

⌐⊸ When your dog is successful staying while you walk quickly, add an additional challenge by jogging around her. When she is successful, click, praise, and treat.

⌐⊸ Then add the additional challenge of waving your hands and yelling "booga, booga," as you run around your dog.

Having Problems?

⌐⊸ Just because you are successful running around your dog in one direction, that does not mean you will be successful running around her the other way. If your dog gets up when you run around, go back to the point where she was successful and incrementally add the more challenging distractions.

⌐⊸ If your dog is distracted, interrupt her with a sound such as "uh-oh," "oops," or "nope" and redirect her attention back to you with a motion such as waving your hand in front of her face (if necessary, with food in the hand).

⌐⊸ If your dog moves as soon as you begin to move, have a friend stand next to you. With your dog in position facing both of you, take a handful of treats and let your dog nibble them out of your hand while your friend walks around your dog. This is a form of counter conditioning as your dog is getting treats while the thing she's afraid of (person moving) is in play. Gradually she will change the way she feels about people moving because it will be associated with treats.

☞ If your dog likes her bed, practice "Stay" with her on her bed.

☞ Location often can also represent security so you might practice in a room where she is most comfortable.

☞ Don't "stalk" your dog by walking slower than your normal pace. Many people walk slowly when they do this exercise, which actually encourages the dog to get up because he thinks you are playing.

The "Automatic" Sit or Lie Down

The automatic sit (or lie down) means that your dog will sit (or lie down) every time you stop and he will stay in that position until he is released. In essence, your stopping will become an additional signal for sit and then stay (or lie down and then stay). This is a good thing to teach your dog to keep her from jumping on people or dogs you meet when on walks.

1. Start in an environment with no distractions, like your backyard. Have your dog walk by your side and take five to ten steps, then stop. Every time you stop, ask your dog to sit or lie down, using the vocal cue, the hand cue, or both. Click, praise, and reward each success. Repeat three to five times.

2. When she will sit eight out of ten times with you using the "sit" vocal cue, see if she has figured out what you are doing by taking a few steps and then stop without saying anything. Wait up to 45 seconds for her to respond. When she sits without your vocal cue, jackpot her. Do a few more repetitions and call it a day (Illustration 14.7).

You can also use the automatic sit (or lie down) to teach your dog boundaries that he should not cross without permission, such as a curb or the edge of your yard. Walk up to the curb, say sit and treat. Instead of going into the street, back up and do it again. Repeat this three times. On the fourth time, stop at the curb and say nothing. Wait. If she sits, jackpot her, then say "okay" and cross the street. (If she doesn't, go back to the step where she was successful.)

Figure 14.7

Automatic sit: Every time you stop, have your dog sit by
your side until she does it automatically.

Sit, Lie Down, and Stand—College Level

In college level you will add even more duration, distance, and
distractions so your dog will sit, lie down or stand wherever and
whenever you ask. You will continue weaning your dog off treats
by using "life rewards" such as going for a walk or a ride, throwing a ball, tossing a Frisbee, getting to say hello to other people
and dogs, getting to sniff a fire hydrant, playing "find it," and so
on. You will also be incorporating the intermittent reward schedule, giving her a treat every other time, then every third or fourth
time, etc. (If necessary, review Weaning Off Treats, page 115.)

By now you are familiar with the step-by-step protocols you
must use whenever introducing a new challenge. The situations
that follow must all be taught using these same protocols, starting in an environment where your dog can be successful and
incrementally building to the more advanced behavior. Asking
for a college level behavior before your dog is ready can seriously impair your progress and very possibly scare your dog.

Add Duration

At high school level, you taught your dog to stay in a sit, down,
or stand for three minutes. Now you will work up to a ten-minute

stay, using the same protocols you used before. When you can do that, begin adding additional challenges such as greater distance and even more distractions. CAUTION: When you're in public places, *always* keep your dog in sight and make sure he is on a leash. (If necessary, review Stay on page 172.)

Add Distance

At high school level, you progressed to having your dog sit, lie down, or stand a distance of 20 feet. College level distance begins there and then increases the distance incrementally until you get to a distance of 100 feet. In addition, college level increases not only the distance component but really challenges your dog by increasing the intensity of the distractions and the duration. Lastly, college level introduces the concept of having your dog do what you ask even though you are not in the room. This is truly the point at which your dog is becoming reliable. In order to reach college level, practice these exercises:

1. Ask your dog to stand, tell him to stay, and leave the room.
2. From outside the room, give the vocal cue for the first behavior listed below, and then reenter the room to see if he was successful. If he was, click, praise, and treat. Then, with your dog remaining in that position, leave the room and ask for the next behavior, and progress to the next behavior, each time returning and rewarding her success with a click, praise, and treat.

   - Ask your dog to sit from a stand.
   - Ask your dog to stand from a sit.
   - Ask your dog to lie down from a stand.
   - Ask your dog to stand from a down.
   - Ask your dog to go to his bed.
   - Ask your dog to come to you.

3. Ask your dog to do all of the behaviors listed in Step 2 above before returning and rewarding. So how will you

know whether your dog was successful? Here's a little trick. Place a mirror against the wall or doorframe in such a way that you can see what your dog is doing.

Add Distractions

In this next exercise you will be adding distractions. Your goal is to keep your dog focused on you so that no matter how close or how intense the distraction is, your dog will still pay attention to you and sit, lie down, or stand *while a person, animal, or object is moving or passing by.* If your dog does what you ask while your friend is running by at a one-foot distance, flailing her arms and yelling "Booga booga," you are on your final lap. The brain pathway is now established, and you can begin the whole process over again with someone your dog doesn't know. If you repeat this with three strangers in three different locations, your dog should begin to generalize, or behave the same way no matter who approaches. You won't have to repeat this process to introduce him to new people. You will, however, have to repeat these steps from the beginning when you introduce dogs.

Person Moving By

1. Ask your friend to stand at least 20 feet away and walk across your dog's path, perpendicular to your position. The person should walk at a normal rate and avoid eye contact with your dog.
2. As your friend begins to walk, ask your dog to sit, lie down, or stand. Click, praise, and treat. That ends the exercise and your friend can stop walking. Repeat this exercise three to five times. If your dog is successful, go to Step 3.
3. Now ask your friend to gradually increase her speed from a walk to a jog, from a jog to a run, while yelling "booga, booga" and waving her arms. Once again, as your friend begins to jog or run, ask your dog to sit, lie down, or stand. Each time your friend increases the intensity of her movements, you are progressing to a new level and will click, praise, and treat each successful attempt. At any point that

your dog isn't comfortable with increased speed or distractions, go back to the intensity at which he was successful.

4. Now you will begin to decrease the distance between your dog and your friend one foot at a time, starting with a walk and then adding intensity by changing the walk to jog, the jog to a run, and so on. Start by asking your friend to walk past at a distance of 19 feet and gradually decrease the distance by a foot at a time. Whenever you decrease the distance, you must return to a walking speed. Repeat three to five times at each distance.

Notes:

🦴 If at any point your dog has trouble, follow the golden rule and go back to the last step at which he was successful.

🦴 If your dog is ultra-sensitive, instead of doing this exercise, go to the Motion Sensitivity protocols, page 277.

Additional Distractions

You will use the same step-by-step protocols as described above whenever you introduce a new distraction. Ask your dog to pay attention to you and sit, lie down, or stand as you introduce the distractions listed below. Use as many of them as possible. Vary your signals by practicing hand signals only and then practicing voice signals only.

🦴 Person with baby carriage
🦴 Person on crutches
🦴 Person with umbrella closed; then open, then twirling
🦴 Person on skateboard
🦴 Person with a dog
🦴 Person bouncing basketball
🦴 Person throwing Frisbee or tennis ball up in the air

Once you've reached the 80 percent mark on visual distractions, ask your dog to sit, lie down, or stand while introducing sound distractions. Practice at the veterinarian's office, the homes of neighbors and relatives, inside the pet store, and at carnivals.

It is imperative you do not frighten your dog by asking for too much, too soon! Gradually build up the sound intensity for each and every individual sound distraction. Remember: *If your dog won't do what you want her to do, go back to the point where she's successful.*

- Loud and sudden noises, such as banging pots, dropping chairs, and whistling
- People shouting and arguing
- Noisy vehicles, such as motorcycles
- Person with vacuum cleaner, first turned off without being moved, then off with movement, then turned on and standing still, then on with movement

Hide-and-Seek Game

Prerequisite: High school level sit/stay or down/stay.

This game is a fun way to combine several different behaviors and it's one of the best ways to obtain an even more reliable stay. The three-step process doesn't apply to this behavior because most dogs will easily grasp it and do it right away.

Hide-and-Seek—Grade School Level

1. Ask your dog to sit or lie down and stay.
2. Now run behind a chair and hide for one second.
3. Stick your head out, say "peek-a-boo!"and hide your head again.
4. When your dog finds you, really praise her and make a big deal out of how clever she was.

Hide-and-Seek—High School Level

Gradually make the basic game more challenging by asking for longer "stays" and making yourself more difficult to find. For example, run into your bedroom and hide in the closet. To make it easy at first, keep the door open a few inches. Get other people involved and have them say, "Find Jane! Where's Jane?" Now jump up—gingerly, of course—on a chest of drawers. Challenge your dog to find you "up in the air." Add distractions.

Find It

This is a great training exercise because it stimulates your dog emotionally, mentally, and physically.

Find It—Grade School Level

When teaching find it, you already know that your dog will take the treat that's offered. Steps 1 and 2 are combined in this behavior because you are already 80 percent sure your dog will immediately be successful.

Prepare: Put your hands in "starting position," holding them close to your chest. Your dog can be sitting, lying down or standing when you ask him to do this behavior.

Steps 1 and 2: Get the behavior and attach a word to it along with the hand signal.

Place a $10,000 treat—like a piece of turkey—on the floor right in front of your dog and simultaneously say "find it." Your hand moving down and then back to your chest again becomes the hand signal for find it. Repeat this several times, progressively moving the treat farther away, but still in plain view.

Note: Step 3 (Use the word only without the hand signal) is not used until high school level when "find it" is combined with "stay." You'll see what I mean as you read the High School steps.

Find It—Junior High School Level

Hide the treat behind the leg of a table or chair or behind a footstool as you say "find it." Let your dog see you place it, but put it out of sight. He'll probably look at you as if you're kidding and it may take him a second or two to figure out what's going on. He now has to find the treat with his nose instead of his eyes. Give him up to 45 seconds to figure it out. When he finally locates the treat and gobbles it up, praise him to high heaven for being such a brilliant dog. Now run across the room and as soon as he looks at you, say "find it" and let him see you hide another treat. Continue this game of moving about the room and hiding treats until you've shown him a dozen or so hiding places. Continue this treat-hiding game throughout the week, running around and showing him hiding spots.

Find It—High School Level

At the high school level of find it, you can actually improve your dog's reliability with other behaviors by linking them together in what's called a behavioral chain. For example, you will ask your dog to sit, then lie down, then stay, then you'll leave the room, then you'll return to the room, and then, at the end of this chain of behaviors, reward your dog. This chain of behaviors will help you to wean your dog off treats, as well as improve your dog's reliability in the "stay" behavior.

1. Have your dog sit, then lay down, then stay, and then walk away from your dog into another room and hide a treat in that room. Return to your dog and say "find it." You no longer have to show your dog where you are hiding the treats. Hence at this level, you only have to give your dog the words for this behavior and he'll know what you mean. If your dog is successful, gradually make it more and more challenging by repeating this exercise and hiding more treats in more places each time you leave the room so your dog has to search for longer periods of time.

    Because your dog hasn't learned yet that "find it" means there may be treats in unfamiliar places, you must hide the treats in the same locations you showed him in junior high school level.

2. Form a more challenging behavioral chain. Have him go to his spot, sit, lie down, stay. Then leave your dog and walk into another room and hide the treats. Return to your dog

but instead of saying "find it," say "come" and have your dog touch your hand. Now say "find it!" and let your dog search for the treats.

Within a week or two, your dog will figure out that "find it" means there's always a treat to be found so you're ready to hide treats in areas you've never shown him before. Send him to his bed, ask him to sit, then lie down and stay. Go to another room and put a big pile of really yummy treats in an unfamiliar location. Return to your dog and say find it. He'll eagerly search for the treats in the familiar hiding spots. Not being able to find any, he might pause and look at you. Say find it again and walk toward the pile of hidden treats. His nose will soon pick up the scent and, voilà, successfully complete his hunt.

Hint

You can also add a treat-filled Kong or a long-chewing treat such as Bully Sticks as one or more of the treats. Then, for the next twenty minutes while your dog is occupied with his reward you can take a shower or have breakfast. Good luck!

Remember to adjust your dog's regular diet to account for daily treats!

Go to Your Spot

This behavior solves virtually every problem behavior your dog has in the house. (It can help with aggression but it's important that you also see a professional when aggression is involved.) By directing your dog to "go to your spot," you are redirecting his attention and giving him something else to do. This can help calm him if he's nervous or distract him when he's doing something you don't want him to do. It is useful when your dog barks at the mail carrier, nudges you while you're on the phone, races to the door when the doorbell rings, begs at the dinner table, or acts fearful about strangers working around the house. It's a great behavior to teach a dog to do for safety reasons, such as whenever a baby or small child enters a room. You can take your dog's spot ("bed") on trips or to your relatives over the holidays and tell him to simply chill there for as long as you want. These go to your spot instructions can be used to teach your dog to go up to a dozen or more places. The methods are exactly the same to teach him to go to his kennel, bed, blanket, mat, den, go outside, get in the house, etc. Be sure to pick a different word for each different location. For instance, you could refer to the kennel as "Kennel" or "Get in your house," or "Go to your den" but, whichever one you pick, always use the same word or phrase for the kennel. Going step-by-step, most dogs will pick up this behavior very quickly; for some it will take three short sessions. Don't rush it, keep the sessions short and stop each session on a high note.

Go to Your Spot—Grade School Level

Prepare: Stand beside the place you want your dog to use as a "spot" and make sure you are no more than one foot away from it. The "spot" can be a bed, blanket, den, or any other place. Start with your dog in a sit position facing you. Put your hands in the starting position on your chest.

Step 1: Get the behavior using a treat (lure) and a hand signal. Let your dog see you throw a $10,000 treat onto the spot. The hand that is throwing the treat is the hand that is closest to the spot (Figure 14.8). For this behavior, the hand pointing to the spot and then immediately returning to your chest is the hand signal for go to your spot. As soon as your dog gets to the spot to get the treat, click and praise (Figure 14.9). Repeat several times. When teaching go to your spot, you already know that your dog will take the treat that's offered. Since the rule is that you go to Step 2 when you are 80 percent sure your dog will be successful, you can now proceed to Step 2.

Figure 14.8

Figure 14.9

Go to Your Spot: Figures 14.8 and 14.9 show teaching your dog to go to his spot with a hand motion.

Step 2: Attach a word to the behavior along with the hand signal.

Say "spot" (or "place," or "bed," or "kitchen," etc.) and use the same hand motion you used while throwing the treat. (Your hand started on your chest, you threw the treat, and your hand returned to your chest.) Click, praise, and treat. Repeat five to ten times.

Progress to putting the treat in your other hand. Give the verbal request and pretend to throw the treat, using the same motion with the now empty hand (from your chest and back again). Click, praise, and treat when your dog is on the spot. The difference here is that you're no longer using the treat as a lure or target. It is now used only as a reward after your dog actually goes to the spot. When your dog is successful eight out of ten times, proceed to Step 3.

Step 3: Use the word only without the hand signal. Keep your hands on your chest. Say the word once. Wait up to 45 seconds. If your dog puts a paw on the bed, effusively praise and jackpot. Repeat ten to fifteen times. If your dog doesn't go to his spot within 45 seconds, return to Step 2.

For shy or hesitant dogs, click the smallest approximation of the behavior. In this case, click and reward when your dog looks at the spot, then click and reward when your dog takes one step toward the spot, then click and reward when your dog puts one paw on the spot, and so on.

Go to Your Spot—High School Level

Add Distance. Begin moving away from the spot, a foot at a time. Move 2 feet away from the spot. Say "spot" and click, praise, and treat every success. With each subsequent attempt, increase your distance from the spot a foot at a time. Click, praise and reward every success. If your dog gets confused, it's a good bet you've gone too far too fast. Go back to the distance you were successful and work at that distance a little while longer.

Once you have begun to move farther from the bed (adding distance) you never throw the treat as a lure again. You only use the vocal signal. The only time you used the treat as a lure was at the very first step when you were next to the bed. After that, the treat is only used as a reward.

Add Distractions. Once you've reached a point where your dog will go to her spot from virtually anywhere, begin adding distractions. When you add a distraction, like someone knocking at the door, go back to standing right by the spot and begin the training process all over. For example:

- ☜ Stand by the door and send your dog to his spot. Click, praise, and treat. Repeat five to ten times.
- ☜ Next, knock or ring the doorbell and immediately send your dog to his spot (bed). Click and treat each time. Repeat ten times. On the eleventh time, knock or ring the bell and say nothing. Wait up to 45 seconds.

The signal for your dog to go to his spot has now been installed as a signal for your dog to run to his spot. With several days, weeks, and months of practice, your dog will automatically go to his spot whenever someone knocks on the door or rings the doorbell.

Go to Your Spot—College Level

As your dog is more successful with go to your spot, gradually add more distance and, over time, wean her off the treats by incorporating the intermittent reward schedule. Give her a treat every other time, then every third or fourth time, and so on. In addition to food rewards, include life rewards such as going for a walk or a ride. "Want to go outside? Go to your bed first." Once he has really got it, you can wean him off treats and his reward can be simply getting to meet someone at the door, going for a ride, or anything else he really likes.

Then you're ready to add additional locations. Identify each location its own individual "label" such as "bed," "mat," "kennel," "kitchen," "couch." Work on these one at a time so each behavior is in place before you teach your dog to go to another place. For every new location, you must start from square one again.

Once your dog knows two or more different locations such as the bed and the kennel, you can then teach him to discriminate between them. To begin, put them at opposite ends of the same room and follow these steps.

1. Stand in the middle, between the two objects and ask your dog to go to the bed. Reward every success. Then repeat ten times.
2. Still standing in the middle, send him to the kennel. Reward every success. Repeat that ten times.
3. Now, with voice only, say the word for one of the locations. See what happens.
4. When your dog goes to the location you've signaled at least 80 percent of the time, start moving one of the objects, such as the bed closer to the other object along the circumference of the circle, so that you are still equal distance from the object. For example, one location can now be in front of you and the other location is still off to your side.
5. Gradually build on success until the objects are next to each other.
6. Once your dog has this two-item behavior figured out, add the third item such as the mat. Repeat the whole process, starting with the mat on the opposite side of the room.

Using Go to Your Spot to Teach Your Dog to Go to the Kennel

Dogs have an inherent dislike of being confined or restrained. Because of this, you don't want to simply stick a dog in the kennel as this can be very traumatic. It's important to get your dog used to the kennel gradually. Learning to go to the kennel is taught exactly the same way as Go to Your Spot. However, because the kennel is enclosed, unlike other locations that you've taught your dog to go to, there's one major consideration to keep in mind. Don't close the gate until you know she's comfortable being in the kennel. For dogs who are sensitive and really hesitant about going into a kennel, there are a number of things you can try:

🦴 If the kennel is the type that is enclosed, take the top off before teaching this behavior.

🦴 Before attempting to teach your dog to get in the kennel, use counterconditioning to change the way she feels about the kennel. There are two ways to do this.

- Lay a bunch of treats in a line from the front of the kennel to the back. You can also try feeding her meals in the kennel. Leave the food just inside the door to begin with and, at each feeding time, put it farther back until, after a week, she has to go all the way inside to eat. It's important not to close the kennel gate during this process.
- When she's not looking, sneak a great treat in the kennel and let her find it on her own. Sometimes dogs are braver when you aren't around. Whenever you notice that she's found and eaten the treat, sneak more treats into the kennel one at a time so she begins to associate the kennel as a magic treat-dispensing haven.

Once you realize that your dog is looking at the kennel as a positive place and starts to explore it without being asked to do so, start using the magnet game. That is, every time you see her going in the kennel, click, praise, and throw her a treat.

Now you can start to teach her to go to her kennel using the Go to Your Spot protocol above.

1. Once you are sure she is comfortable going into the kennel, send her to the kennel and close the gate for one second. Immediately give her a treat through the gate. Then open the gate and let her out. Repeat this three to five times, opening the gate immediately after treating.
2. Gradually progress to keeping the gate closed for longer periods of time for up to fifteen seconds, adding a second at a time before giving her a treat. This may take several sessions over days, weeks or even months depending on your dog's sensitivity. When she's comfortable with the gate being closed for fifteen seconds, go to Step 3.
3. Begin to add distance by moving away from the kennel and returning to it a step at a time. In other words, send your dog to the kennel, close the gate, back up one step,

come forward one step, give your dog a treat, and open the gate. Each time you increase your distance from the kennel and return to your dog, give a treat and then open the gate again. Progress to the point where you leave the room for short periods of time and gradually increase to longer periods.

If you are training a young puppy, confinement won't be as much of a problem as that issue doesn't get triggered until a dog is a few months old. Puppies are more adaptable and accept things as they are more easily. That being said, every dog is an individual and, if your puppy is having extreme difficulty with being confined, don't confine him. Call a professional dog trainer for advice.

Hint

For this and all exercises that require your dog to move, your attitude can help tremendously. If it's fun for you, it's fun for your dog. So if your dog stands around or seems bored, get happy! Dance around; use different vocal sounds from kissy sounds to howls. Pretend to eat food and exaggerate with "hmmmmmm . . . look what I have!"

Having Problems?

🦴 Relax your expectations. It isn't necessary for your dog to get it in one session.

🦴 Leave treats on the bed (or wherever) throughout the day. Within a very short time, your dog will actually go to the spot and search for the treat. When that happens, use the Magnet Game. Instantly click, praise, and throw an extra treat to your dog the moment he places a paw on the bed (or kennel, spot, etc.).

🦴 Look at the spot after giving the signal. Dogs have a tendency to follow your gaze.

🦴 Make sure you wait a full 45 seconds for your dog to figure out what you want.

Using Go to Your Spot as a Problem Solver

I mentioned at the beginning of this section that the Go to Your Spot exercise can be used as a substitute behavior to solve virtually every problem behavior you have in your home. Once your dog will go to his spot (or bed, kennel, etc.) from a distance of 15 feet, you can now assign several different signals to the same behavior.

Barking

Dogs bark much less when they are in a down position because it is a more subordinate position and a more relaxed position. If your dog starts barking, simply tell him to run to his bed and lie down. Tell him to stay. When he's quiet, release him.

Begging

If your dog begs at the table, use this behavior as a substitute.

1. Teach your dog to go to his bed while you are standing at the dining room table. Click and treat each time. Repeat five to ten times.
2. Next, sit in the chair and give the signal. Click and treat each time. Repeat five to ten times. On the eleventh time, sit in the chair and say nothing. Wait for up to 45 seconds. Your sitting in the chair will now be installed as a signal to go to his bed. Every time you sit, your dog will go to his spot (bed).
3. When your dog will automatically go to his bed every time you sit in your chair, you will then ask him to lie down and reward him. With several days of practice, whenever you sit at the table to eat, he will automatically go to his bed and lie down. You can throw him treats from the table or occasionally get up to pet and treat him. To keep your dog on the bed, you can give him a favorite chewie such as a Bully Stick, chicken strip, or a treat-filled Kong.

Bolting Out the Door

If your dog bolts out the door, use this behavior as a substitute.

1. Teach your dog to go to his bed while you are standing by the door. Click and treat each time. Repeat five to ten times.
2. Next, put your hand on the doorknob and say "bed." Click and treat each time. Repeat ten times. On the eleventh time, put your hand on the doorknob and say nothing. Wait up to 45 seconds.

Your hand on the doorknob will now be installed as a signal for your dog to go to his spot. So instead of bolting out the door, your dog will go the other way. Then ask him to lie down and stay. The reward will be you calling him to go for a walk. With several days, weeks, and months of practice, he will automatically go to his bed and lie down whenever you go to the door.

CAUTION: Most dogs are much quicker than their human. Always have a leash on your dog when you practice this in case he tries to escape.

Chewing

Put the bed in a social area and teach your dog that while he's in the house, he has to stay on it. You can do this by keeping him tethered while at the same time giving him a great chewie that will take a while for him to finish. You are teaching him which objects are appropriate for chewing while, at the same time, preventing him from chewing on inappropriate objects.

If one of the inappropriate objects he chews is his bed, bring the bed out only when you are practicing the Go to Your Bed behavior. When you are done teaching, pick up the bed so he doesn't have a chance to chew on it. After a few weeks, he will only chew the appropriate objects you give him.

REMINDER: Only tether a dog when you are in the same room to supervise. If you are unable to stay in the same room with your dog, use a baby gate to keep your dog segregated in a safe location instead of tethering.

Jumping
If your dog jumps on you or your guests, use this behavior as a substitute.

1. Teach your dog to go to his spot (bed) while you are standing by the door. Click and treat each time. Repeat five to ten times.
2. Next, stand on the other side of the door. Open the door and say "spot." Repeat ten times. On the eleventh time, open the door and say nothing. Wait up to 45 seconds. You walking in the door has now become installed as a signal for your dog to go to his spot. With several days of practice, he will automatically go to his spot and lie down whenever you walk in the door. Then ask him to lie down and stay.
3. Now ask a friend to help in the next stage. Stand with your dog by the door. Have your friend come in and as she does, send your dog to his spot. Repeat ten times. On the eleventh time, say nothing. The signal for your dog to go to his spot will now be installed whenever someone walks in the door. The reward is you saying "Okay" and then your dog gets to greet the person.

Reacting to Doorbell or Knock at the Door
If your dog runs to the door and barks whenever someone knocks or rings the doorbell, use this behavior as a substitute.

1. Teach your dog to go to his bed while you are standing by the door. Stand by the door and send your dog to his spot. Click and treat. Repeat five to ten times.
2. Next, knock or ring the door bell and immediately send your dog to his spot Click and treat each time. Repeat ten times. On the eleventh time, knock or ring the bell and say nothing. Wait up to 45 seconds. The signal for your dog to go to his spot has now been installed as a signal for your dog to run to his spot. (If your dog doesn't do what you've asked in 45 seconds, go back to the step where she was successful.) Then ask him to lie down and stay. With several

days, weeks, and months of practice, your dog will automatically go to his spot whenever someone knocks on the door or rings the doorbell.

3. Now ask a friend to help in the next stage. Stand with your dog by the door. Have your friend ring the doorbell or knock and as she does, send your dog to his spot. Repeat ten times. On the eleventh time, say nothing. The signal for your dog to go to his spot will now be installed whenever someone knocks on the door or rings the bell.

Come When Called

The benefits of a reliable come when called behavior, also referred to as recall, don't really need to be enumerated. The key to its usefulness is how reliable you get it to be. There is simply no shortcut to reliability, which is based on three things: repetitions, consistency, and improvement through ever increasing challenges. That's it.

Remember the number one rule: Never call your dog to you unless you are 80 percent sure she'll respond; in other words, don't use the word "come" if there's a chance she won't. Also, don't call your dog to you if you're going to yell at her or if you're leaving for the day. (In positive training we don't yell anyway, so you should be okay.) If you do yell or leave after calling her, your dog will very quickly learn that there is a negative consequence whenever she hears the word "come"; hence, she won't come when called. Unless she's at a strong High School level, never call her if she's running away. She might inadvertently learn that the word "Come" is irrelevant or that "Come" means run the other way. (See the 80 Percent Rule on page 127.)

Come When Called—Grade School Level

I teach come when called, which is also referred to as recall, as a targeting exercise because it is so easy for both humans to use and dogs to learn. For this behavior I always emphasize incremental training or teaching in baby steps. What we are looking to do is form an automatic response. This means that as soon as we give the signal our dogs are so conditioned that they will stop whatever they're doing and run to us. They won't even think about it. The key to success is to do thousands of repetitions over a long period of time.

Prepare: Rub some turkey, chicken, or cheese on the fingers of one hand and hold a treat in the other hand. Put your hands in "starting position," holding them close to your chest.

> **Step 1:** Get the behavior using a treat (lure) and a hand signal. With your hands in starting position on your chest, bring the treat-smelling hand down to your side, palm forward, two inches in front of your dog's nose. The hand signal for come is your hand moving from your chest to your side. As soon as he touches your hand, click, praise, and reward with the treat that you're holding in the other hand. Repeat ten to fifteen times. When your dog will do this successfully 80 percent of the time, you are ready to proceed to Step 2. (See Figures 14.10, 14.11, and 14.12)

Figure 14.10

In start position, you have your hands on your chest.

Figure 14.11

Say "come," and put your hand down by your side to get your dog to walk toward you.

Figure 14.12

The final part of come when called is your dog touching your hand with his nose. Then its time to click, praise, and reward.

Step 2: Attach a word to the behavior along with the hand signal. Say "come" and present your treat-smelling hand four inches away from your dog's nose. For each repetition, add an inch or two of distance. Progress to a distance of 20 feet. The goal is that no matter how far away you are, your dog will immediately rush over to you to touch your "magic hand." This targeting method will prove very helpful in the "leave it" (page 220) and "heel" exercises (page 202) that follow.

Hints
Use everyday opportunities and life rewards to practice "come" such as:

🦴 Feeding time. Have your dog touch your hand before you put the food down.

🦴 Going outside. Have your dog touch your hand before you open the door.

🦴 When you take your dog for a walk, periodically ask your dog to touch your hand (come).

Note: For this behavior, Step 3 (use word only) will not be used until you get to college level, which is taught as part of The Triangle Game on page 224. For now, continue to have your dog touch your hand whenever you say come before giving a treat.

Come When Called—Junior High School Level

1. Form a triangle with other members of the family, each about 6 to 10 feet apart. Ask your dog to sit and stay in the middle. Have person A say with a happy, excited voice, "Jackson, come." As he arrives and touches her hand, click, reward with a treat, affection, praise and petting, and say, "What a wonderful dog you are!" Then person B immediately calls, then person C calls, and then each person takes random turns calling "come."
2. Repeat Step 1, but this time ask your dog to sit in front of you after touching your hand. When he does so, click, praise, and reward. Repeat five to ten times.
3. Add challenges and distractions, such as:

🦴 Practice with your back turned.

🦴 Practice while you're lying on the ground.

🦴 Practice while you're sitting on the floor.

🦴 Practice saying "come" while you're in another room.

🦴 Form a behavioral chain. Ask your dog to sit and stay. From a standing position 10 feet away, say with a happy, excited voice, "Jackson, come." As he arrives and touches your hand, ask your dog to sit again, then lie down, then, at the end of all these behaviors, click, praise, and reward him with a treat.

🦴 Take it all outside and start from the beginning. Remember, whenever you change environments, you have to go back to the beginning. (See Context Learning in Chapter 10 on page 117.) So when you take your dog outdoors, go back and repeat Grade School Level. Start in a relatively low distraction environment like the backyard early in the morning.

High School Level

Now you really start adding distractions. Here are two more exercises to integrate:

1. Interrupt your dog's dinner and ask her to come to you. She has to stop eating, sit in front of you, and then go back to eating. Teach this by putting just a low-valued food in the bowl to start. Kibble is best for this exercise. Stand a foot or two away and call her. Reward her with several $10,000 treats like pieces of turkey or liver. Let her return to her bowl of kibble. Repeat this three to five times. Then gradually add more food in the bowl so she really gets into eating before calling her. Then progress to adding special treats like turkey and liver to the food bowl. Last, progress to the point where you have nothing in your hand when you call her. At this point, you will no longer have to lure and reward her from your hand. The food in the bowl will be the reward, even though she stopped eating it to come to you.

2. Have a friend hold a treat a couple of inches from your dog's nose and say, "Look what I've got!" As your dog anticipates getting the treat from your friend, put your target hand just to the side of your dog's face (about three inches) and say come. As soon as your dog turns his head, praise him and say "okay!"

Then have your friend stick the treat in your dog's mouth. Repeat this exercise five to ten times, each time increasing the distance of your target hand. Your goal is to have your dog walk all the way across the room to touch your hand and then return to your friend to get the treat. What happens if your dog refuses to turn his head away? Lower the value of the treat in your friend's hand and hold a more valuable treat in your hand. Then go back to using a hand signal without the treat.

Having problems?

🦴 For puppies who can't see really well at a distance, crouch down and open your arms and with a happy, excited voice say, "Jackson, come."

🦴 Turn your side to your dog and crouch down when you offer your hand. This works with rescue dogs who are a little skittish.

🦴 Run the other way after saying "come" to make it a happy game.

🦴 Play hide and seek. (See the "Hide and Seek Game," page 181.) Your dog will always run to find you if you make it a game.

🦴 Do a few repetitions with a treat in the hand that's signaling. Then go back to using a nontreat hand signal.

🦴 Practice the Triangle Game (see page 224).

Quiet

(Also see "Barking" in Part 4, Resolving Problem Behaviors, page 253.)

Teaching your dog to be quiet can be confusing. This is because the opposite of quiet—barking—is a behavior that really lends itself to being unintentionally trained. (See Unintentional Training on page 251.) In other words, it's easy to inadvertently teach your dog to bark, which is the opposite of the behavior you're looking for. Therefore, it's important to really watch what you're doing when you interact with your dog in day-to-day situations. For example, if you're on the phone and your dog is barking to get your attention and you finally get fed up and yell "shut up," you may have unintentionally trained him to bark because you gave him the attention he was looking for. Remember, dogs learn "what-happens-when." It's as if they say to themselves, "What happens when I bark?" If the answer is, "I get rewarded by my person paying attention to me," you've just *taught* your dog to bark. So watch how you respond when your dog barks.

Here is the protocol for teaching quiet. This behavior is not taught in the traditional three-step process.

1. Believe it or not, a method of teaching your dog to be quiet is to teach her *to bark* first. You do this by giving her a lower value reward, such as praise, whenever she barks. Then teach her to be quiet by interrupting her barking. Do this with an unexpected short, crisp "quiet," followed by a higher value reward, such as a $10,000 food treat as soon as she stops barking. She quickly learns that "quiet" gets better rewards. This method of training is referred to as putting a behavior "on cue." (See "Put the Behavior on Cue" in Chapter 12 on page 138.) While your dog is barking, use a word like "sing" or "speak." Click, praise, and treat. Do this often enough and pretty soon your dog will have linked barking with the word or signal. Please note: In this case, you are labeling the behavior right away. This is because your dog is already doing the behavior.

2. Now that your dog is barking on signal, interrupt the barking with another sound, like the word "quiet" or "enough." As soon as she stops barking, click, praise, and then, this time, reward with a $10,000 food treat. Then get her singing again; reward with praise. Then say "quiet" once more and click, praise, and reward with a food treat. Repeat five to ten times in each session. When your dog is successful eight out of ten times, go to Step three.

3. Stretch the length of "quiet" time by delaying the food treat for two seconds, then three seconds, and so on until you have progressed up to several minutes. Progress to a point where you will stop giving treats for singing and only give them for being quiet. Because you're only using praise to reward the barking, your dog will gravitate more toward silence, where the $10,000 treats are.

Heeling

To many people, the term "heeling" means walk without pulling. However, they are really two separate behaviors. Let's look at the differences:

> *Heeling* means the dog walks or stands by your side within an imaginary boxed area by your leg—not too far ahead of you, not too far behind you, not too far from your side, and not too close to you. The idea is that he stays within the perimeters of this imaginary box, without bumping your leg.

> *Walk without pulling* means just what it says. While the dog is on a leash, he can go ahead of you, behind you, or to your side, but he immediately stops pulling whenever he feels the slightest tension on the leash.

First we'll deal with heeling and then walk without pulling.

In Grade School Level Heeling, there are several methods you can use to teach your dog to walk by your side. You can pick and choose from them or use them in combination. I primarily use methods two and three in my classes and in-home training sessions. Heeling doesn't follow the usual three-step process (get the behavior, add the word, then use the word only) because your dog will figure this out quickly. Therefore, you are already 80 percent sure your dog will be successful in doing the behavior and there is no need for step one.

Heeling—Grade School Level

There are two methods in beginning heeling. Try them both and see which works best for you.

Heeling—Method 1: The Traditional Method

This behavior is taught with a slight variation on the three-step process.

Prepare: In a nondistracting environment, have your dog sit by your side.

Steps 1 and 2: Get the behavior using a treat (lure) and attach a word to the behavior along with the hand signal. With your hands in starting position on your chest, say "heel" and, using the hand that is closest to your dog, stick a treat in her mouth. Do not walk forward while you do this. Stay in one place and don't move. Repeat this ten to fifteen times. The hand signal for heel is similar to the hand signal for come. Your hand will move from your chest down to your side. This works because both come and heel are targeting behaviors. In other words, wherever the target hand is, that's where your dog is supposed to be. The only difference between come and heel is that in the come behavior your dog is coming toward you and facing you. In the heel behavior your dog is facing the same direction as you.

Step 3: Add motion. Your dog will now be looking up at your hand anticipating another treat. At this point, begin to walk and treat at the same time. As you continue to walk, the hand next to your dog brings the treat from your chest to your dog's mouth. Just before you give it to your dog, say "heel." Then bring your hand back to your chest each time. Repeat ten to fifteen times.

Step 4: Say the word only. Keep your hands on your chest. Say the word "heel" one time and begin walking. Take four or five steps, then stop and say "sit." (Use the sit hand signal—hand up over the dog's head—if you need to.) When your dog sits, praise, and then give her the treat. Begin again and each time gradually add more steps before stopping and asking your dog to sit. For example, take eight or nine steps and then ask your dog to sit. Then twelve or thirteen, and so on. Whenever you come to a stop, click, praise, and treat. If you practice this heeling exercise and add the distance of one additional house-length each day, you'll be around the block in a month or two with your dog remaining in heel position.

HAVING PROBLEMS?

If your dog wants to come in front of you when you stop, that is natural as she's used to getting rewards while standing in front of you for all the other behaviors. To resolve this, bring the treat close to her nose as you prepare to stop. *As you stop*, use the sit hand signal by bringing the treat slightly over her head and then give it to her when she sits. If you repeat this ten to fifteen times, that should solve the problem.

Method 2: Spontaneous Heeling

This method is a variation of the Magnet Game (see page 159). It is so easy that the three-step training process does not apply to this method.

Step 1: In a nondistracting environment, meander around an enclosed area or yard with your dog off the leash. If you don't have an enclosed area in which to work, put him on a twenty-foot leash so he can't wander off.

Step 2: Whenever your dog happens to walk by your side, click, praise, and treat. You can encourage (prompt) him to do this more and more often by patting your leg, taking quick little steps, and praising even the slightest interest in staying by your side. Every time he starts going off in another direction, you should abruptly turn and go the other way, being careful, of course, not to jerk him if he's on lead. Every time he happens to come up to your side, once again, click, praise, and treat. If he stays there, continue to praise and treat.

Hint

If your dog is pulling and he is one of those extra powerful dogs or if he was abused before you got him—as is the case with many rescue dogs—it may be helpful to use an Easy Walker or NewTrix harness or a halter-style collar with these methods. The combination of an anti-pulling collar with a bungee leash often gives 50 percent more control of your dog immediately.

Heeling—High School Level

At this point your dog is successful at heeling using one of the methods taught in grade school level.

1. Ask a friend to stand 10 or 15 feet away from you and your dog. With your dog in heel position, walk up to the person and have your dog sit. Then shake the person's hand and ask the person to walk away. Click, praise and reward your dog.
2. Repeat the previous step with this difference. This time you and your dog will stay in position and your friend will approach you. The other person walks up to you, shakes your hand, and walks away. Click, praise and reward.
3. Start at a distance of about 30 feet from another person. With your dog in heel position, walk toward the other person as the other person walks toward you. When you meet, have your dog sit, then shake hands with the other person. Then you and the other person should continue to walk in opposite directions. As you are walking, click, praise, and treat.

Hints
- Make sure your dog has had plenty of exercise before heeling.
- Start with a person your dog knows and have her say hello to your dog before practicing.
- If your dog gets up each time the person approaches, keep your foot on the leash.

Heeling—College Level

Most dogs must be between 18 and 24 months of age to reach a college level proficiency in heeling. Even with mature dogs, it usually takes at least six months of consistent work to attain this level. For college level, you will be repeating the high school level exercises and adding new locations, people, and dogs.

1. Take your dog to town and ask him to heel as you walk up and down the sidewalk among pedestrians, other dogs, and noisy traffic. Walk over grates, under ladders, and by delivery people who are wheeling carts into stores or restaurants. Remember to keep these sessions short and use $10,000 rewards.
2. Ask for longer periods of heeling. At this level your dog is riveted to you no matter what and will not leave your side unless released.

Having problems?

🦴 The key to success while heeling a dog in a heavy distraction area is, you guessed it, incremental training (baby steps). So if your dog can't handle a lot of people, heel her across the street where there are less people. Keep the sessions short and make sure you have exercised her before going to town.

🦴 Try the "horse feedbag" trick. If you think your dog is going to get really distracted by something or someone, put a bunch of treats in your hand and, as you walk your dog past the distractions, allow your dog to nibble the treats from your hand. She will then be happily eating the food from your hand and the distractions will be less significant to her. This is an especially good thing to do when you are walking your dog past houses and yards with barking dogs who go nuts whenever you pass by.

Walk Without Pulling

The only difference between "walk without pulling" and "heeling" is that you're allowing your dog a greater freedom area or "envelope." In heeling, you click when the dog is right by your side. In walk without pulling, your dog can be anywhere as long as the leash is loose. You teach this by clicking and treating whenever your dog slackens the leash.

To teach your dog to walk without pulling, I use a combination of five methods. You will note that the usual three-step training process is not applicable for methods 1 through 4. The five methods are:

1. The Start/Stop Method
2. The Voluntary Return Method
3. The Reversal Method
4. The Walk/Release Method
5. The Get Behind Me Method

Any of these methods works fine by itself but your progress can be greatly enhanced if you use two, three, or even all five of them. They are all powerful communications to your dog that scream: "Stay by my side (or close to it) without pulling and you'll be forever free to walk wherever you want to go."

Walk Without Pulling—Method 1:
The Start/Stop Method

Have you ever seen a dog straining on a leash, pulling the human along? What's happening here is that the person has inadvertently taught his dog that the freedom to go forward is actually a reward for pulling. This is the exact opposite of what you want your dog to do.

Step 1: The next time your dog pulls, creating a taut leash, stop in your tracks. Your dog will sniff for a while and eventually he'll wonder what's going on. (See Figure 14.14.)

Step 2: When he turns his head to look back at you, you'll feel the leash slacken a bit. Immediately click, praise, and begin walking again. (See Figure 14.15.) You are rewarding the relaxed muscle tension by walking forward. This gives him the freedom to explore again. Now your dog is learning that a taut leash (muscle tension) means stop and a loose leash (relaxed tension) means go. Each session should be done at a predetermined distance. I suggest you use the length of your neighbor's house to start.

Step 3: Every day or two extend the distance you practice by the length of an additional house, until you can walk around the block without a problem. If your dog pulls and you haven't yet mastered walking without pulling for any distance to speak of, go to Method 4: The Walk/Release Method.

Figure 14.13

In the stop/start method of walking without pulling, when your dog pulls, creating a taut leash, stop in your tracks.

Figure 14.14

When your dog turns back to look at you and the leash slackens a bit, immediately click, praise, and reward and start walking again.

There is a critical juncture you must be aware of to make this method work. Within a ten-minute session, your dog will figure this out. You have to be aware of his recognition. Here's what will happen. Let's say you've done a dozen or so stop-go's . . . there will now come a point where your dog will back up or relax his shoulders as soon as he feels the leash go taut. This will happen so fast that you won't have a chance to come to a complete stop. This is the critical point where you effusively praise and, if possible, click and treat him. He has figured out he can keep you moving if he doesn't feel any pressure, so he stops the pressure. If you don't acknowledge this point, he'll say, "Well, that wasn't it" and just keep pulling. I sometimes tell people to close their eyes so they can feel it rather that look for it. Just be careful you don't walk in to a phone pole.

Walk Without Pulling—Method 2:
The Voluntary Return Method

Imagine what would happen while you're practicing Method 1, the Start/Stop Method, if your dog voluntarily comes all the way back to you whenever the leash goes taut. In this method, your dog gets rewarded not only for keeping a loose leash; she gets an additional reward for staying close to you. In the Start/Stop Method, your dog was rewarded for slackening the leash with praise and the freedom to continue walking. Let's say that instead of pulling ahead again, she waits for you to catch up, and now she's by your side. She will quickly learn that she can keep you walking as long as she keeps the leash loose . . . but she will also figure out that if she's by your side, she'll get an additional bonus of food treats.

So it looks like this: Practice the Start/Stop Method given above but now be ready to add an additional reward if your dog.

- 🦴 Waits for you to catch up; or
- 🦴 Walks back to you a step or two.

This also works if your dog stops to investigate something. You keep walking and quickly pass her. As she finishes her sniffing and quickly catches up to you, click and treat her the moment she is at your side. This is a form of the Magnet Game as you didn't *ask* her to walk by your side, but you "captured" her doing it with a click and treat.

Walk Without Pulling—Method 3:
The Reversal Method

If you have a more challenging dog, start out with the Start/Stop Method but add another twist. Your new rescue dog, for example, with his desire to walk ahead of you, will constantly try to shoot by you. Anticipate his frolic to the front and just as he passes you, turn and walk the other way, being very careful not to jerk him. He will now be behind you, wanting to catch up. (See Figure 14.15.)

Now, just as he gets to your side on his way to the front, click, praise, and treat. This click once again marks the position you're looking for. This method works because dogs really don't like to retrace familiar ground as much as they like to explore new territory. So he learns he can keep you going forward if he doesn't walk ahead of you. And he also learns that he gets treats if he stays by your side.

Figure 14.15

In the reversal method of walking without pulling, just as your dog passes you, turn and walk the other way, being very careful not to jerk him.

Walk Without Pulling—Method 4:
The Walk/Release Method

As I've mentioned, if you practice Heeling and Walking Without Pulling at a rate of adding one house length per day, it may take some time to get around one block. So how do you exercise your dog if that's the case? The anti-pulling harness will certainly help and it is necessary if your dog is stronger than you are. If you want to continue walking your dog and still give him the message that "tight means stop, loose means go," use this method.

1. Use a four-foot leash. When your dog pulls and the leash goes taut, don't come to a complete stop. Keep your arm stationary so your dog can't move (see Figure 14.16).
2. Hold your dog in place while you continue to walk forward (see Figure 14.17).
3. As soon as you've gotten to your dog's side, release the tension on the leash. If he immediately pulls again, repeat the process of holding him in place while you walk up next to him. Again, once you are by his side, release the tension on the leash and continue walking. This all happens in a fraction of a second (see Figure 14.18).

Figure 14.16

In Step 1 of the walk/release method of walk without pulling, your dog pulls, making the leash go taut.

Figure 14.17

Step 2: Hold your dog in place while you continue to walk forward.

Figure 14.18

Step 3: As soon as you've gotten to his side, release the tension on the leash.

Walking Without Pulling—Method 5: The Get Behind Me Method

This is one of the easiest methods to practice and is super effective.

1. With your dog by your side (either side is fine), say "Get behind me" and throw a food treat behind you. As your dog goes back to retrieve the treat, click and praise. Whatever side your dog is on, that's the hand you use to throw the treat. When you throw the treat behind you, you should throw it between you and your dog. Repeat five to ten times. When your dog is successful 80 percent of the time, go to Step 2 (see Figure 14.19).
2. Now when your dog moves to get in front of you say "Get behind me" without throwing the treat. Your dog will begin searching for the treat behind you. When he does, click and then treat him. You are now rewarding the behavior rather than luring him with the treat. Over time, he will begin hanging out behind you in anticipation of the occasional treat.

Figure 14.19

The get behind me method of walking without pulling.

Hints for Successful Walk Without Pulling

I've mentioned the use of life rewards, which are anything that your dog wants other than food, such as going for rides, coming in the house, being petted, chasing a ball, and so on. You can use three ready-made life rewards to help teach your dog to walk without pulling:

1. Investigating the neighborhood
2. Marking the neighborhood
3. Saying hello to other dogs

If your dog has a strong desire to sniff and investigate every bug, bush, and bottle, use these doggy desires as rewards for not pulling instead of a food treat. For example, if your dog wants to leave a calling card for his pals in the hood, or if your dog really wants to greet his pals that are also on a walk, use these as rewards for not pulling. The moment your dog stops pulling and turns to look at you, expecting a food reward, instead say "okay" and let him investigate or mark the hydrant he was eyeing or release him to say hello.

As vigilant as we are in trying not to jerk our dogs or put them in the position of jerking themselves, there are times when your dog will simply lunge forward, such as when he tries to chase a squirrel or another dog. In these emergencies, you must have the ability to stop him. This is another good reason to use the bungee leash and an anti-pulling harness to minimize the chances of your dog escaping or hurting himself.

Stop

There's a term in animal training called stimulus control. It basically means an animal will reliably do what you ask virtually every time in every situation. For example, when whales and dolphins at water parks hear a particular underwater sound, they are trained to stop whatever they are doing and go to their pens. Water park trainers have a terrific sense of anticipating potential problems. If a dangerous situation is even hinted at, the buzzer sounds and all of the marine mammals swim to their respective pens.

All of that being said, there's no such thing as 100 percent reliability with any animal . . . or human, for that matter. As mentioned before, in most cases 80 percent reliability is considered good. To train your dog to 90 percent reliability and above takes a little more commitment of time and energy. I suggest you take the time to train your dog to a very high level of probability for at least one life-saving behavior such as "stop" or "come" or "down" or "leave it." If you have trained your dog to this high level of reliability for even one of these behaviors, it might save her from running in front of traffic or keep her from other dangers, such as being sprayed by a skunk. For example, if you teach your dog "stop" and raise this behavior to this level of behavioral reliability, you are then virtually assured that she will freeze in her tracks when you ask her to stop, no matter what she is doing.

Stop—Grade School Level

Grade School Level of stop is to teach your dog to stop while coming toward you.

Prepare: Begin in a nondistracting environment. Put a treat in one hand and hold the clicker in your other hand. Place your hands in the starting position on your chest. Have your dog sit and then walk about 6 feet away and turn and face her.

Step 1: Get the behavior using a treat (lure) and a hand signal. Call your dog. When she gets halfway to you, take a half-step forward and simultaneously use the hand signal by shooting the palm of your hand toward her like the signal for "stay." If you move forward with your right foot, use your right palm—or use the left foot and left palm. (See Figure 14.20) The purpose of moving forward is to help stop the forward motion of your dog. When she stops, click, praise, and treat. Repeat ten times. When your dog is successful eight out of ten times, proceed to Step 2.

Step 2: Attach a word to the behavior along with the hand signal. Have your dog sit and then walk about 6 feet away and turn and face her. Then call her. When she gets halfway to you, say "stop" and, once again, move your right (or left) foot forward and simultaneously shoot your right (or left) palm toward her. When she stops, click, praise, and treat. Repeat five to ten times. When your dog is successful 80 percent of the time, go to Step 3.

Step 3: Use the word only without the hand signal. Call your dog and say "stop" without giving the hand signal or moving toward her. Repeat a thousand times . . . well, do several anyway . . . When your dog stops eight out of ten times after hearing the word stop, gradually add more distance between you and your dog. Increase to a distance of 7 feet, then 8 feet, and so on.

Figure 14.20

In Step 1 of Grade School Level, face your dog from a distance of about 6 feet. Call her to you. Step toward her and shoot your palm in front of her and say "stop."

Add Additional Challenges:

1. When your dog is successful and stops the moment you say the word at a distance of 20 feet from you, increase the challenge by having her stop while she is moving more quickly. You can get her to move more quickly by simply using a happy voice and moving away from her as you signal "Come."

2. Progress to stopping her while she is running at full speed.

If at any point your dog is not successful, go back to the step and/or distance or speed where she was successful.

Having Problems?

Because you've asked your dog to come and then stopped her in her tracks so many times, she may now be anticipating this. She may take the easy way out and just stand there anticipating that you're going to ask her to stop anyway. When you notice this happening, you need to re-strengthen the come when called behavior by allowing her to come all the way to you ten to twenty times without interruption, clicking, praising, and treating each time. Then you can put the two behaviors—come when called and stop—together again. This is done by introducing a random schedule of reinforcement. Randomly select three times out of ten when you will interrupt your dog as she is coming to you by saying "stop" and allow her to reach you without interruption the other seven times. With this random schedule in place, you will keep your dog motivated to come to you while at the same time installing the stop behavior. In other words, each time you call her to come to you, she'll learn to either: a) stop after she's started coming to you; or b) come all the way to you depending on what you've asked. Both behaviors will then be strengthened.

- If your dog continues to move forward after you have given the signal to stop, decrease the distance between you and your dog before saying "come." This catches your dog from gaining any momentum.
- If your dog is still moving forward, put her on a leash and attach it to a stationery object behind her to inhibit her movement. Just be careful to avoid her from jerking herself. Jerking is avoided by maintaining a short distance of 3 to 5 feet between you and your dog when using this technique.

Stop—High School Level

Prerequisite: Grade school level of reliability for heel.

High school level teaches your dog to stop by your side while remaining in a standing position. Your dog does not have to sit when she stops. However, if she does sit or lay down when she stops, that is okay.

1. Start walking with your dog by your left (or right) side. Keep your hands on your chest with a treat in one hand. (It really doesn't matter if you do this with your right or left foot; however, most people choose to have their dog on their left.)

2. Take five to seven steps and say "stop" while simultaneously putting your left (or right) palm in front of your dog's nose as you come to a stop. This is the same hand signal for stay. When she stops, click, praise, and treat. Repeat ten to fifteen times.

3. Take five to seven steps with your dog and then say "stop" while signaling with your hand as before. Keeping your hand in front of your dog's nose, continue your forward motion by taking one extra step past your dog with your right foot. (See Figure 14.21.) Return to your dog, click, treat, and praise. Repeat ten to fifteen times.

   If your dog is on your left side, take a half-step forward with your right foot after you signal "stop." If your dog is on your right, move forward with your left foot.

4. Walk with your dog and say "stop" and give the "stop" hand signal as before. Keeping your hand in front of your dog's nose, continue your forward motion but this time take two steps forward . . . right foot forward, then left. Return to your dog, click, praise, and treat. Repeat ten to fifteen times.

5. By now she's getting it. Even though you are walking past her, she realizes that you are always going to return to her as long as she stays in position. Now walk with your dog and say "stop" as before and take three steps (right, left, right), then progress to four and so on. After each progression, come back to your dog, click, praise, and treat. You no longer have to keep your hand parked in front of your dog's nose once you are taking three steps. Simply say "stop" and give the hand signal and bring your hand back to starting position on your chest.

6. When your dog is successful and stays put while you walk twenty steps away, increase your speed. Begin by walking

quickly, saying stop, and continuing to walk briskly away from your dog. If successful, make it a little more challenging and jog with your dog, then say "stop," give the hand signal, and bring your hand back to starting position on your chest. Then progress to running. Remember that after every progression, return to your dog and click, praise, and treat. If at any point your dog is not successful, go back to the step where she was successful. Repeat that step several times before adding the more challenging speeds.

Figure 14.21

In Step 3 of the high school level of stop, say "stop" and continue your forward motion one extra step past your dog. Return to your dog and reward.

Having problems?
- 🦴 Give your dog extra exercise before doing this so she is less motivated to keep moving.
- 🦴 Try taking smaller strides when you step away from your dog.

Stop—College Level

Now your dog is ready to learn to stop while you are standing behind her and she is moving away from you. For example, when you're out for a walk, sometimes your dog is—with your permission, of course—out ahead of you. What happens when she sees a squirrel? We need to teach her to stop, no matter how enticing a distraction is. This is a tricky stage but if you've dotted your i's and crossed your t's in the first two levels, your dog will respond to this level too. The protocol used for this stage is exactly the same as the one used in the Post Graduate Level in the Triangle Game, so go to page 224 and have fun with it!

Leave It

Leave it means: "Dog, don't touch whatever you are eyeing." This could be the Thanksgiving turkey, your shoes, the children's stuffed animals, the remote (God forbid), his poop, road kill, or my Portuguese Water Dog's favorite—dead fish. You can also use "leave it" to keep your dog from approaching other dogs, cats, and people. You'll notice an exception to the three-step process with this exercise because I don't use a lure or a hand signal with "leave it." If you want to, you can use the same signal used for "stay" and "stop" but it isn't needed.

There's only one level of leave it because I teach the advanced levels of leave it in the Triangle Game, which follows.

Step 1: Get the behavior. Put a treat in your hand and close your fist. Put your fist, fingers facing your dog, at your dog's nose level about two inches away. Your dog will really go after your fist, licking and mouthing. Stay still. (See Figure 14.22.) Within 90 seconds, your dog will either back up and turn her head to the side OR lower her head beneath your fist. The instant your dog moves her nose off your hand, even if it is only an inch away, click and immediately give her the treat from your fist. (See Figure 14.23.) Repeat this ten to twenty times. Your dog will have a "wait a minute, something's happening here" moment somewhere between ten and twenty repetitions. You will present your fist but your dog will hesitate and not come forward. This hesitation may only be for a fraction of a second but when it happens, click and treat and really praise your dog. You have rewarded your dog for not approaching the treat. Now proceed to Step 2.

Figure 14.22

In Step 1 of the leave it behavior, put a treat in your hand, make a fist, and place it two inches in front of your dog's nose.

Figure 14.23

The instant your dog moves her nose off your hand, open your hand and give your dog the treat.

Step 2: Attach a word to the behavior.

    ☞ Add the words "leave it" and present your fist as before. If your dog doesn't move to your fist, click and treat. Repeat this ten to fifteen times.

    ☞ Lower your hand an inch or so closer to the floor with each presentation. Progress to the point where you can place the treat on the floor with your hand covering it.

    ☞ With your hand covering the treat, say "leave it" as before and give your dog the treat if he doesn't move toward it. When your dog is successful eight out of ten times, proceed to the next step.

    ☞ Place the treat on the floor, covered by your hand as before. Say "leave it" and uncover the treat. Keep your hand close to the treat and if your dog tries to grab it, snatch the treat away. Try again. If she stays put for a fraction of a second, click, praise, and give her the treat. Now progress to uncovering the treat for two seconds, then three, etc. Once your dog will leave the treat for ten seconds, go to the next step.

    ☞ Say "leave it" and then drop the treat on the floor (instead of placing it) from a height of two inches off the floor and a distance of 2 feet from the dog. Count one second, click, praise, and give your dog the treat that you dropped. Progress having your dog stay for ten seconds after the treat has dropped.

    ☞ Next, increase the distance between you and your dog. Say "leave it,'" drop the treat, take one step away, return and click, and give your dog the treat that you dropped. Then say "leave it," then drop it and move two steps away, return, and so on.

NOTE: Do not release your dog and allow her to get the treat herself. Always pick up the treat that you dropped and then give it to your dog. This method will really help when you accidentally drop a piece of food on the kitchen floor. Your dog will have a powerful habit installed that she can never touch something unless you give it to her.

Using Leave It to Solve Food Stealing

Use the "Leave it" behavior to keep your dog from stealing food from the dining table or the kitchen sink.

1. Show your dog a treat while standing next to the dining room table or kitchen sink. I like to use string cheese because I can lay it on the surface and it will hang over the edge so the dog can see it. Say "leave it" and place the treat on the table. Wait one second and click and give her a piece of the cheese. Adding a second for each repetition, progress to having her wait ten seconds before rewarding.
2. Add distance. Say "leave it,'" place the cheese, take one step away, return and click and treat. Then two steps and so on. When you reach ten steps, go to Step 3.
3. Place the treat on the table and say down. (You don't have to say "leave it" any more.) Click and treat when she goes down. Repeat ten times.
4. Place the treat on the table and say nothing. Wait up to 45 seconds. Because of your previous training, your dog will realize that she has to lie down and will do so without your asking. Click and treat. Incrementally move farther from the table after placing the food on it. As you add more and more distance after placing the food on the table, you'll eventually place the food and leave the room. You'll then return and click and treat as before. Now begin to stay in the other room for longer periods of time, starting with one second, then two seconds, etc. Eventually, whenever your dog sees food on the table, she will simply lie down and wait for you to return from wherever you are because she knows that you will eventually give her what she's waiting for. Your dog will also learn that if you don't return after a period of time, she will just simply walk away because she isn't rewarded for staying there. Either way, you've established the behavior.

Notes

Until your dog becomes reliable with leave it, you may find her climbing up to steal food from the table or kitchen counter. To interrupt this behavior, you can startle her with a sound intense enough to get her to stop what she's doing and get her back on all fours. Whistle, shake a can, or clap loudly. . . . but startle, don't scare! Then do three practice "leave its" to remind her that she'll be given the treats if she lies down and waits. Until your dog figures this out, use prevention and management by using tethers or baby gates to keep her from stealing food and hence being self-reinforced!

The Triangle Game

Imagine this: Your dog escapes from your yard and you see him chasing a squirrel. You run out the door and see the squirrel dart in the street with your dog close behind. You yell "Stop!" or "Come!" or "Down!" or "Leave it!" and, because of your consistent training, your dog does so immediately. How do you get your dog to be this reliable? The Triangle Game is a step-by-step training program that can show you how to get this kind of postgraduate level of control. It is comprised of the behaviors down, stay, leave it, come when called, and find it. It is the easiest and simplest way to acquire high levels of reliability for every one of these behaviors. And it is great fun for your dog.

I suggest you read through all of these steps before actually trying it. Once you understand the concept, it is very easy to practice. Pay attention to the distances I've suggested. The more consistent you are, the quicker your dog will learn this. If you have any problems with the individual behaviors, review those sections.

The Triangle Game—Grade School Level

Before attempting the Triangle Game, your dog must have mastered "leave it" to the extent that you can drop a treat on the floor and he doesn't move for at least ten seconds.

Your dog will be at one point of the triangle, the treat on the second point, and you will be on the third point. You can teach this behavior while you're sitting on the ground or in a chair if you like.

1. Ask your dog to sit or lie down and stay.
2. Say "leave it" and place the treat off to your side about 3 feet from your dog.
3. Place your hands in starting position on your chest. Say "come" and move your hand from your chest to about two inches to the side of your dog's head so your dog has to turn away from the treat to touch your hand. As soon as your dog turns her head and touches your target hand, click and say, "Good! Find it!" or "okay" and let her get the treat. Now you are teaching your dog that if she turns her head away from the treat and comes to you first, then and only then will she be given permission to get something on the floor or ground.

The major difference between this exercise and the "leave it" exercise you were doing before is that now you are giving your dog permission to get the treat. Previously, if she stayed put, you then picked up the treat and gave it to her as a reward. Now you are teaching her that if she turns her head away from the treat and comes to you first, she be given permission to get the treat herself.

4. Now repeat the same exercise. Ask your dog to sit or lie down and stay, place the treat off to your side about 3 feet from your dog. Place your hands in starting position on your chest, say "come" and move your hand from your chest to a position of an additional inch from your dog's nose. If she touches your hand, click, praise, and allow her to get the treat. The next time, place your hand four inches away, then five, etc. After each exercise, click, praise, and allow her to get the treat.

5. Progress to the point where your target hand is as far away as the treat but on the other side of your body. This is the Triangle.

Once your dog will do this three times in a row, add another challenge, which you will do by standing up while you teach the behavior.

The Triangle Game—High School Level

1. Ask your dog to sit or lie down. Say "leave it" and drop a treat about 6 feet from your dog. Move to the other point of the Triangle so that you are 6 feet from the treat and 6 feet from your dog (an equilateral triangle). Remind your dog to stay. (Figure 14.24.)
2. Place your hands in the starting position on your chest. Say "come" and use the hand signal for come by bringing your hand down from your chest to your side with your palm facing the dog. If your dog comes to you and touches your hand, click, praise, and allow your dog to get the treat. Repeat ten times.

Figure 14.24

In the Triangle Game, you form an equilateral triangle with your dog at one point, you at another point, and the treat at the third point.

Hints

☞ If your dog starts toward the treat instead of your hand, quickly step between your dog and the treat and say "ahh-ahh." And then, do it again. This time, put your dog back in position but instead of standing 6 feet from your dog, stand 3 feet from your dog along the same line of the triangle. If 3 feet is too far and your dog is still going to get the treat when you say come, move to a distance of 2 feet or 1 foot. In other words, find the distance where the dog will come to you and touch your hand. At that point of success, gradually add more distance until you reach 6 feet. Gradually increase your distance until you, your dog, and the treat are equidistant.

☞ When you ask your dog to "come," use the hand that is on the other side of your body, away from the treat. If you signal "come" with the hand closer to the treat, your dog will be more tempted to veer off and snatch the treat.

The Triangle Game—High School Level

Once your dog will reliably come to you at the 6 feet distance, you will begin moving the treat closer to the center point between you and your dog.

1. Ask your dog to sit or lie down and stay.
2. Say "leave it" and drop the treat about 12 inches closer to the center point between you and your dog.
3. Place your hands in the starting position on your chest.
4. Say "come" and present your target hand as before.
5. If your dog comes to you and touches your hand, click, praise, and allow your dog to get the treat.

Now move the treat 12 inches closer to the center and follow the same steps. If your dog is successful and always comes to you and touches your target hand, continue moving the treat closer to center until there is a straight line with you and your dog facing each other, the treat right in the middle . . . 3 feet from your dog and 3 feet from you. When you say "come," your dog should walk around the treat, touch your hand, and then be given permission to get the treat. Repeat ten times.

The Triangle Game—College Level

1. Ask your dog to sit or lie down and stay.
2. Say "leave it" and drop the treat about 12 feet in front of your dog.
3. Walk behind your dog and stand 3 feet away.
4. Place your hands in starting position on your chest.
5. Say "come" and present your target hand as before.
6. If your dog turns around and comes to you and touches your hand, click, praise, and allow your dog to get the treat. Repeat five to ten times.
7. With each successful repetition, place the treat 12 inches closer to your dog. Your goal is to be able to place a treat right between your dog's paws and have him ignore it when you say "come."

Hint

If your dog goes for the treat instead of coming to you, put a leash on your dog to prevent that from happening.

The Triangle Game—Post Graduate Level

1. Ask your dog to sit or lie down and stay.
2. Say "leave it" and drop the treat about 12 feet in front of your dog.
3. Walk behind your dog and stand 3 feet away.
4. Place your hands in the starting position on your chest.
5. Say "find it!" As your dog gets up to get the treat, immediately say "come" and present your target hand as before. If your dog turns around and comes to you and touches your hand, click, praise, and allow your dog to get the treat. (See Figure 14.25.) Repeat five to ten times. Now your dog is in motion and you are interrupting her and having her turn around and come to you. The reason you say "come"

as soon as your dog gets up rather than waiting for her to gather a head of steam is that it is harder for a dog to turn around once she gets going. Also, the treat becomes more motivating as she gets closer to it. It is important to build on small increments of success. If necessary, attach a leash to prevent her from getting the treat.

6. Follow these steps and progress to allowing your dog to get closer and closer to the treat before saying "come."

7. Now get a Frisbee or a motorized mouse. These toys are often advertised in pet magazines. Throw the Frisbee and/or let the mouse roll past your dog, say "go get it," and, just as she gets going, say "come." When she returns, click and treat. This is a huge test. If your dog is successful here, you've just about got it. If not, go back to the point where she was successful.

8. The final step is to take your dog to a park with distractions such as squirrels and rabbits and do the exercise in that environment. If you can call your dog to you while she is chasing a squirrel, you should be writing your own training book.

Figure 14.25

In Step 5 of the post graduate level of the Triangle Game, you stand behind your dog. Send her forward toward a treat and, as she's walking say, "come." Remember to click, praise, and reward after each repetition. Gradually progress to have her take more and more steps away from you at a faster and faster speed.

Having Problems?

Because you are repeatedly asking your dog to turn around and come to you before allowing her to get the treat, at a certain point you may notice that your dog will simply stand there when you say find it. If this happens, allow her to get the ball or Frisbee ten times without interruption. Then put the two behaviors together by introducing a random schedule of reinforcement. Select three times when you will interrupt your dog while she's moving toward the ball or Frisbee and have her come to you. Allow access to the ball or Frisbee without interrupting her the other seven times.

Take It and Drop It

Although my dog Molly is in retirement now, she used to help me with a program in elementary schools called Paws for Peace. In this program we teach children the principles of kindness, respect, and responsibility toward animals and each other. The highlight of the program was a trick that Molly used to do which employed the "take it" and "drop it" behaviors. I told the children to ask Molly to "answer the phone," which she did, picking the receiver up in her mouth. Then, on cue, when I told her it was a bill collector, she ceremoniously dumped the handset in a wastebasket. It was a real crowd-pleasing trick. Service dogs employ the use of "take it and drop it" when they help disabled people by picking up objects, answering the phone, opening doors, and so on.

There are several methods you can use to teach these behaviors. In fact, a whole chapter could be written on the various ways to do this. However, the following method is as good as any and better than most. Some dogs pick up this behavior extremely quickly. This is especially true of retrievers. So it's a good example of knowing your dog's learning baseline. (See Learning Baseline on page 151.) Always start at the point where your dog is successful and build from there.

Take It—Grade School Level

I teach take it and drop it as one behavior with two separate parts. Take it is taught first and then, when your dog is actually holding the object in his mouth for three seconds or more, you will teach drop it in junior high level.

Steps 1 and 2, get the behavior (use a lure) and add the word, are combined because most dogs will immediately respond and touch the object. (There is not a hand signal for this behavior.)

Steps 1 and 2: Get the behavior using a treat (lure) and attach a word to the behavior.

Rub a piece of turkey on the object you want your dog to take, such as a pencil, a glove, a ball, a dollar bill, etc., and then hold the object in your hand one inch away from your dog's nose. As you do this, say "take it." As your dog comes forward to examine the object and touches it with his nose click, praise, and treat with a $10,000 treat. Repeat five to ten times. Once your dog is touching the object whenever you present it, begin to lower the object an inch closer to the floor with each presentation. When you get to the point that your hand is on the floor when you say take it, proceed to Step 3. This may take several sessions over several days.

At this point, your dog is not actually "taking" the object, he's just touching it with his nose. However, some dogs may immediately put the object in their mouth, which is your ultimate goal.

Step 3: Use the word only without the hand signal. Place the object on the floor and say take it. Do not reward when your dog touches the object as you were doing in Steps 1 and 2. Wait until your dog licks the object. When he does, then you will click, praise, and treat. Repeat five to ten times. Here's what's happening: Up to this point, the object has been used as a target similar to the process you used to teach your dog to come when called when he had to touch your hand. In this case, when your dog touches the object and is not rewarded, he will try to figure out why the reward did not follow. In essence, he's thinking to himself, "Wait a minute, we had a deal! You're supposed to give me a treat every time I touch the object. Well, I'll show you!" He will then naturally escalate his intensity by either licking or nudging or mouthing the object. Wait for that to happen. It is that escalation that you are now rewarding. Repeat five to ten times with that escalated behavior—the licking, the nudging or the mouthing. Do several sessions over several days so your dog really understands what you're asking.

Step 4: Add progressions.

- Now place the object on the floor, say take it and wait for your dog to pick the object up with his mouth, if only for a second. Lavishly praise this behavior, click, and treat.
- Now place the object on the floor, say take it and ask your dog to hold onto it for longer and longer periods of time, rewarding each subsequent success. This is done by delaying the reward, first for one second, then two seconds, then three seconds, and so on. When your dog will hold the object for three seconds, go to Junior High School level where you will teach your dog to Drop It.

Hints

- As you are teaching take it, be sure to use the same object until your dog is reliable. Then, you can begin to teach your dog to take new objects. When you do that, go back to Steps 1 and 2 and follow the same step-by-step protocol with each new object. Eventually you won't have to repeat all of these steps because your dog will "generalize" and learn that "take it" means take whatever object you are pointing to. Some objects are more difficult for dogs to put in their mouths, such as metal objects, soda cans, or eating utensils. You may have to spend more time with Steps 1 and 2 with those types of objects.
- You can hurry this whole process along by using the words "take it" at other times during the day. For example, throw a $10,000 treat or a favorite toy, like a tennis

ball or squeaky toy off to the side and say "take it." Repeat these steps over and over again. Your dog will quickly associate the words "take it" with something orally terrific.

Take It and Drop It—High School Level

Now you're ready for the "drop it" part of take it and drop it.

Steps 1 and 2: Get the behavior using a treat (lure) and attach a word to the behavior. Once you've asked your dog to "take it" and your dog is reliably holding the object in his mouth for three seconds or longer, present a $10,000 treat. Say "drop it" as you present the treat. When he drops the object from his mouth, reward him with the treat. Repeat five to ten times. In other words, ask your dog to take the object and then ask your dog to drop the object for each repetition.

Step 3: Use the word only without the hand signal. As your dog is holding the object, say "drop it," without presenting any food. When your dog drops the object, click, praise, and treat.

Throughout the day, whenever you see your dog carrying something like a favorite toy in his mouth, present him with a treat and say "drop it." This will speed the process up. After he drops the toy, remember to always give it back to him.

Emergency "Drop It"

If you have to open your dog's mouth in an emergency situation, gently cup one of your hands around the dog's upper or lower jaw. Then, with your fingers on one side of the jaw and your thumb on the other side, gently roll your dog's lips over his back teeth. Most dogs will open their mouths when they feel the skin on their teeth. Say "drop it" while you are doing this and reward your dog even though he was forced to let it go. You do not have to use any force to open your dog's mouth. Remember to be gentle so you don't hurt your dog.

 **Chapter 15**

Tricks

Your training sessions will be the most productive if you have an attitude of fun. Dog trainers have different names for various tricks. For example, sit up can also be referred to as beg, sit pretty, or prairie dog, while play dead can also be called go to sleep, relax, or "gotcha." There are no rules, so have a good time and give the tricks whatever names you want.

Adding tricks to your dog's repertoire is simply another way to bond with your dog—and perhaps impress a few friends with your training prowess. In addition, teaching your dog tricks helps to build your confidence as well as your dog's. Another benefit is that you will raise your dog's stress-management threshold, which will help her cope with life's challenges. In turn, this will strengthen her immune system which will keep her healthier and help her to live longer. And, as you know, how you treat your dog is linked to how you treat yourself and others, so you, too, will reap all of these same benefits. The other great thing about teaching your dog these particular tricks is that they all have practical uses. There are many ways to teach tricks:

The Magnet Game: If you use the Magnet Game, simply wait for your dog to do something and as soon as she does, click, praise, and treat. (See Magnet Game, page 159.) I taught my Portuguese Water Dog, Molly, to sneeze on cue using the Magnet Game. Whenever she would sneeze, I would immediately praise her and give her a treat. Then I added a vocal signal, "Geshunheidt!" and she would dutifully sneeze on cue.

"Molding" the Behavior: Another way to teach a trick is to "mold" the behavior. This has to do with physically manipulating the dog to get what you want and then rewarding once the dog is in the final position. The way I teach "shake" is a form of molding.

"Shaping" the Behavior: Shaping is the process of forming a behavior using baby steps, otherwise known as increments or successive approximations. Each approximation is a successful behavior in and of itself which ultimately leads to the final position you are looking for. A good example of the use of shaping is teaching your dog to play dead.

Luring: All of the behaviors in this book are obtained through luring and the aforementioned Magnet Game and shaping. Luring entices a dog to do something without touching him, such as a dog following a treat to lie down or come when called.

If one of these methods doesn't work for you or your dog, simply try another tool. There is no one way to get a behavior.

So be safe, have fun, live long, and prosper, as you teach your dog some or all of the tricks below!

Sit Up—Also known as Beg, Sit Pretty, or Prairie Dog

Caution: This trick is not viable for large dogs or dogs who have weak or bad backs.

Practical Application: Builds confidence and improves temperament as physical balance is directly linked to helping promote emotional balance.

It's very easy to teach your dog to sit up as it's just a matter of using baby steps (incremental training) to teach your dog to balance while sitting on his behind. Some dogs figure this out immediately. If so, you can skip all of these steps.

Step 1: Get the behavior using a treat (lure) and a hand signal.

🦴 Face your dog and ask him to sit.

🦴 Hold a treat over his nose just far enough that he has to look up to get it. The hand signal for sit up is similar to the hand signal for sit in that you are placing your hand directly over your dog's head. The difference is that for sit up, your hand goes no more than an inch *over* the crown of your dog's head and then you move your hand up in the air another inch *above* your dog's head. When he takes the treat, click, praise, reward.

🦴 Hold the treat a little higher. As he stretches his head a little farther, you'll see him come up on his toes a little. When he takes the treat, click and praise. If his behind leaves the ground, take the treat away and don't place your hand so high the next time.

🦴 Hold the treat a little higher so one paw (or both paws) lift off the ground, even if only for a split second. Click, praise, reward.

🦴 Hold the treat over his nose at the same point as Step 4 and keep it there while he lifts his front legs a little higher and begins to balance. Click, praise, reward.

   NOTE: If the treat is too high, your dog will get off of his behind. If it is too far forward, he won't be able to balance. If it's too far back, he'll fall over backward. I like to keep the treat a half-inch or so over my dog's nose and move it up and back an eighth of an inch at a time.

🦴 Hold the treat above his head and keep it there for longer periods to let your dog find his balance. (See Figure 15.1.)

Step 2: Attach a word to the behavior along with the hand signal.

🦴 Add the word of your choice to label this behavior, such as "sit up," "beg," "sit pretty," or "prairie dog," along with the hand motion. Repeat five to ten times. Reward after every attempt.

Step 3: Use the word only without the hand signal.

🦴 Use the word that you have chosen for the behavior and then wait up to 45 seconds for your dog to respond. Reward success. Return to the previous step if not successful.

Figure 15.1

In Sit Up, hold the treat above your dog's head and let your dog find his balance. Gradually extend the length of time that he's sitting up.

Play Dead—Also Known as Go to Sleep, Relax, and Gotcha

Practical Application: Teaches a dog to relax and builds trust.

Step 1: Get the behavior using a treat (lure) and a hand signal. Face your dog and have her lie down. For this behavior, she needs to be lying on her hip to one side. If she isn't already doing this, you can:

🦴 Wait for her to do so;

🦴 Physically (gently and playfully) nudge her over; or

🦴 Use the treat in your hand to lure her to curl over on her side. This is done by moving the treat, starting at her nose, in a tight semi-circle around the side of her body, so she has to turn her head and shoulders to get it. This movement of your hand is the hand signal for play dead. When she rolls over on her hip, click and release the treat.

Once she is on her side, the steps look like this:

🦴 Move your hand from her nose to her side a quarter of the way to her mid-back, click, praise, reward (see Figure 15.2).

🦴 Move your hand a little closer to her mid-back, click, praise, reward. Continue with this routine in quarter or half-inch increments until you get to about six inches from touching your dog's back. You should then see that her opposite shoulder (the one on the floor) is more relaxed. Now move the treat in a straight line from its current position and continue over her nose to the floor. Her head will follow the treat and lay on the floor. (See Figure 15.3.) Click, praise, reward. Repeat five to ten times.

Step 2: Attach a word to the behavior along with the hand signal. Say your selected word such as "Gotcha!" and simultaneously move the treat, starting from her nose, around to her back, up in a straight line, and continue over her nose to the floor as you did in Step 1. Her head will follow the treat and lay on the floor. Click, praise, and reward. Repeat five to ten times. At some point during Step 2 your dog will not come all the way back to her original down position but will hesitate a second or two in the relaxed position or maybe just lift her head. Reward that with many treats and then go to Step 3.

Step 3: Use the word only without the hand signal. Put your hands in the starting position and say "gotcha!" or the word you chose. Wait 45 seconds. If she moves a little, as if to say "Is this what you're looking for?" click, praise, and reward. On each attempt, reward any moves that are closer to the final position. Finally, after you've said the word or given the signal "Gotcha!" and she's completely relaxed laying on her side, with both head and body on the floor, add the word stay to keep her in that position. Ask for a one-second stay, click, praise, reward. Then progress to two seconds, and so on.

Figure 15.2

To get the Play Dead behavior, with your dog on her side, move your hand from her nose to her side a quarter of the way distance to her mid-back, click, praise, reward.

Figure 15.3

Move the treat in a straight line and continue over her nose to the floor. Her head will follow the treat and lay on the floor.

Having Problems?

☞ Whatever side your dog is on, that's the direction you want her to go. Don't "go against the grain" and try to get her to shift over and Play Dead on the other hip.

☞ Position your body so your treat hand and arm don't get in your dog's face. If your dog is on her left side to start, use your left hand to do this. If your dog is on her right side to start, use your right hand.

☞ If your dog refuses to roll on her shoulder and gets up the moment your hand gets close to her back or, if her leg is so planted she refuses to roll onto her side, you'll have to shape this position in micro-mini steps: Click, praise, and reward a head turn of two inches. Next time, click, praise, and reward a turn of three inches, and so on. When you get to the point where you know she won't go any further, click, praise, reward that position five to ten times and end the session. In the next session, do the same. You will notice that within three days, she will relax a little more each time and you'll finally be able to complete the behavior.

☞ In between sessions, whenever you see her on her side resting, go over to her and stroke her and talk with her softly. Her body will remember these experiences and help you when you practice.

☞ Practice this exercise during the day when she is a little more tired and relaxed.

Spin—Also Known as Twirl

Note: The steps below are for a Left Spin. Repeat the same protocol on the other side when teaching a Right Spin.

Step 1: Get the behavior using a treat (lure) and a hand signal. Stand with your dog facing you. Position your left hand with the treat in front of your dog's nose, no more than two inches away. Begin moving your arm to the left and leading your dog to turn her head and body around in a circle. As your dog follows the treat, move your arm in a complete 360-degree circle, maintaining your hand position at your dog's nose level. The movement of your hand in a 360-degree circle over your dog becomes the hand signal for spin. Complete the circle and click, praise, and reward. Repeat five to ten times.

Figure 15.4

Figure 15.5

Figure 15.6

Figure 15.7

Step 2: Attach a word to the behavior along with the hand signal. Now simultaneously say "left turn" or "left spin" (emphasizing the word "left") while you lead her around in the circle. Repeat five to ten times and click, praise, and reward after every completion.

Step 3: Use the word only without the hand signal. With your hands in starting position say "left turn." Wait up to 45 seconds. If your dog makes an attempt, as if to say "Is this what you're looking for?" click, praise, and reward. If she simply stands there or walks away in frustration or boredom, return to the previous step.

Hints

For Spin and all exercises that require your dog to move, your attitude can help tremendously. If it's fun for you, it's fun for your dog. So if your dog stands around or seems bored, get happy! Dance around, use different vocal sounds from kissy sounds to howls. Pretend to eat the dog's food treats and exaggerate with "hmmmmmm . . . look what I have!" Drop to the ground and pretend you found something interesting. Use a tennis ball or another of your dog's favorite toys in order to generate interest.

Shake, High Five, and Wave

These three behaviors are simply variations on the same theme and are taught in sequence.

Practical Application: These behaviors help desensitize dogs to being handled by veterinarians and groomers, especially for nail clipping.

This is a behavior that can actually be "captured" with the Magnet Game as some dogs, like Boxers, have a natural tendency to hit you with their paw to get your attention. So whenever you happen to see your dog lift a paw, click or praise and reward and your dog will do it more often. If you do enough "captures," you can then add a signal like "shake" because you will be 80 percent sure your dog is going to lift his paw. That being said, I teach "shake" by molding the behavior.

Shake

Step 1: Get the behavior using a treat (lure) and a hand signal. Have your dog sit facing you. With one hand, hold a treat to your dog's mouth and let him nibble it if necessary. This will keep his attention so he doesn't follow your other hand. It also serves the purpose of forming a positive association to his paws being touched. As your dog is nibbling the treat, reach for your dog's paw. Gently lift your dog's paw off the ground and release the treat from your other hand. The hand signal for shake is presenting your hand in front of your dog's body, as if to shake hands. Repeat ten to fifteen times.

Figure 15.8

In Step 1 of Shake, gently lift your dog's paw off the ground and release the treat from your other hand.

Step 2: Attach a word to the behavior along with the hand signal. Repeat Step 1 but add the word "shake" as you lift your dog's paw. Repeat ten to fifteen times.

Step 3: Use the word only without the hand signal (slight variation). With one hand on your chest in the start position, offer your other hand as if you are going to pick up your dog's paw but don't actually grab it. Say "shake." Wait up to 45 seconds. If your dog makes an attempt, as if to say "Is this what you're looking for?" and lifts her paw an eighth of an inch . . . even if it looks like she is just shifting her weight, click, praise, and reward. Repeat. With each repetition, your dog will lift her paw higher and higher. When she actually places her paw in your hand, "jackpot" her by clicking, praising, and giving five to ten treats.

Hints

- 🦴 If she simply sits there or lies down instead, return to the previous step. This behavior may take three sessions so try not to do too much too fast.
- 🦴 You might experiment by using your dog's other paw. Although it still hasn't been proven whether dogs are "left-handed" or "right-handed" like humans, many do seem to favor one side over another.
- 🦴 Also, watch your dog throughout the day and if she lifts her paw without asking, make sure you praise and treat.

High Five

When your dog will reliably shake at least 80 percent of the time when you ask her to, you can do a High Five. All you do is offer your hand as if to ask for a shake, but as your dog lifts her paw, say "High Five" and quickly turn your palm so it is facing your dog, fingers pointing up. Your dog will automatically exert a tad more effort to reach your open hand. That's all there is to it.

Wave

Once your dog is used to exerting a little more effort in the High Five, you can introduce Wave. Present your hand as if you are asking for a High Five. As your dog goes to hit your palm with her paw, say "wave" and quickly withdraw your hand about three to six inches and make a wave good-bye motion with your hand. (Flap it forward and back.) Your dog will try to swat your hand once or twice and that's a wave. Click, praise, and treat.

Figure 15.9

To get a "High Five," offer your hand as if to ask for a shake, but as your dog lifts her paw, quickly turn your palm so it is facing your dog, fingers pointing up.

Figure 15.10

To get your dog to wave, present your hand in the High Five position. As your dog goes to hit your palm with her paw, say "wave" and quickly withdraw your hand about three to six inches and make a wave good-bye motion with your hand.

Congratulations! You've read a lot. Treat yourself to a movie or read a great novel like *Replay* by Ken Grimwood.

PART 4

Problem
Behaviors

Chapter 16

Identifying the Causes of
Problem Behaviors

From a dog's perspective, there is no such thing as problem behavior. He's doing what he's doing because it feels good. To look at it from another perspective, a behavior you don't consider a problem might be one to other people. You might like your dog jumping on you when you get home while others don't. If your dog's behavior is harmful to him, the environment, other people, other animals, or you, it deserves immediate attention.

Physiological and neurological problems can impact your dog's behavior. Therefore, before implementing any behavioral modification program, ask your veterinarian to do a thorough exam including a comprehensive blood panel. You are especially interested in any imbalances with the thyroid gland or the liver functioning. If health problems exist, work closely with your veterinarian and/or a professional trainer who uses positive training methods.

Aggression and fearful responses are often related to a dog's sensitivity to touch, sound, and motion. These topics are covered in Chapter 18, Help for Your Sensitive Dog.

An Imbalance in the Nine Ingredients for
Optimum Health and Growth
Basil, a three-year-old male German shepherd, got off the family sofa and walked toward his handler, April, as she was teaching her year-old baby girl to walk. Without hesitating, Basil walked

around April and suddenly bit the baby in the face. I got the call the same day. The dog was now locked in his kennel and April was in tears, wondering if there was anything she could do so her baby would be safe with Basil around. Would Basil always be a threat to children? Would it be necessary to have him euthanized?

On investigation, I learned there several factors had contributed to Basil's behavior. First, there was an obvious lack of training—Basil had never been taught what was expected of him when the baby was in the room. In addition, the veterinarian found Basil was developing an arthritic condition and therefore was probably in some pain. And, finally, Basil may have been protecting his toy, which April later found hidden under the couch.

This story illustrates the severe problems that can develop when one or more of the nine ingredients for optimum health and growth are imbalanced or missing in your dog's life. In Basil's case, he had not been provided with sufficient play, socialization, exercise, employment, or positive reinforcement training. Basil was being himself, a dog who was behaving with the hand that he was dealt. He viewed himself as head of the house and was willing to assert his authority, guarding his territory and his possessions.

Fortunately, there was a happy ending to this story and, with a watchful eye and resolute commitment by the family, Basil is growing old alongside them. The baby sustained only superficial cuts that healed quickly and there were no scars.

In most cases, problem behaviors are caused by an imbalance in the nine ingredients. Exceptions are those cases where physical or neurological influences are involved. Let's look at some of the ways in which these imbalances could be occurring:

High-quality diet: Is your dog chewing things or misbehaving because of hunger? Or is his diet low in essential nutrients? Sometimes a dog chews on objects because the body, in its own wisdom, is seeking nutrients that are missing or underprovided in the diet. For instance, if your dog chews on grass, eats feces, or eats from a cat's litter box, his body may be looking for missing nutrients. While a little bit of grass can be okay, it can be problematic if the lawn has been sprayed with pesticides or if chemical fertilizers have been used. Is your dog "hyper" because of all the salt and sugar he's being fed due to a low-quality pet food? Is he having problems "holding it" while in the house? Maybe he's been drinking more water than usual because of too much salt in the rawhide bones and other chewies he's been fed.

Play, exercise, and socialization: Many dogs are simply bored and frustrated because they're not getting enough physical, emotional, and mental stimulation. They don't get enough exercise. They don't get to socialize with their dog pals and other human beings. They are bored because they haven't been presented with anything new and exciting lately.

Employment: Does your dog have a job to do? If you don't provide an environment for him to express himself, he'll chew, or bark, or jump just to keep himself "employed."

Rest: Is your dog getting enough rest? Many problem behaviors, including snapping or growling, can manifest because your dog is exhausted.

Training: Some people think their dogs are stubborn or dumb, but many dogs are simply confused because they haven't been trained in different situations or because they haven't successfully repeated the behavior you're asking for enough times. (See Chapter 6 for a discussion of the concept of context learning.)

Quiet time: Does your dog have a place to "get away from it all" for quality quiet time? Maybe his jumping and chewing are simply stress relievers.

Health care: Does your dog have a physical problem that might be contributing to the chewing problem?

Unintentional Training

As well intentioned and diligent as you might be during your dog's training process, certain situations may crop up in which her behavior is the opposite of what you intended. In many cases, you are directly responsible for eliciting the problem behavior in the first place.

Let's say you want to calm your nervous dog that is shaking and pacing from the sound of fireworks on July Fourth or the lightning and thunder from a summer storm. When the fireworks start to blast or the thunder rumbles, you might soothe your dog by stroking him and murmuring, "It's okay, Benjie. Everything's fine. Good dog." In these cases, you may be inadvertently practicing unintentional training because your dog views the praise as a reward for the behavior. In other words, you are actually rewarding behavior you are trying to discourage.

Or let's say you are talking on the phone and your dog starts barking for attention. A normal response is to interrupt the call and yell at the dog, "Be quiet!" Once again, you may be rewarding the undesirable behavior. In this case, you are giving your dog what he wants—your attention.

Another classic example of irrelevant and unintentional training is yelling "Come" as the dog runs across the street chasing a squirrel. If you say the word "Come" often enough while your dog is running away from you, she might begin to think that it means to run the other way. After all, that's when she hears it the most. To make the word you're using relevant, don't use it unless you're 80 percent sure your dog will actually do what you're asking.

Remember the rules of reinforcement—your dog's behavior can be increased or decreased by your response to that behavior. In other words, in these examples listed, your actions could actually be reinforcing the behavior you want him to stop. Telling a dog "It's okay" while he's shivering because of the fireworks or thunder may actually be reinforcing the nervousness!

Giving your dog attention, whether positive or negative, while he is barking may actually reinforce the barking. Stop *reacting* and remember to *respond* instead, as discussed in Chapter 1.

When considering what do to with your dog's "problem" behavior, try to look at the situation from your dog's point of view. Take a mental snapshot of the environment at the time of the problem behavior. Become aware of what your dog is actually learning from the people and events around him. Changing the environment is the most important consideration. In order to modify your dog's behavior, it's helpful to begin by reviewing the following steps:

1. Take a step back from the situation and pause (unless you, the dog, or the environment is in danger).
2. Do a round of three complete breaths (see page 74).
3. Ask yourself, "What do I want my dog to do?" rather than "What do I want my dog to stop doing?" Write down your goals.
4. Review the Tools of Dog Training in Chapter 12 and pick one or two or three that you think would work for the situation.
5. Make an outline, plan the steps you are going to take, and create the environment necessary to implement your plan.
6. Practice.
7. Review the results and amend your actions as necessary. If you're not sure how to proceed, a private class with a nonviolent dog trainer may be necessary.

Aggressive Behavior

If your dog exhibits aggressive behavior, it's important that you consult a behavioral specialist and be willing to spend the time necessary to resolve the problem by overhauling your own daily routine. Aggression should be taken seriously and handled right away. The ramifications are serious, ranging from injury to financial liabilities. The treatment of aggression and other serious behavioral problems is beyond the scope of this book.

Chapter 17

Resolving Problem Behaviors

This chapter will offer resolutions to your dog's problem behaviors. The trick is to use one or more of the tools that are offered until you find one that works. If one tool doesn't work, try another.

Barking
When your dog barks, try one or more of these options:

1. Ignore it. Many behaviors simply disappear when they are not reinforced.
2. Teach a substitute behavior like "be quiet." First, distract your dog with sound or movement and then give a "quiet" signal. (See Quiet on page 200.)
3. Get up and walk around. Reward your dog when she looks or even glances at you.
4. Take a walk. If you lead your dog around a chair, you will be taking her mind off the reason for the barking and the barking will stop.
5. Counter-condition your dog to the stimulus that is prompting him to bark by giving him treats while he is hearing another dog barking. For example, if your dog is barking at another dog, move your dog away from the other dog to a distance that is a little more manageable and then give your dog treats as he is barking. Remember, classical conditioning trumps operant conditioning. If your dog will take treats while the stimulus is in sight or earshot, you are not

rewarding your dog's barking, you are changing the way your dog feels about what is triggering his behavior . . . like the other dog.

6. Make sure your dog has eliminated. Maybe your dog is over his stress threshold. If he needs to eliminate but hasn't had the opportunity, that is yet one more stress. Lightening his stress load in this way might help him move more comfortably and also deal better with other stresses.

7. Identify the trigger, that is, whatever is causing your dog to start barking, such as a mail carrier coming up the walk, a or child skate-boarding by, and re-direct your dog to a substitute behavior such as going to his bed and lying down. (See Go to Your Spot, page 184.)

8. Block your dog's view so he can't see whatever it is that's triggering him.

9. Put some peanut butter or caramel on the roof of your dog's mouth.

10. Hold your dog firmly but gently until quiet. Release when his muscles relax, even slightly. Say "okay," or another release word.

Begging at the Table

The trick to solving a begging problem is to teach your dog to go to his spot. (See Go To Your Spot, page 184.) Until he has learned this behavior, practice prevention and management by tethering your dog away from the table. While your dog is at his spot or tethered, give him something to chew like a chicken strip, Bully Stick, or treat-filled Kong.

Bolting Out the Door

If your dog is prone to bolting out the door, take extra precautions while you're trying to resolve the issue. Safety is paramount. Try one or both of the methods below. (Also see the Triangle Game on page 224 to increase behavioral reliability.)

Figure 17.1

Holding a dog to your chest to quiet him: One arm is firmly, but not roughly, wrapped around the back of the dog while the other hand is placed on his head. Note that the thumb is on one side of the dog's ear while the fingers are on the other side. Caution: Use this method only if your dog is at point E on the learning baseline for handling (see page 270).

Method 1—The "Door Fan" Method

1. Say nothing. Then open the door two inches and let Fido think he's going out. When the door doesn't open all the way, he'll back off and perhaps walk around a little. As he backs off, open the door wider. He'll scoot back, ready to bolt, but as he moves toward the door again, quickly close it back to the two-inch mark. Repeat over and over until your dog backs away and then sits. Then say "okay" and open the door wide. (Keep your dog on a long leash while doing this exercise if your yard is not enclosed.) Please be careful not to catch your dog's nose in the door!
2. Progress to opening the door but telling him to stay. Go through the door first, return to your dog, then say "okay."

3. Progress to having him stay while you walk to the end of the driveway, return to your dog and then release him by saying "okay."

Method 2—Substitute the "Go to Your Spot" Behavior (see page 184)

Chewing

When dealing with any problem behavior, the first thing to do is review the nine ingredients (Chapter 2) and determine how you can upgrade and balance them. With the chewing behavior, this is especially evident. Dogs chew furniture, holes in walls, wires, sticks, clothes, and virtually everything else. Teaching your dog what to chew on and where to chew it keeps your belongings safe and also protects your dog from dangers. Try one or more of the tips below to help with the chewing problem.

1. Schedule two fifteen- to thirty-minute quality-with-doggie times a day to play, exercise, and socialize your dog. A dog that is stimulated is less likely to vent his boredom and frustration in ways that create problems for his human family. Run with your dog and play fetch, hide-and-seek, and find it. Train him to sit, lie down, stand, stay, and come when called. Teach him tricks such as sit up, roll over, play dead, and answer the phone.
2. Give your dog "legal" chew toys such as the Nyla Bones, Bully Sicks, Chicken Strips or a smart toy, such as a Kong, Buster Cube, or a plastic treat ball.
3. Teach "leave it" (see page 220): Put several objects in the middle of the floor. Watch for your dog to check them out for "chewability." Interrupt him while he's thinking about it with the words "leave it," and then click, praise, and reward with a legal chewy.
4. Re-direct the dog to a substitute behavior such as going to his bed and laying down. (See Go to Your Spot, page 184.)

5. Above all, practice prevention by creating an environment where your dog can be successful. Remove illegal objects so your dog can't get to them in the first place and use management methods such as tethering, baby gates, and a kennel so your dog is not tempted to chew on the wrong items.

Eliminating in the House (Housetraining)

It's important to follow a strict set of rules when teaching a puppy to eliminate where and when you want.

1. Set a schedule. Puppies up to about three months of age need to eliminate eight to ten times a day. Scheduled times should include:

   🦴 First thing in the morning when you get up
   🦴 15 to 30 minutes after each meal
   🦴 After play or other excitement
   🦴 When you get home from work or school
   🦴 Early evening
   🦴 Just before bed
   🦴 During the night (if necessary)

2. Always take the puppy or dog to the same location to eliminate.
3. Mark or label the elimination behavior with a word. For instance, encourage him with a friendly voice saying "hurry up" or "outside" or "go potty." As soon as your dog finishes, praise and reward him with a treat.
4. Manage your environment. Keep your dog in a kennel or tethered so she can't make mistakes. If you tether her, make sure it's in a social area. Never leave a dog tethered alone. You can tether her to you by attaching her leash to your waist.
5. Keep the elimination time envelope short. Give your dog ten minutes to "go." If she doesn't eliminate within the ten-minute timeframe, bring her back in the house and put her in her kennel or tether her. Try it again fifteen minutes later.
6. Remember the one-second rule. If you walk in the room three seconds after your dog has peed on the carpet, she

won't associate a reprimand with the behavior. So don't reprimand her at all. If you catch her in the act, startle her with excitement but don't scare her. Shout "Oh, my gosh" and run to her. The idea is to have her stop what she's doing without freaking her out. Pick her up or head her outside all the while shouting, "Oh, my. Oh, my." As soon as you get outside, act thoroughly relieved. Relax your voice and body. Then encourage her with "go outside" or "hurry up."

7. Don't give your dog any food or water after eight o'clock in the evening. Leave a couple of ice cubes for her.

8. Although some puppies and dogs can "hold it" all through the night as young as eight weeks, many need to eliminate during the night so you'll have to set your alarm to take her out. The elimination needs of each individual puppy or dog will vary; however, here are some guidelines for puppies eight weeks and older. If the dog is younger than three months old, take her out every 4 to 5 hours. This means if you go to bed at 10:00 P.M., get up at 2:00 or 3:00 A.M. and take her out again. Keep adding fifteen-minute increments every two or three days until you're confident she can make it for seven to eight hours. You'll know you've gone too fast if you find she's eliminated in her kennel or pen area.

If you bring your dog in the house after she eliminates and then immediately leave for the day, your dog will quickly learn that eliminating is associated with your leaving. As a result, she'll start procrastinating while she's outside. Instead, once you're back in the house, let her spend five to ten minutes playing with you or a chew toy before you leave.

When your dog eliminates in the house:

🦴 Clean the urine with an enzymatic cleanser. There are several on the market.

🦴 Don't let her see you clean it up. There's still a debate about this, but some experts think you might be giving your dog a message that you're accepting her little "gifts."

Get Off the Couch

Use one or more of these options to teach your dog to get off—and stay off—the furniture.

1. To teach your dog to get off the couch or your bed or any other furniture, use the exact same process as go to your spot (see page 185). First, encourage your dog to get up on the couch or bed. You can do this by saying "couch" or "up" and patting the couch. However, don't use a treat to get him on the couch. Once he's on the couch, stand next to it and go through the same steps listed for go to your spot, but instead of saying "spot," say "off."

2. Give your dog his own chair. Allow him to get on one chair and one chair only. Throughout the day, do "appropriate chair" training. This means set up sessions where you teach your dog to get on the "okay" Chair. Simply follow the protocol for "Go to your Spot" and substitute the word "chair."

3. Practice prevention so your dog can't get on any chair you don't want him to be on. To keep your dog off the chair when you are out of the room, a simple preventive measure is to put sheets of aluminum foil across the chair or couch cushions as dogs dislike the feel and sound of aluminum foil. Your dog will soon learn to avoid the foil-covered furniture and you can discontinue using it.

4. If you see your dog about to get on a chair or couch that is forbidden, you can interrupt him with "Ah, Ah" and redirect him to the acceptable chair or spot.

5. Practice management, keep a short tether on your dog when he is in the house so if you ever have to move a stubborn dog off the furniture, you can simply grab the cable and

gently pull him off. It's okay to pull a dog if necessary as long as you are gentle and don't jerk him. Gently pulling him off avoids any possible negative association of being grabbed by the collar. NOTE: Never let your dog wear a leash (tether) if you are not around to supervise!

Grabbing the Leash While Heeling

Try one or more of these options:

1. Teach your dog to "go get the leash" before every walk. (See "Take It" on page 230.) Sometimes a dog will learn not to put the leash in her mouth unless she knows it's associated with a walk.
2. Teach your dog spontaneous heeling using a target stick before teaching her to heel on a leash. (See Heeling on page 205.)
3. If she's looking at you, then she's not chewing on the leash. Reward her whenever she happens to look at you. Practice more "pay attention" exercises. (See Pay Attention on page 162.)
4. Teach your dog to release the leash on command. (See Take It and Drop It on page 230.)
5. Anticipate the undesirable behavior of chewing the leash while walking before it happens; distract your dog, and train him for another behavioral response, such as heel or sit.
6. Use a halter-style collar.
7. Teach your dog to carry another toy.
8. Soak the leash in bitter apple or Listerine mouthwash. If neither or those work, try bitter orange. (Bitter apple can be purchased in pet supply stores; bitter orange must be prescribed by your veterinarian.)

Jumping on People

When your dog jumps on a person, try one or more of these options:

1. Turn away from your dog and give her no attention.

2. Interrupt your dog from even thinking about jumping by interjecting some sound or motion and then put her in the sit or down position before the jumping occurs.

3. When at home, lower the greeting effect when leaving and returning. Simply say a soft "hello" when you come home and "later" or "see ya" when you depart. Don't act excited. Praise and pet your dog only when she is sitting or lying down or generally more relaxed.

4. Give him something else to do whenever you walk into the room like going to his bed. This behavior can then be linked to the cue of you entering the room. (See College Level Go to Your Spot, page 188.)

5. Just before the dog reaches you, throw a treat to the side, saying "find it." If you do this enough times, within a week your dog will start holding back in anticipation of the thrown treat.

6. Teach your dog to jump on signal. In other words, have her sit, then have her jump up on you as a reward for sitting.

Lunging Aggressively at Other Dogs

Of all the behavior problems listed, this one most often reflects how you are feeling and what you are communicating to your dog. Many dogs are taught to be aggressive because the person at the other of the leash is anxious and communicates that anxiety to the dog. In essence, you're saying, "That approaching dog or person is a threat. Protect me!" If this is the case, change your attitude first, then change your dog's behavior.

A number of suggestions are offered here; try one or more of them.

Caution: A professional trainer is required to deal with aggressive behavior. Be sure you find a trainer who uses nonviolent methods.

1. Management is a key to handling this problem. A halter-style collar or an Easy Walk harness will help.

2. Anticipate the problem before it happens and walk across the street or down a driveway if necessary. A distance of at

least 20 feet is recommended. Step on your dog's leash at a distance that doesn't pull his head down but is not long enough that your dog can jerk himself if he jumps. This will keep him by your side rather than in front of you. Give your dog as many treats as you can as the other dog passes by. However, if you have a dog with severe issues or if you have a large dog, do not stop and do this.

3. Have a friendly dog walk by at a distance that does not bother the aggressive dog as much. Ask your dog to lie down and stay. Give your dog treats as the other dog passes by. Progress to saying stay, waiting for your dog to look at the other dog, then turn to you without your asking. See Motion Sensitivity on page 277.

4. Anticipate the lunging behavior before it happens and distract your dog with a sound or motion while she's thinking about it.

5. Whenever another dog appears, get happy and friendly and give your dog a treat. This will help change the way your dog feels about the other dog.

Spay or neuter your dog. Lunging at other dogs is often reduced when your dog is spayed or neutered. An intact male dog is three times more likely to attack than a neutered dog. A spayed female will not have the same maternal protectiveness and is also less likely to mouth or nip. Because she doesn't have to protect her young, she doesn't have to protect the territory around her.

Mouthing and Bite Inhibition

Puppies learn at a young age to modulate the degree of pressure they use when they play with each other. This is called bite inhibition. But if a puppy is taken away from the litter too soon, he never learns this. As a result, many older dogs use their mouths to grab a person's arm or leg or skirt. It's your job to teach your dog to control his impulse to bite and chew you and other people.

Try a number of these methods. Do two or three repetitions of one method, then alternate with another method.

1. Practice "ouch" training. When you feel so much as a tooth for whatever reason, immediately make a sound like a puppy yelping, like the word "yipe." This holds true whether it's a playful puppy nipping at you or an older dog mouthing your arm. When you make this sound, most dogs and puppies will immediately back off. When your dog does back off, give praise. Note: If your dog gets more excited when you do this, this is not the technique for him. Don't do it.

2. Use the "aaaah!" method. Lower your vocal pitch and interrupt the mouthing with a quick "aaaah." To some dogs this is perceived as a low-intensity growl. We use it simply as an interrupter—to interrupt the behavior. Note: If your dog gets more excited when you do this, this is not the technique for him. Don't do it.

3. Give a "yipe" or "aaaah" and then leave the room or put the puppy or dog in a two- to five-minute time out. A good way to handle the time out is to put him behind a baby gate. Then, after the time is up, return his freedom and let him know that everything between you is now okay and there are no hard feelings. The combination of making a sound and giving a time out is very powerful.

4. Before your dog has a chance to chew on you, give him something legal to chew on like a Bully Stick or Nyla bone. Or give him a treat-filled Kong to play with.

5. Before your teething puppy has a chance to mouth or nip you, give him an ice cube or a piece of frozen canvas. Or put one of the aforementioned bone toys in the freezer for ten minutes or so and then give it to him. This helps numb the gums for a while, alleviating the discomfort of emerging teeth.

6. Put the puppy on the floor whenever a nip occurs and walk away.

7. Teach the dog to lick on signal instead of nipping you. Rub some turkey, peanut butter, or cream cheese on your hand. As your puppy licks it off, say "lick." Then click, praise, and treat with turkey. Another variation of this tip is

to simply lick the palm of your hand and then let your dog lick your saliva.

8. Put the dog's kennel in a social area or tether him so nipping can't occur. Reward calm behavior.

9. Immediately hold the dog gently but firmly until her body relaxes. Then say "okay" and release. (See Figure 17.1 on page 255.)

10. Practice management methods (see Leashes and Tethers on page 90) and use a halter-style collar.

11. If the dog is nipping ankles or feet, have her sit or lie down when you are approaching and/or use a leash tied around your waist to lead the dog away from your feet.

12. Ask your veterinarian if it's okay to give a teething pup one-quarter of an aspirin before class to reduce inflammation and soreness of gums.

Separation Anxiety

Dogs are social animals. A dog with separation anxiety is, in essence, in panic due to feeling alone and unsafe, being confined, and his inability to predict an end to his suffering. Dogs in this situation will do everything they can to try to escape and to relieve their anxieties. People have come home to find holes chewed in their walls, couches torn to shreds, linoleum ripped up from the floor, and their dog's mouth and paws bloodied from frenzied attempts to escape.

A number of elements and methods can be used to help resolve your dog's separation anxiety, including making him feel more safe and secure, creating routine and predictability in his life, and building his confidence.

Safety and Security

If your dog exhibits signs of separation anxiety, the first thing to do is to create a safe environment for him while you're away. Put him behind baby gates or in an exercise pen or dog run and make sure there's nothing in his environment that he can destroy or that will hurt him. Do not put your dog in a kennel unless you are absolutely sure that he is comfortable in it. Remember, safety is paramount. In extreme cases of separation anxiety, a professional should be called and it's mandatory for someone to take a week off from work to help your dog with the beginning stages of this process.

Create Routine and Predictability in Your Dog's Life

A first step in resolving separation anxiety is to ease your dog into a greater sense of security when left alone by teaching her the depart and return lesson below. This lesson will convince your dog that your departure always means that you will eventually return. If your dog *knows* that your leaving is *always* followed by your returning, and that neither occurrence is a very big deal, much of the stress associated with being left alone will be alleviated.

The "Depart and Return" Lesson

Because dogs have an anticipatory response, the first thing you'll want to do is to stay relaxed. If you have a high level of energy when you depart and return, your dog will pick up on that and begin anticipating you departing or returning. His excitement level will feed off yours. It's a vicious circle. So stay calm and relaxed. Give him a simple "see ya" when you leave. Then, on your return home, ignore him totally until he relaxes even a little bit, at which point you will reward him with petting and affection. He'll learn that if he remains calm, he gets rewarded. In essence, you're telling him that being separated or alone is no big deal.

1. Act as though you are preparing to leave the house (put on your shoes, find your keys, and so on).
2. At the door, give your dog the verbal signal "See ya." Open the door but do not go through it—stay in the same spot. Close the door, click, and treat. Repeat five to ten times and end the session. Repeat this simple process until your dog redirects her focus from your actions at the door to the treat in your hand.

3. Begin adding intensity. After giving the verbal signal "See ya," open the door and go through without closing it. Come back inside immediately, click, and treat.

4. Increase the intensity. Repeat the process but close the door behind you. Count "one thousand one" and come back inside. Click and treat. Repeat five to ten times, and end the session.

5. In subsequent sessions, begin to gradually increase the time you stand outside the closed door. Your goal is for your dog to remain calm and relaxed while you are outside. If at any point she begins to exhibit signs of anxiety, return to a shorter increment of time and continue more slowly. Continue in this way until you can stay outside the closed door for ten seconds while your dog remains quiet and calm inside.

6. As your dog progresses, add distance. Take two steps away from the door while you are outside, count to ten, then come back in, click, and treat. Gradually add more distance, taking three steps, four steps, and so on.

7. Add distraction by getting in your car and closing the door. (The distraction here is the sound of your car door opening and closing, a sign of departure that your dog knows well.) Immediately return to your dog, click, and treat.

8. Continue in this way at your dog's speed, eventually starting the car, staying in the running car for longer periods, and then taking car out of driveway for longer periods. Click and treat your dog each time you return.

If your dog is less anxious, you may not need to do any of the steps except the one in which you get into your car. Some severe cases of separation anxiety require all of these steps and more.

Confidence Building

Building a dog's confidence builds a sense of security. Although it's recommended that you stay home to help a new canine family member make his transition to new surroundings, it's equally important to lessen his "neediness." In other words, you need to show him that being alone is okay too. You can help your dog gain confidence and security by giving him smart toys to play with (such as the Buster Cube); teaching the "find it" behavior (page 182); and implementing the "depart and return" described above.

Emotional health is also encouraged and promoted through advanced training in the "Sit" and "Lie down" behaviors, such as increasing your distance from your dog and leaving her sight. These behaviors should initially be taught indoors, then progress to teaching them outdoors.

In addition, I highly recommend enrolling in socialization classes and agility, herding, water work, and/or tracking classes, depending on your dog's sensitivity level. In these classes, other handlers will work with your dog and you will work with other dogs. All of these behaviors and activities communicate to your dog that everything's okay and that he can adapt and be safe.

Additional Helpful Hints
Here are a few more tips for dealing with separation anxiety:

Set a schedule. Dogs thrive on routine. Once they know when you're going and coming, they relax more because they are able to predict the future.

Just before you leave, give your dog a special toy or treat. Having something to chew on such as a Kong, Buster Cube, Bully stick, or a treat ball will take his mind off you being gone. Alternatively, hide a dozen treats around the kitchen. As you're leaving tell your dog to "Stay" and then, as you walk out the door, say "find it."

Turn on a radio or television. Choose a channel that you normally listen to. Soothing classical or New Age music, such as Steven Halpern's "Inner Peace Music" series, is best. I suggest that you turn it on as soon as you awaken and leave it on when you leave. That way your dog will associate this music with your presence.

Use herbs, flower essences, aromatherapy, and homeopathic remedies. Consult a holistic veterinarian for recommendations on natural treatments such as herbs, flower essences (such as Bach Flower Remedies), aromatherapy, and homeopathic remedies to help your dog deal with separation anxiety and other emotionally based issues. You can also consult books like *The Natural Dog,* by Mary Brennan, D.V.M.; *Beyond Obedience,* by April Frost; and *Four Paws, Five Directions,* by Cheryl Schwartz, D.V.M.

Consider medications. Several pharmaceuticals are used in conjunction with behavior modification programs for separation anxiety, as well as other behaviors. Contact a behaviorist who uses nonviolence methodology and your veterinarian if you want to look into pharmaceutical alternatives.

Exercise your dog before you leave. If you get your dog a little tired, he'll have less energy to burn off while you're gone.

Identify your dog's triggers. Separation anxiety is often triggered by a specific event. For example, if you pick up your keys and then leave, your dog quickly learns that the sound of the keys means that you are going to leave. Other triggering events might be putting on your shoes, combing your hair, and so on. By desensitizing your dog to these events, your dog's anxiety will be lessened. There are two ways to do this:

- Counter-condition your dog to the "meaning" of the event, such as picking up the keys. Throughout the day, pick up your keys and give your dog a treat.
- Change your routine. For example, if you usually get up in the morning and take a shower, then comb your hair, then do your exercises, then put on your shoes, then have breakfast, then pick up your keys, and then leave . . . mix this routine up. Change the order of these events so your dog won't be able to predict which event is associated with your departure. This will keep him from accumulating stress.

Chapter 18

Help for Your Sensitive Dog

If your dog is ultra-sensitive, it's important to identify his learning baseline for touch, sound, and motion—that is, the point at which he will interact with you without being distracted by environmental stimuli. Dogs who were poorly socialized in their youth never had a chance to acclimate to the sights, sounds, and touch sensations of everyday life. These ultrasensitive dogs will find even grade-school level training too much to handle. If your dog belongs in this category, you'll need to go slowly and follow the step-by-step training process described in this chapter so your dog can achieve a basic level of confidence and trust. Then you'll be able to use the basic training procedures given in Chapter 14.

If your dog has extreme sensitivity, hiring a professional trainer is mandatory. In cases of extreme fear issues, it's also essential to have a professional on board.

Before you begin training, look at your environment from your sensitive dog's point of view. Think about how the sights, sounds, and physical sensations of the world might be influencing his behavior. Is there another dog barking in the distance? Are tree branches moving, leaves blowing, or dirt swirling? Are airplanes flying overhead?

Touch Sensitivity

Handling is an important aspect of socialization—one that helps teach your dog adapt to her environment. Your dog's acceptance of being handled is an important part of her training. It teaches her to enjoy being stroked, touched, petted, and held. Handling is especially important for sensitive dogs because it helps desensitize and habituate them to being touched. Handling is important not only for vet-friendly visits, so your dog will allow an examination, but also to create a safe environment. This is especially important if there are children in your home. If a dog has not learned to be handled or touched and a child should happen to step on her tail or accidentally fall on her, the dog might react by biting.

We have all heard the stories of children being bitten or even severely mauled by family pets. These tragedies could potentially have been avoided if the dog had been socialized and taught how to behave around a child. Regardless of how well your dog is trained or socialized, never leave a child alone with a dog.

When I work with families, I always stress the importance of training the dog what to do when a child enters the room. For example, you can teach your dog to go to her bed and lie down. With enough repetitions, this will become an automatic behavior. I also stress the importance of getting the dog used to being touched as a child might touch him. Both of these suggestions can be used as added safeguards in the child-dog dynamic.

Establish the Learning Baseline

When beginning the training process it's up to each handler to ascertain to what degree the dog is comfortable being touched, if at all. This is true whether you're working with a puppy or an adult dog. It's at this point, which I call the handling baseline, that you begin to work with tactual socialization with your dog. The chart on page 271, The Learning Baseline for Handling (Figure 18.1), is your guide to the process. As the chart indicates, the handling baseline ranges from Point A, in which a dog allows minimal interaction to Point F, in which a dog is supremely secure in his interactions with you. When other people

Figure 18.1
The learning baseline for handling

The *learning baseline* refers to the point at which the dog is motivated to interact with you. This chart illustrates the learning baseline for handling, ranging from Point A in which the dog has minimal interaction to Point F in which the dog is supremely secure in his interactions with you. You never want to distress your dog by asking her to do more than is physically, mentally, and emotionally possible. Looking at this chart, where would you begin to successfully touch, hold and handle your dog?

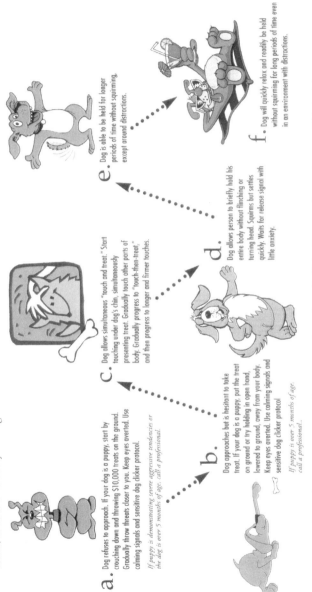

a. Dog refuses to approach. If your dog is a puppy, start by crouching down and throwing $10,000 treats on the ground. Gradually throw threats closer to you. Keep eyes averted. Use calming signals and sensitive dog clicker protocol.

If puppy is demonstrating severe aggressive tendencies or the dog is over 5 months of age, call a professional.

b. Dog approaches but is hesitant to take treat. If your dog is a puppy, put the treat on ground or try holding in open hand, lowered to ground, away from your body. Keep eyes averted. Use calming signals and sensitive dog clicker protocol

If puppy is over 5 months of age, call a professional.

c. Dog allows simultaneous "touch and treat." Start touching under dog's chin, simultaneously presenting treat. Gradually touch other parts of body. Gradually progress to "touch-then-treat," and then progress to longer and firmer touches.

d. Dog allows person to briefly hold his entire body without flinching or turning head. Squirms but settles quickly. Waits for release signal with little anxiety.

e. Dog is able to be held for longer periods of time without squirming, except around distractions.

f. Dog will quickly relax and readily be held without squirming for long periods of time even in an environment with distractions.

Caution: If your dog is sensitive to touch or motion, shy and stand-offish, please exercise caution to avoid being bitten. Please consult a professional dog trainer.

touch the dog, each person must begin at an earlier handling stage and gradually progress.

Most dogs with a high degree of sensitivity and shyness are equally sensitive to sound. For this reason, it's important to use the clicker protocol for sensitive dogs to keep from making the situation worse. (See the tips for using a clicker described on page 125.)

Acclimating Your Dog to Touch

Point A on Figure 18.1 illustrates the type of dog who stays well outside the tactile arena. She wants nothing to do with being touched. This is generally the result of poor socialization. You can't expect a dog who has been poorly socialized to immediately accept a human's touch, let alone enjoy being held for any length of time. Yet she will interact. She will accept food, but on her own terms.

A poorly socialized dog does not like the following:

- Being touched on the head
- Having a person reach over her body or touch her back
- Being picked up
- Having a person reach out to her, especially if she is retreating
- Having her paws or tail touched

In order to socialize such a dog for handling and move her from Point A to Point F, start by sitting on the ground about 6 feet away from her, keeping your side to her, and using body language that communicates a nonthreatening demeanor. This body language includes looking away, scratching, blinking, licking your lips, yawning, and so on. Next, toss a $10,000 treat like a piece of turkey toward the dog, but off to the side. Then toss several more treats, one at a time. During each session, toss the treat so it's a little closer to you and your dog will gradually gravitate toward you.

NOTE: Using a clicker can speed the touch sensitivity training process along. If you are using a clicker, you would click as the dog is taking the treat. But a word of caution: Since most touch-sensitive dogs are equally sensitive to sound, it's important to use the clicker protocol for sensitive dogs on page 125 because you don't want to make the situation worse.

Please use a behavioral specialist if your dog is exhibiting truly "standoffish" behavior such as indicated in Points A and B on the Learning Baseline chart for Handling. Always err on the side of safety to avoid being bitten or the possibility that a member of your family, especially a child, might be bitten.

At Point B on the chart we have a dog that will take a treat close to you but whose back end seems to be straining to stay away at the same time that the front end leans forward to take the treat. Gradually, treat by treat, inch by inch, entice the dog to reach over your body to take the treat from your open hand. Never reach for a dog. Always let the dog choose to come to you except, of course, in an emergency where you might have to grab your dog.

At Point C touch is added to the equation. However, it's important that you don't rush the process. Ask the dog to lean toward you and take the treat from one hand while you simultaneously touch him with the other hand. Always start touching under the chin because, as I mentioned earlier, some dogs don't like it when people reach over their bodies. (See Figure 18.2.) Gradually, over several sessions, begin touching other parts of the body, going from the chin to the side of the dog's head, then to the top of the head, down the back, to the tail and paws. Simultaneously give a treat with every touch.

Once your dog is comfortable being touched all over his body, little by little begin keeping your hand on his body for longer periods of time. For example, if your hand is on your dog's back, keep it there for two seconds, then give a treat. Then three seconds and treat. And so on. When you reach the point where you can keep your hand on your dog's back for ten seconds, begin adding pressure to your touch. For example, put your hand on your dog's back, squeeze a little more firmly for one second, then release and treat. Then continue and progress a second at a time until you are firmly grasping his back for ten seconds. NOTE: When you began adding firmness to your touch, you went back to holding your dog for only one second and gradually progressed from there.

Figure 18.2

Figure 18.3

Handling: Figures 18.2 and 18.3 show Point C of the Handling Baseline. In the first photo, handling consists of a simultaneous touch and treat beginning under the dog's chin. In the second photo, the handler is progressing to touching over the dog's head. This progression will take several sessions with a dog that will interact at this level and is not too stressed.

Figure 18.4

In Illustration 18.4, the dog is now at Point D.

Figure 18.5

Illustration 18.5 represents a dog that is at Point F.

Once you become successful with the simultaneous touch and treat, start to touch and then treat, beginning with a one-second delay. In other words, touch your dog and immediately treat. Then touch your dog, hold your hand there for two seconds, then treat. Next, count three seconds then treat, and so on. Each session should include ten repetitions and then stop. As your dog relaxes, begin touching for longer periods of time with longer delays between the touches and the treats. Then progress to firmer touches, and gradually touching all over your dog's body. Remember to reward your dog after every touch. If at any time your dog seems uncomfortable by drawing away or flinching, return to the point where he is more comfortable.

The next stage, Point D, is a dog that allows someone to touch and hold his body without flinching or turning his head. At this point, the dog can be held for several seconds and briefly lifted off the ground. In order to do this, present another treat but don't release it. Hold it between your fingers so your dog will have to nibble it while you are still holding onto it. Simultaneously, take your other hand and slip it underneath your dog's chest between his front legs. Repeat this five to ten times. If your dog is comfortable, proceed to the next part of Point D.

As before, let your dog nibble a treat from between your fingers as before and simultaneously lift the front legs off the ground an inch or two and then lower him back down to the ground. Repeat this five to ten times until your dog feels comfortable having his front legs lifted off the ground. In the next part of Point D, you will lift your dog's front legs off the ground, lower them back, and *then* give him the treat. Do several sessions of five to ten times until your dog is comfortable having his front legs lifted off the ground. Next, begin lifting and holding your dog in the air for longer periods of time until he is comfortable having his front paws off the ground for ten seconds.

At Point E, the dog has lost his anxiety about being held or lifted and has shifted his focus onto the reward. The occasional squirm or tenseness is triggered again when major distractions come up but, at this point, the dog will quickly settle down again. Now he has begun to look at most touching and holding as enjoyable.

At the final stage, Point F, the dog really loves being touched and held and welcomes every friendly fondle. Now touch has become its own reward.

Motion Sensitivity

Some dogs are secure and relaxed no matter what's going on around them, while others are so fearful that they flinch at even the slightest distraction. Dogs who jump, cower, or hide at the movements of everyday life require extra consideration. If your dog gets nervous when a person gets up from a chair; a leaf blows in the wind; shadows dance on a wall; or traffic, joggers, or other animals pass by, the exercises below will help build confidence and teach him how to relax.

The keys to resolving motion-based sensitivities are:

- Learning to identify the exact trigger for the dog's fearful response
- Maintaining enough distance to keep the stimulus from triggering that response

🦴 Changing the way the dog feels about the stimulus (counter-conditioning) and systematic desensitization

🦴 Increasing behavioral reliability and your dog's confidence through training (operant conditioning)

Acclimating Your Dog to Motion

Begin this training in a low-distraction environment such as your living room or back yard at a time of day when the world is still waking up. You will use two exercises to acclimate your dog: the perpendicular walk and the direct approach.

The Perpendicular Walk

In the first exercise, you are desensitizing your dog to other people. By associating a movement, like a person passing by, with a food treat, you change the way he feels.

Have lots of $10,000 treats ready, as well as a clicker. (Refer to page 124 for a description of how to use a clicker.) Ask another member of your family or someone else your dog knows to help you out.

Note: There are three levels to this exercise. *Your dog may accomplish all three levels within one session or it may take multiple sessions per level, depending on how sensitive he is.*

Level One

1. Position your dog beside you and stand on his leash so he is unable to walk away. The leash should be just loose enough that it doesn't pull his head down. Allow your dog to sit or lie down if he wants, but do not ask him to.

2. Ask your friend to stand at least 20 feet away and walk across your dog's path, perpendicular to your position. The person should walk at a normal rate and avoid eye contact with your dog.

3. As your friend is walking, feed your dog treats one at a time as fast as he will eat them. Be happy and exuberant as you do so: "Yay! Look at Susie walking in front of you! Isn't she great!" You might give your dog twenty treats in that short time period. (Note: If your dog refuses the treats, your

friend is too close. Increase the distance to 30, 40, or even 50 feet.) When the dog takes the treats, you are at the right distance. After about twenty paces, your friend should halt. Repeat this exercise at least three to five times (more is fine if your dog doesn't seem to mind). End the session.

Level Two
1. Warm up by repeating the process described for level one.
2. Now, ask your dog to lie down and stay. Once again repeat the process of level one. If your dog is successful, go to Step 3.
3. Ask your dog to lie down and stay. This time as your friend walks by, do not feed any treats, and offer no praise. Just wait and say nothing. When your friend comes to a halt, your dog should look at your friend and then turn and glance at you. Exuberantly praise, click and treat. Two things have happened: you have changed the way your dog feels about someone walking by and you have taught him what you want him to do . . . lay down, relax, and look at you. Repeat this step three to five times. End the session. (If he isn't successful—meaning he isn't turning his head to look at you, go back to step two and repeat three to five times; then try again.)
4. In subsequent sessions, ask your friend to gradually increase her speed from a walk to a jog, from a jog to a run, while yelling "booga, booga" and waving her arms. Always wait for your dog to turn his head away from your friend and look at you before clicking, praising, and treating.

Hint: At any point that your dog isn't comfortable with increased speed or distractions, go back to giving him food treats *as* your friend goes by. The bottom line is that you want to link any increase in speed or distraction with food.

Level Three
At this level, you will decrease the distance between your dog and your friend by one foot at a time. Start by asking your friend to walk past at a distance of 19 feet and repeat all the steps

in Level Two. Whenever you decrease the distance, you must return to a walking speed. Repeat three to five times at each distance and then end the session. In subsequent sessions, continue to decrease the distance.

The Direct Approach

When your dog is successful with the perpendicular walk, it is time to move on to the more challenging direct approach.

Level One

1. Ask your dog to lie down and stay. From a distance of 20 feet, your friend should walk directly toward you, avoiding eye contact with your dog. Do not give treats while your friend is approaching. Have your friend stop when she is 10 feet away from your dog. Wait for your dog to look away from your friend and look at you. Click, praise, and treat. Repeat three to five times. End the session.

2. If your dog is relaxed, have your friend gradually increase the intensity of her speed and movements as she approaches by going from a walk to a jog, to a run, to a run while waving her arms and yelling "booga, booga." Each time she will stop at a distance of 10 feet from your dog. With each increase in speed, repeat the exercise three to five times, always clicking, praising and treating every successful attempt. Keep your progress slow and steady—it may take several days or weeks to reach this level. If at any point your dog seems anxious, have your friend return to a slower pace.

Level Two

1. Warm up by repeating the steps described for level one. When your dog remains relaxed with your friend approaching at a run, waving and clapping (always stopping 10 feet away), you are ready to decrease the distance a foot at a time. Ask your dog to lie down and stay. Have your friend approach at a walk, stopping when she is 9 feet away. Repeat three to five times.

2. With each practice session, you will ask your friend to get closer to your dog, adding intensity with each step, until she is running all the way up to you and your dog, stopping at a distance of one foot. For a sensitive dog, this may take several days or weeks. Do not decrease distances until you are sure your dog can handle it.

Generalizing the Behavior

If your dog stays relaxed while your friend runs up to the one-foot distance, flailing her arms and yelling "Booga booga," you are on your final lap. The brain pathway is now established, and you can begin the whole process over again with someone your dog doesn't know. If you repeat this with three strangers in three different locations, your dog should begin to generalize, or behave the same way no matter who approaches. You won't have to repeat this process to introduce him to new people. You will, however, have to repeat everything from the beginning when you introduce dogs.

Running directly toward a dog while flailing your arms may be too much for some dogs to handle, no matter how small your progressive steps. If this is the case with your dog, hire a professional to monitor your training.

If at any point your dog has trouble, follow the golden rule and go back to the last step at which he was successful. Build success by taking incremental steps. In her excellent book, *Help for Your Fearful Dog,* Nicole Wilde stresses the importance of incremental training this way: "That might mean that instead of going from 'walks at a normal pace' to 'walks faster, swings arms,' you should insert a step where the person walks faster but does not swing arms." Progress more quickly or make the speed or intensity increments smaller depending on your dog's comfort level.

Before adding more challenging distractions, check your dog's body language for signs that he's okay. Are the ears relaxed? Tail relaxed? Does your dog look in anticipation for the treat or is he panting and darting his head back and forth as if looking for an escape? Make sure that you see the relaxed state a few times before adding intensity or more challenging distractions.

Sound Sensitivity

If your dog is fearful of sounds, the following exercises will help desensitize her to sudden noises and increase her confidence and trust.

Level One

Ask your dog to sit and stay. Have your friend stand 20 feet away. Ask him to drop a cooking pot from a distance of two inches from the floor. As soon as you hear the sound, stick a high-value treat such as chicken or turkey in your dog's mouth and praise profusely. You might say something like, "Yay! We love sounds!" to reinforce a positive attitude about the loud sound. Repeat three to five times. Repeat this exercise several times a day until you see your dog is staying relaxed. This may take several days or a week.

NOTE: If you find that your dog is extra sensitive to sounds, increase your distance and/or decrease the intensity of the sound (put a towel on the floor, use a book instead of a pot). Do only three repetitions.

Level Two

1. Warm up by repeating level one.
2. Then ask your dog to lie down and stay and drop the pot but this time, do not treat. Wait. Your dog should turn toward the sound but then look to you for the treat. When that happens, click, enthusiastically praise, and give him a jackpot of treats! Repeat three to five times and end the session.

Level Three
1. Warm up by repeating level two.
2. Then increase the intensity of the sound by having your friend drop the object from a greater height. For example, four inches from the ground, six inches from the ground, etc. Repeat three to five times and end session. Always wait for your dog to turn his head away from the sound and look at you before clicking, praising, and treating. If your dog seems anxious, return to an intensity at which he is successful. When you get to a height of 3 feet and the pot is really clanging, it's time to kick it up to level four.

Level Four
1. Warm up with three repetitions of level three.
2. Then have your friend move one foot closer and drop the pot. Follow the steps above of incrementally adding more intensity by first dropping the pot from two inches, then three inches, etc. After each exercise, click, praise, and treat when your dog looks to you. Repeat each intensity three to five times.
3. When your dog is successful with the louder sounds at the decreased distance, repeat the exercise by having your friend move one foot closer. Your eventual goal is to have your dog stay relaxed while a pot is dropped a foot away from him from a height of 3 feet. You want your dog to look at you as if to say, "So what else ya got?" In other words, the sound is no longer a big deal. This might take weeks or months, depending on your dog's sensitivities and your skills.

NOTE: If you happen to accidentally drop a pot or your dog is startled by a car backfiring, a police siren or a motorcycle zooming by, don't coddle her, although that's what you'll want to do. Be a good actor or actress and immediately exclaim: "Yay! The pot dropped! Here's some turkey!" By linking the treat to the disturbance, your reaction will have an affect on your dog's future behavior and change the way she feels about unexpected and scary sounds.

Index

About the Authors

Paul Owens is featured on the DVD *The Dog Whisperer: Beginning and Intermediate Dog Training*. He is certified by the **Association of Pet Dog Trainers** (APDT) and the **Delta Society's Animal Assisted Therapy Program**. He is an endorsed member of **The National Association of Dog Obedience Instructors** (NADOI). Paul began training dogs in 1972. He is a leading proponent of positive, nonviolent animal training in the United States. Paul is the director of the nonprofit educational organization **Raise with Praise,® Inc**. and the founder/director of the children's afterschool violence-prevention program, **Paws for Peace**. His specialty is in the evaluation and behavior modification of aggressive dogs and he is frequently consulted and referred by veterinarians. His public service work includes bite prevention programs for children and monthly dog training seminars at area Humane Societies and shelters. Paul has practiced and taught yoga in the United States and India for more than 30 years. He lives in Los Angeles with his three dogs: Molly, Grady, and Buddy.

Norma Eckroate is the co-author of *The New Natural Cat, Complete Holistic Care and Healing for Horses,* and *Switched-On Living,* among other books. She lives in Los Angeles.